CW01655121

HAN

The aim of this book is to show that handwriting can be legible, speedy, and pleasing to the eye, and that such writing is within the capacity of anyone who cares to spend a few hours acquiring the necessary skills.

TEACH YOURSELF BOOKS

This book is planned for the intelligent adult who wants to change his handwriting for the better and will give him excellent advice and guidance. It is systematic and comprehensive, and has plenty of illustrative material.

Education

HANDWRITING

John le F. Dumpleton

TEACH YOURSELF BOOKS
Hodder and Stoughton

First printed 1955
Twelfth impression 1975
Fourteenth impression 1977

ISBN 0 340 05612 6

Printed in Great Britain for
Hodder and Stoughton Paperbacks, a division of
Hodder and Stoughton Ltd, Mill Road, Dunton Green,
Sevenoaks, Kent (Editorial Office: 47 Bedford Square,
London WC1 3DP)
by Richard Clay (The Chaucer Press), Ltd., Bungay, Suffolk

CONTENTS

ILLUSTRATIONS

Figure

Chapter One

INTRODUCTION

In recent years there has been a re-awakening interest in the art of handwriting. Many business men are deploring the illegible scrawls of their clerks, and the undecipherable signatures cf their correspondents. Commerce has been reprieved from ultimate disaster by the ubiquitous but impersonal typewriter. However, there are still occasions when this machine is not the most appropriate or convenient writing instrument. A quick glance through personal correspondence serves to remind us of the sad state into which most handwriting has fallen. Some people are so ashamed of their own hand that they even use the typewriter for personal notes. Many of us are only too conscious of our indifferent scripts, but shrug our shoulders and resign ourselves to what appears to be an unavoidable deficiency.

The aim of this book is to show that handwriting can be legible, speedy, *and* pleasing to the eye, and that such writing is within the capacity of anyone who cares to spend a few hours acquiring the necessary skills. It should be clearly understood that throughout this book the author has in mind the development of a swift correspondence hand. Far too many people have the erroneous notion that really good handwriting can only be written slowly. All the examples of contemporary hands which are illustrated here have been written at an unconstraining speed. It is not suggested that writing can be done at great speed without suffering some deterioration, but by following the model set forth in the following pages the reader may acquire a hand which still retains the essential qualities of clarity, fluency, and comeliness.

Although re-forming handwriting habits requires a certain amount of application and practice, the busy reader should not be deterred. If time is precious study can be restricted to those chapters which deal with the practical business of learning a new hand, but the enthusiastic student of handwriting will find much useful supplementary information in the remainder of the book.

No attempt has been made to give an exhaustive survey of the history of handwriting, as this has been competently done in various books which are already available. They are listed in the Bibliography at the end of this manual.

Finally, a word of warning: handwriting is a series of movements, and movements are very difficult to demonstrate by printed diagrams. The development of unselfconscious rhythmic movement is essential to the acquisition of a really successful cursive hand. For this reason do not scamp the pre-writing exercises, which are specially designed to condition the hand to the necessary rhythms.

Chapter Two

THE NATURE OF HANDWRITING

THE existence and purpose of handwriting are very largely taken for granted, but it is necessary to start off with a clear idea of what handwriting is, and where it came from.

What Is Handwriting?

Handwriting can be defined as a visual record of thought made by prescribed movements of a hand-controlled instrument designed to mark a surface. It is generally accepted that the traces left by the writing instrument should be commonly understood, although there are not a few cases of cryptic writing being used in order to conceal the writer's thoughts from any eye but his own. However, in this manual we are concerned with that writing which is mainly used as a means of communication, and where the prime necessity is to be intelligible.

Legibility

The first essential, then, is that writing should be legible. The writer must use symbols which are easily recognisable, arranged in an accepted way. These symbols which we call the alphabet can, in fact, differ quite a lot, but a glance at Fig. 1 will show that such differences are not so great as to destroy their legibility. However, it is desirable that most written matter should approximate in appearance as far as possible to that of the printers' types

1. abcdefghijklmnopqrstu
2. abcdefghijklmnopqrst
3. abcdefghijklmnopqrstuvw
4. *abcdefghijklmnopqrstuvwxy*
5. abcdefghijklmnopqrst
6. *abcdefghijklmnop*
7. *abcdefghijklmnop*
8. *abcdefghijklmnopqrstuv*

Fig. I.—Printers' Alphabets and Handwriting Alphabets Compared

used for books and periodicals. This is a reversal of the situation five hundred years ago at the birth of printing, when it was necessary for the printer's types to emulate as closely as possible the handwritten letters used in the writing of books. That with which we are most familiar must set the standard. With that condition in mind, look again at the alphabets in Fig. 1. The first four are modern printers' types used in the printing of books, newspapers, and notices, and the last four are handwriting alphabets. Which is the most suitable of the latter from the point of view of easy identification with the former? The choice of a suitable writing alphabet cannot rest on the question of legibility alone, though. Ease and speed of writing must also be taken into account.

Fluency

Handwriting, if it is to be of any practical use, must be capable of easy and swift execution, but at the same time such fluency must not detract from its legibility to any degree. It seems to be a contemporary fallacy that as long as handwriting is done as quickly as possible it does not matter whether it is also readable. The present concern about the state of handwriting arises mainly from the result of this false assumption. Look at Fig. 2; what other virtue has it other than that it is swiftly written? Many hands which show a similar deterioration fail because they are based on a handwriting alphabet

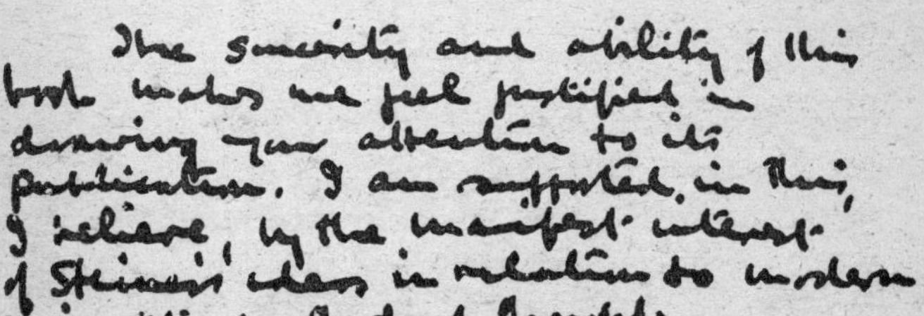

Fig. 2.—Bad Handwriting

that is not cursive. The print script shown in Fig. 1 (5) is of this type, and if taught to young children has to be replaced at some stage by another alphabet which is more easily adapted to the requirements of speed. This requirement needs not only a script composed of letters which easily join, but also a script whose letter forms are conducive to fast writing. Round, upright letters are not cursive, and if used in handwriting, degenerate under the stress of speed. Alphabet No. 8 in Fig. 1 is the only one which is truly cursive, and yet is closely identifiable with printers' type. It is this script which is demonstrated in the present handbook.

Beauty

There is yet one more pre-requisite of good handwriting that is not always recognised as such, and that is beauty. To some people there seems to be something indecent about this word, but there is something deep within each of us which responds to beauty when it is experienced. Unfortunately, this experience is far too infrequent with many of us, and in self-defence we pretend that it does not matter. Nevertheless, if we can manage to create, by means of our handwriting, something which gives pleasure to the beholder, without the expenditure of undue labour or affectation, we shall find that it is worthwhile.

The Qualities of Handwriting

It is suggested, then, that the qualities of handwriting are clearness, swiftness, and comeliness, in that order of precedence. These qualities may be expressed more succinctly perhaps as legibility, fluency, beauty. A study of calligraphy will show that this trinity is in fact indivisible, each member sustaining the other two.

The pre-requisite of good handwriting, and by good writing is meant that which contains these three qualities, is a sound model, an irreproachable handwriting alphabet. This is the staple of which a good hand is contrived; the development of legibility, fluency, and beauty being entirely dependent on it.

The Choice of an Exemplar Alphabet

There are two alternatives which might be adopted when searching for the exemplar alphabet: the first is to choose from those used before, and the second is to create a new one. It would be a very hardy person who would enter on the second course, and the majority of us would prefer to find a ready-made pattern, if such a one exists.

During the last half-century or so much scholarly research has been done into the writings of the past, from the calligraphic point of view, and the one thing which has become most obvious is that writing, like all crafts, is the product of the tools and materials used. It is clear, therefore, that for pen writing we should seek out the best that has been created by the pen, and as we are concerned with the Western alphabet we need look no further back in time than two thousand years, when the Romans were in the process of perfecting the alphabet they had acquired from the Greeks, and which we still use today. For the satisfaction of knowing why the model chosen for this book is considered the best it will be profitable to consider a brief account of the development of handwriting from Roman times to the present day.

The Development of Handwriting

Probably the most useful and the most enduring thing which the Romans bequeathed to posterity was their alphabet. They had acquired the framework of this from the Greeks, but improved upon it and adapted it to suit their own requirements. Since that time, roughly two thousand years ago, very little alteration has taken place. One or two letters have been added, and a minuscule (small-letter) alphabet has developed from it, but it is basically the same alphabet that we use today. The letters shown in Fig. 3 are easily recognisable to us, although the inscription is in Latin. The photo-

Fig. 3.—Trajan Column Inscription

graph shows part of an inscription on the Trajan Column in Rome, which was erected in 114 A.D., and it should be borne in mind that these letters were incised in marble with mallet and chisels. It is thought, however, that they were probably set out on the stone first with a flat brush, so that the incidence of thicks and thins was determined by the movement of the square edge, as shown in Fig. 4.

Fig. 4.—Laying Out Roman Inscriptional Letters with a Brush

The Romans had no small-letters, and no spaces were left between words. The same capital letters were used for the writing of books, but owing to the fact that a pen on parchment found curved strokes easier than straight, the square capitals gradually changed their shapes. The only means of book production at that time, and for the next 1,400 years, was by handwriting and copying. As the scribe was strictly trained to copy exactly what he saw in front of him, any modifications of letter-shapes were perpetuated, and often aggravated by the copyist's own calligraphic idiosyncrasies. So that by the sixth century an alphabet of small-letters, now called half uncials, had evolved.

The Influence of the Writing Tool

As has been stated already, the writing tool at this time was the pen; a pen cut from a goose quill by the scribe himself. The word *pen* comes from the Latin *penna*—a feather, and the use of the word quill to describe such a pen seems to be of more recent origin.

It should be clearly understood that the pen of the early Christian scribes was cut with a square edge at the tip, and not a sharp point. The effect of this was to produce those thick and thin strokes which have already been mentioned in connection with the Roman inscriptions. Such variations of strokes were achieved without any alteration of the pressure on the pen during writing: a most important consideration, as will be seen later (Fig. 5). The appear-

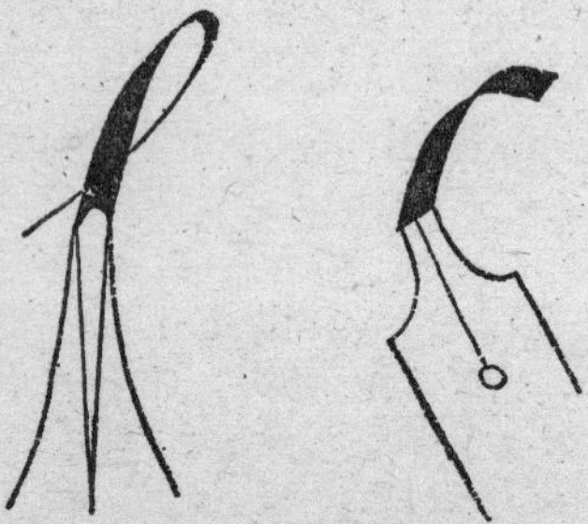

Fig. 5.—Comparison of Edged and Pointed Pens

ance of the writing was greatly affected by the angle at which the pen was held, but by the tenth century it was generally accepted that the most convenient angle was one diagonal to the writing line. The scribe was able to write faster in this manner, and furthermore he was able to get more words on a line, which was a great consideration, as parchment was expensive even in those days.

However, the excessive angularity which crept into handwriting through extra speed and compression led to a degeneration of legibility, and in the eighth century the Holy Roman Emperor Charlemagne ordered a general reform of handwriting. This resulted in the development of an extremely legible and pleasant-looking script, which is now called Carolingian.

Handwriting and the Italian Renaissance

By the fifteenth century handwriting had again become over-compressed and angular, and Italian scholars translating the rediscovered classics were greatly impressed by the clear script in which they were written. This was the Carolingian hand, and stimulated yet another reform of handwriting. The clear, round script which resulted (Fig. 6) was in use in Italy at the time of the invention of printing, and consequently the early Italian printers modelled their types on it. Thus the fifteenth century Italian book-hand became the foundation of the "Roman" small-letters which have superseded all others for the printing of books.

Cursive Handwriting

The scripts so far discussed were those used for the writing of books, but there existed through the ages a less formal hand which was used for correspon-

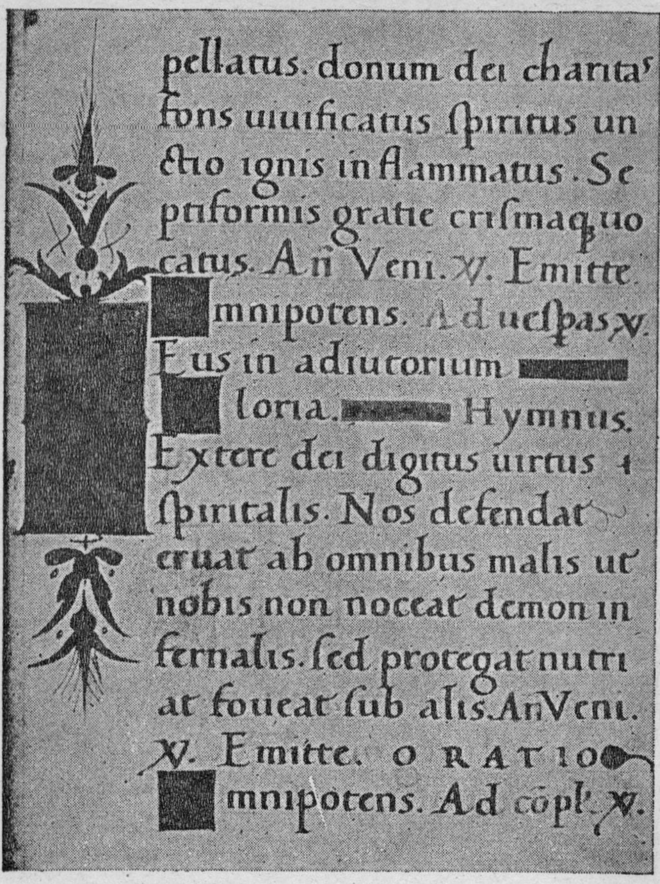
pellatus. donum dei charitas
fons uiuificatus spiritus un
ctio ignis inflammatus. Se
ptiformis gratie crismaque uo
catus. An Veni. ℣. Emitte.
mnipotens. Ad uespas ℣.
Eus in adiutorium
loria. Hymnus.
Extere dei digitus uirtus et
spiritalis. Nos defendat
eruat ab omnibus malis ut
nobis non noceat demon in
fernalis. sed protegat nutri
at foueat sub alis. An Veni.
℣. Emitte. ORATIO
mnipotens. Ad copl. ℣.

Fig. 6.—An Italian Renaissance Book-hand

dence and personal memoranda. In earlier days, when few but the scribes could write, these cursive scripts had little influence, but with the rebirth of learning in the fifteenth and sixteenth centuries, more and more people were becoming literate, international trade and affairs of state were growing in importance, and in consequence there arose a greater need and use for correspondence hands. The informal writing used in the Apostolic Chancery at the Vatican for the less-important correspondence was, at the latter end of the fifteenth century, a rapid version of the clear, round Roman book-hand. Written at speed with a slanted pen, it became more compressed, and the pen often ran on from letter to letter, forming ligatures. This expeditious hand was known as *Cancellaresca corsiva*, or Chancery cursive.

Owing to the international influence of the Vatican, the Chancery cursive became widely known, and influenced handwriting in many countries. In England this hand became known as Italic, because of its country of origin, and as there were diverse chancery scripts appertaining to many different royal chanceries throughout Christendom, it is convenient to call the Chancery cursive by that name today.

The Decline of Handwriting

In order to supply an increasing demand for writing instruction several of the Papal scribes produced handwriting manuals, the first of which, by a certain Arrighi, appeared in 1522. The diagrams for these manuals were engraved on wood blocks, and printed by the new process. The intervention of the engraver between the scribe and the pupil was

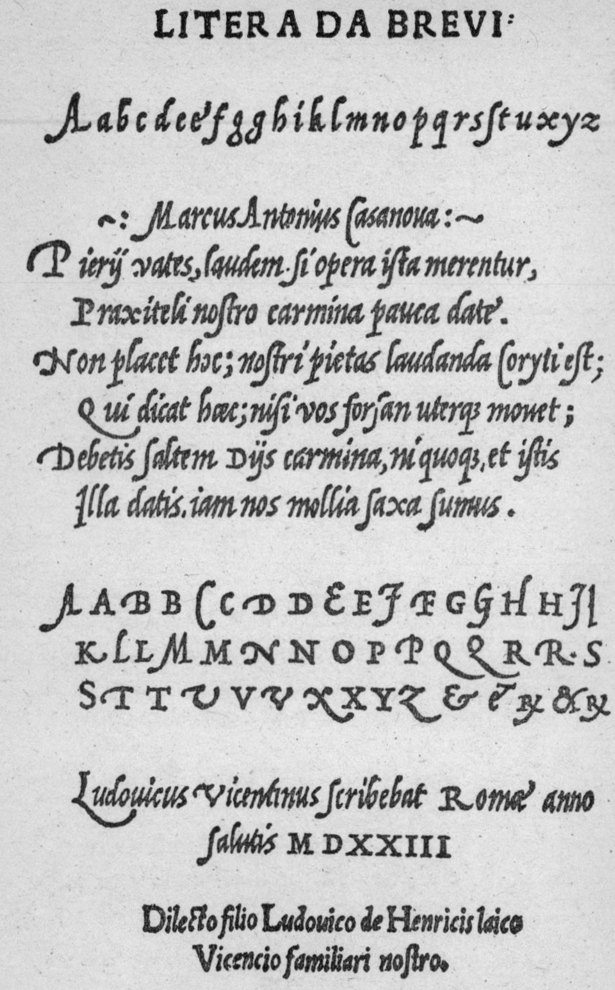

LITERA DA BREVI:

Aabcdeefgghiklmnopqrsſtuxyz

~: Marcus Antonius Casanoua :~

Pierij vates, laudem si opera ista merentur,
Praxiteli nostro carmina pauca date.
Non placet hoc; nostri pietas laudanda Coryti est;
Qui dicat hæc; nisi vos forsan uterq; mouet;
Debetis saltem Dijs carmina, ni quoq; et istis
Illa datis. iam nos mollia saxa sumus.

A A B B C C D D E E F F G G H H I I
K L L M M N N O P P Q Q R R S
S T T V V V X X Y Z & &

Ludouicus Vicentinus scribebat Romæ anno
salutis M D X X I I I

Dilecto filio Ludouico de Henricis laico
Vicencio familiari nostro.

Fig 7.—A Page from the Writing Manual of Arrighi
(1523)

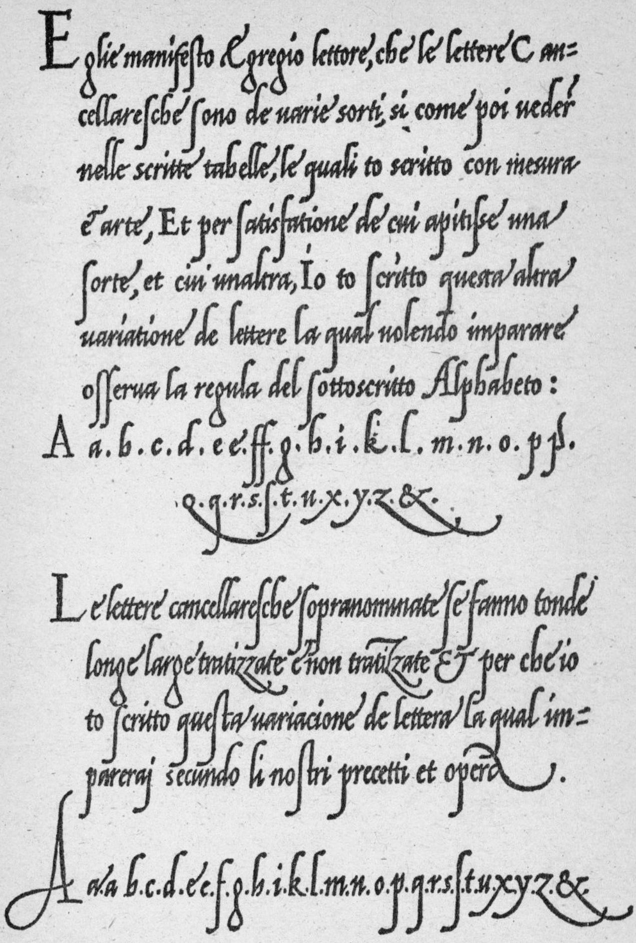

Fig. 8.—A page from the Writing Manual of Tagliente (16th cent.)

unfortunate, although highly-skilled wood engravers faithfully reproduced the pen-written scripts of the master (Figs. 7, 8, 9). Nevertheless, italic letter-forms were the product of the rightly-handled pen, and were therefore foreign to the graver.

As methods of printing progressed during the sixteenth century, the use of wood blocks was discontinued in favour of metal plates, which were more durable, and by 1600 handwriting manuals were being engraved on silver, which soon gave place to copper.

The method of printing from engraved metal plates was different from that used for wood blocks. With the latter, the cut-away areas printed white, only the raised portions holding the ink and making an impression on the paper. With the introduction of metal plates it was found more convenient to use the intaglio method of printing. This meant that the paper was printed from the ink retained in the incisions made on the plate, the surface of the plate being wiped clean after the inking. Now, by its nature metal is not conducive to large, wide cuts, and the intaglio method can only be used if the lines on the plate are reasonably fine, so no attempt was made to produce the kind of print shown in Fig. 9. This was made from an engraved wood block, the letters being cut away, leaving the surrounding area to print black.

When the copper engraver came to execute plates for a handwriting manual he was forced to modify the variations between the thick and thin strokes. The cuts in the metal were made with a sharp, lozenge-pointed steel tool called a burin, and the engraver could produce fine lines by lightly scoring the metal, and wider lines by pressing the burin deeper into it. The characteristic stroke of the burin was an anti-clockwise curving cut gradating from thin through thick to thin again, and in order to facilitate this the engraver pivoted his plate on a small sandbag, on which he revolved it whilst working. The intervention of the copper engraver's techniques in the reproduction of handwriting models turned writing away from the influence of the pen towards that of the burin.

Printing had resulted in the virtual disappearance of the scribe, and in his place flourished the writing master, who aimed to instruct all who wished to learn the art of handwriting. Competition was keen amongst these professionals, and their writing manuals were more often intended to dazzle their customers and confound their rivals than to set forth a rational hand. Many of the writing masters of the seventeenth and eighteenth centuries were master engravers, and the striking and flourishing which abounded in the pages of their manuals were more a demonstration of their skill with the burin than with the pen (Fig. 10).

The development of copper-plate writing models, produced by the varying pressures of the burin, led to the use of a sharp-pointed pen. The invention of the steel pen in the first half of the nineteenth century perpetuated this custom, and the rapid growth of industry and commerce at this time led to the publication of many utilitarian copper-plate copy-books.

The twentieth century has seen a great speeding-up of everyday life, and most people find that they have

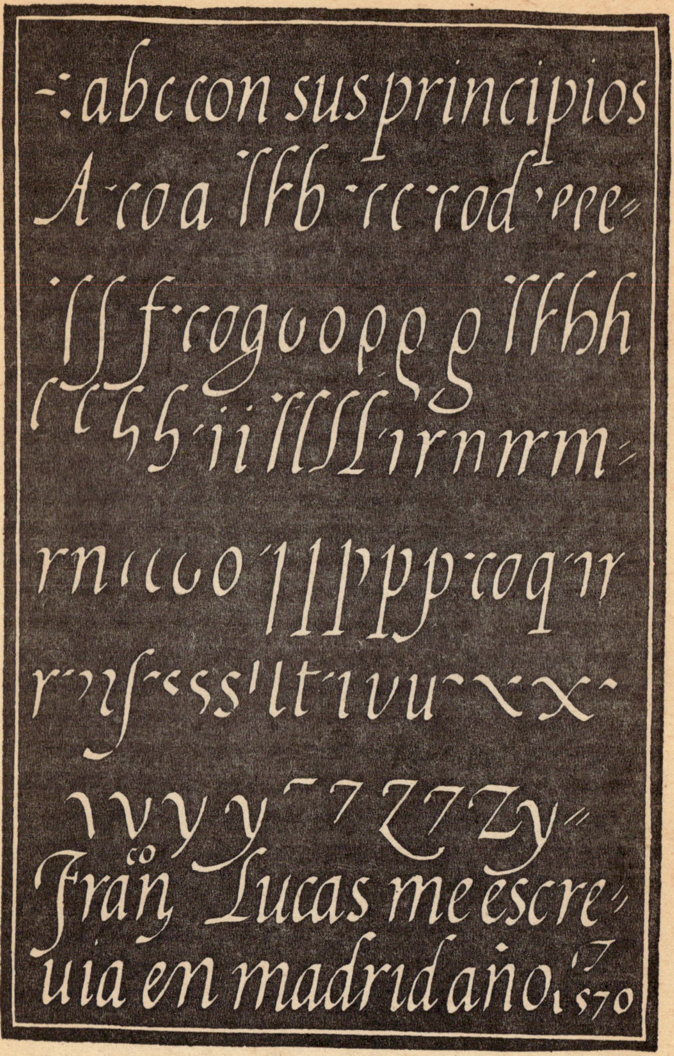

Fig. 9.—A page from the Writing Manual of Lucas (Spanish 1570)

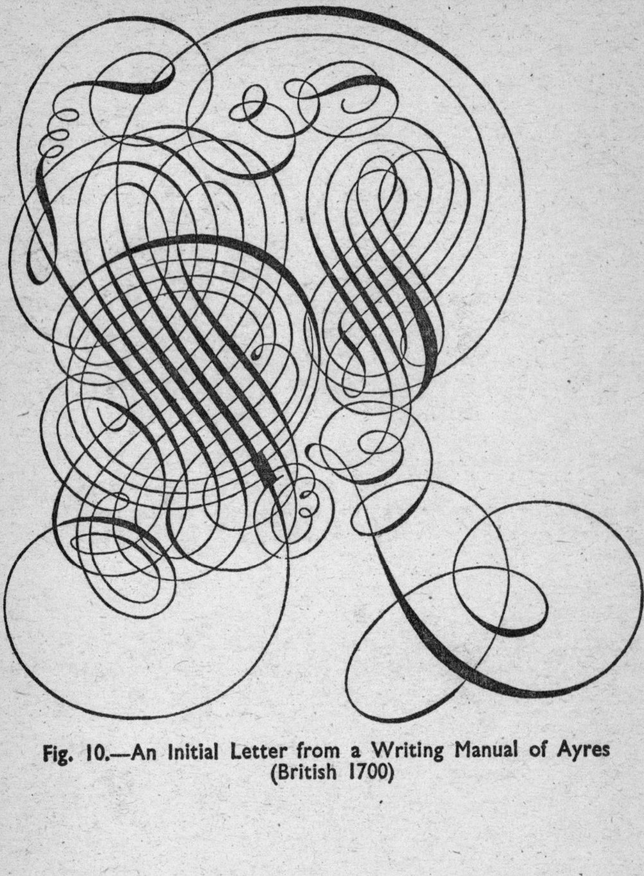

Fig. 10.—An Initial Letter from a Writing Manual of Ayres (British 1700)

I should say sincerity, a deep,
great; genuine sincerity, is the
first characteristic of all men in
any way heroic THOS CARLYLE

A:

I should say sincerity, a deep,
great, genuine sincerity, is the
first characteristic of all men
in any way heroic. T. CARLYLE.

B

Fig. 11.—Comparison between Shaded and Unshaded Writing

not the time to write slowly enough with a sharp-pointed pen to produce a clear, shaded, round hand. The result has been a change-over to fountain pens tipped with a blob of iridium, and to ball-point pens, which both produce a uniform stroke. A comparison will show that writing which is composed of strokes of varying thickness gains in character and readability (Fig. 11).

The modern problem is how to achieve an expeditious hand and at the same time retain this desirable quality of variety of stroke. It will be found that a good modern equivalent of the scribe's edged pen is the answer. There are on the market now a variety of steel and alloy nibs, and also fountain pens, which have been designed to meet this requirement. Details of these will be found in Chapter 3.

Things to do

1. In order to appreciate the principles of the square-cut pen it is worth making, if you can find the time, a simple home-made one which can be used for initial practice.

Take a length of dowel about as long as a pencil and make a half-inch saw cut across one end (Fig. 12). Then break up a wooden matchbox, and taking

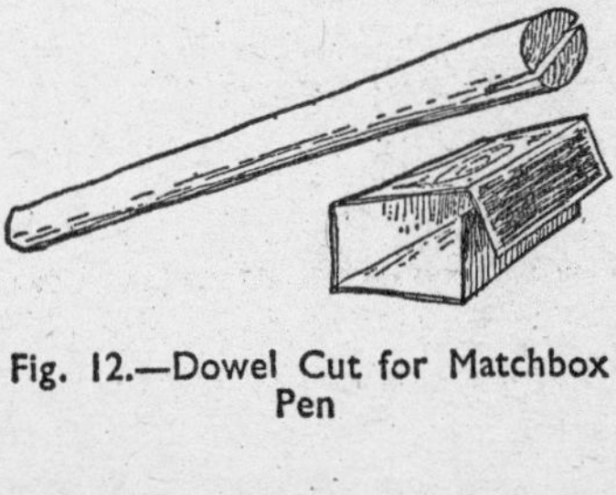

Fig. 12.—Dowel Cut for Matchbox Pen

a piece about half an inch wide from it, insert it into the saw-cut (Fig. 13). This piece of thin wood is the nib. Dip it in some writing ink, and then let it 'take a line for a walk' across a sheet of paper—

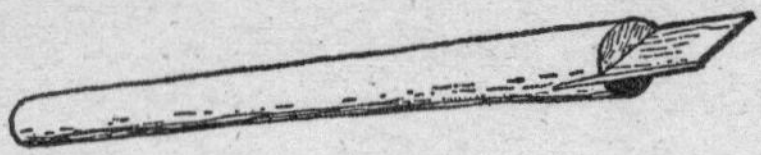

Fig. 13.—Matchbox Wood Inserted in Dowel

newspaper will do. This 'walk' needs to be a meandering one, exploring most parts of the paper. Make sure that all the time the pen is writing you are holding it at an angle of about forty-five degrees to the top edge of the paper. You should then find that the line you have drawn varies in width according to whether the pen was being pulled, pushed, or sidled. These variations of stroke, which the penman calls shading, are entirely independent of pressure. The pen should always be manipulated with the *least* pressure possible. Try another wandering line, this time not pressing on the pen at all. Allow the pen to 'skate' across the surface of the paper. It will soon be obvious that with a pen as wide as this small movements produce blobby, incoherent results. One factor that has to be considered in relation to the edged pen is the matter of *scale*. Use a wide pen for practice, in the initial stages, but a much narrower one for ordinary writing.

2. It is instructive to collect as many different examples of handwriting as possible. It is helpful when trying to be critical—in the best sense—to have some form of methodical examination. The

following questions applied to each piece of writing will help observation:

What sort of tool was used? (pointed, rounded, square, pencil, dip pen, fountain pen, ball pen, etc.).

How legible is the writing? (very, reasonable, poor, bad).

Are the letter-shapes well formed?

If not, have they deteriorated through speed, or is it just an immature hand?

Was it written at speed or not?

Is it an attractive hand?

If so, why?

If not, why?

Is it a truly cursive hand? (does the writing flow rhythmically).

3. For those interested in the historical development of handwriting there are several good books on the subject. These are listed at the end of this volume.

Chapter Three

WRITING TOOLS AND MATERIALS

ALTHOUGH the matchbox pen is an interesting experimental tool, it is obviously of no use for practical writing purposes. As was stated in the previous chapter, the instruction in this book is based on the use of an edged pen, and a number of suitable metal pens of this type are on the market. There are also a number of fountain pens which have been specifically designed for italic writing, some rather more expensive than others.

Before finally deciding on the most satisfactory nib it is as well to try as many different kinds as possible, but it is worth bearing in mind the old axiom that a bad workman blames his tools. The pen should not be held responsible for all the shortcomings of a piece of writing.

Most of the pens in the following list are made in a variety of widths, and although eventually a narrow pen may be preferred, it is most important to use a broad one for practice, until the making of the letter-shapes has been properly mastered.

Dip Pens

Wm. Mitchell's "Cursive"—a stiff steel pen made in a number of widths, suitable for practice.

Geo. Hughes' "Durador"—a gilt alloy pen made in one width only, suitable for normal writing.

Geo. Hughes' "Flight Commander"—a gilt alloy pen which can be obtained in Broad, Medium, and Fine widths.

Wm. Mitchell's "Italic"—a range of gold metal pens from very broad to fine, and with equivalents in each width for left-handed writers.

Geo. Hughes' "Violin"—a stiff steel pen useful for practice, in several widths.

Fountain Pens

Swan-Biro Ltd. "Calligraph".
"Calligraph Prefect".

Mentmore Pen Co. "Platignum Quick-Change" (Italic).

E. S. Perry Ltd. "Osmiroid 65" (Italic).

The last two have interchangeable nib-units, and the "Osmiroid" can be obtained in Medium or Fine, with equivalents for left-handed writers. There is a choice of nib-widths in the "Calligraph" range also. The prices quoted here are those ruling at the time of writing, and include purchase tax.

Ink

Any good writing ink is suitable, but for those who may prefer black the following are suggested:

Swan Old English Manuscript Ink—a jet-black ink intended for use in fountain pens.

Parker Quink Permanent Black—not so intensely black as the Swan ink, but flows more freely.

Stephens' Fountain Pen Black: Waterman's Midnight Black—neither of these are quite so black as the Quink.

It will be found that some writers like to use a

brown ink, such as Waterman's Aztec Brown; other manufacturers market a similar ink.

Paper

For practice, a smooth unglazed paper such as cream wove or bond are quite satisfactory. Good-quality typing paper can be very pleasant to use, and so can plain foolscap. If lined paper is preferable at first, use either ruled foolscap or a ruled guide such as is provided on some writing pads.

There is a considerable number of good note-papers available, some of which are much more expensive than others. The following are of particular interest:

Basildon Bond—a good inexpensive paper.

Spicer's Calligraphers' Paper—a pleasant paper, but rather more expensive.

Whatman Writing (11 lb.)—a quality paper which is very expensive.

Things To Do

1. *Pen Practice*

Start with a stiff nib such as the "Italic" or the "Violin", and have it broad. Make a zigzag line across the narrower width of the paper, as continuous as possible. It should not be built up stroke by stroke, but an effort should be made to keep the zigzags all the same height, and the same distance apart (Fig. 14). The pen should be held as before,

Fig. 14.—Zigzag Stroke showing Pen Position

so that the writing edge is always at an angle of forty-five degrees to the writing line.

However, left-handed writers will find that they produce the reverse result by doing this. It is essential that the up-stroke be thin, and the down-stroke thick, as the construction of the letters is based on this premise. The left-hander can produce the same strokes either by tilting the paper, or by using a reverse-oblique pen as shown in Fig. 15.

The zigzag line should be repeated until it can be written evenly and quickly.

Fig. 15.—Reverse-oblique Pen and its Angle of Writing

2. *Loosening-up Exercises*

Having mastered the zigzag, it would be as well to do some loosening-up exercises. Most adults who have years of writing habits behind them tend to press much too hard on the pen. This is probably due to early instruction with a flexible, pointed nib, but it is also partly attributable to nervous tension. It is most necessary to break this habit, as it hinders rhythm and fluency, as well as tiring the muscles of the hand.

Probably the easiest way to overcome this difficulty is to allow the pen to 'skate' across the paper in any direction, without attempting to produce any particular shapes. The pen should be allowed to glide over the paper in all directions, producing all sorts of curves, loops, and twists (Fig. 16). There are two rules for 'skating' which apply to writing generally:

1. Always hold the pen at an angle of 45° to the writing line.
2. *Never* press; hold the pen as lightly as possible.

That eminent calligrapher, Edward Johnston, advised his students to hold their pens so lightly when writing that they could be lifted from their fingers by another person, without any resistance. This is probably the counsel of perfection, but it is worth aiming at. Examine the fingers gripping the pen. Is the index finger sharply bent and strained? Is the thumb pressing the pen hard against the middle finger? If so, the grip should be relaxed. This may result in an apparent loss of control over the pen, but confidence is easily regained with practice.

3. *Writing Patterns*

Before starting on the alphabet, practise the writing patterns shown in Fig. 17, starting with number 2. All these patterns contain basic movements and rhythms which occur over and over again in writing, and it is important to master these at the outset. It should never be forgotten that writing consists always of *movement*. A printed shape on a page can be very misleading, unless it is borne in mind that it is made by a certain movement. This may seem like stressing the obvious, but it is surprising how often it is overlooked. If the movement is weak and unsatisfactory, so will be the writing.

Fig. 16.—Loosening-up Exercise

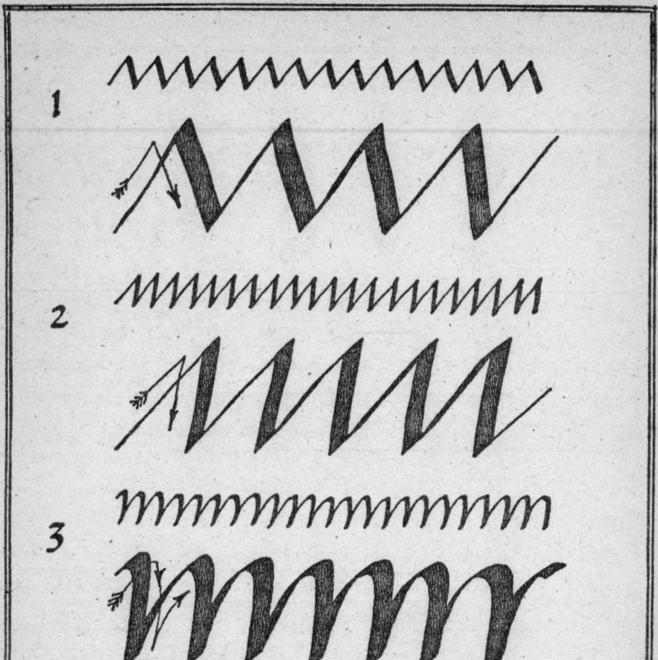

Fig. 17.—Writing Patterns

Time for Practice

The elementary exercises mentioned above may seem rather tedious and time-wasting, but it is absolutely essential to commence with a fluent rhythmic pen-action, otherwise the writing will be stilted and disjointed, and difficult to write quickly. Some of the mechanical exercises can be done at odd times, as a form of doodle; when the radio is on, or when someone is talking. A certain high-ranking Civil Servant has admitted doing this at departmental conferences. Nevertheless, it would be wrong to regard all handwriting practice in this casual manner. When practising actual writing, odd scribbles here and there can do more harm than good.

Chapter Four

THE ALPHABET

THE alphabet displayed on the following pages is based on that used by the Vatican scribes in the fifteenth and sixteenth centuries, the Chancery cursive or Italic. Apart from the fact that it is written with an edged pen, it is distinguished by a complete absence of loops. Contrary to common opinion, loops do not necessarily give greater speed in writing. In many cases the pen has to travel further in order to make the loop (Fig. 18). Although

Fig. 18.—Looped Word compared with Unlooped Word

there is a complete absence of loops in the pure exemplar, it will probably be found that when a speedy hand has been acquired occasional loops will occur, but they are not part of the letter-shape, and should not be thought of as such. In speedy writing the pen often slurs from one word to the next, but such links are not looked upon as belonging to the letter-forms.

It is most important that the illustrations of personal correspondence hands at the end of this volume should not be used as models for other writers. They merely illustrate what can be achieved and show the influence of their writers' personalities, as do all hands as they mature. Character in handwriting cannot be taught; it is something which develops naturally in unselfconscious writing. The primary aim must be to acquire a legible, speedy, and comely hand, and it is necessary to accept the hard fact that in the initial stages of learning the writing will appear rather formal and characterless. Perseverance will develop self-confidence, and in due course the writing will become characteristic of the writer.

Practising the Alphabet

It was stressed in the last chapter that writing is movement, and the alphabet diagrams should be examined with that firmly in mind. Furthermore, they attempt to illustrate the result of swift movement, so that when the letter-shapes are practised they should not only be written accurately, but also as quickly as possible. As with the patterns, it is important to make the movement in the right direction, starting in the right place and finishing in the right place. Economy of movement is essential to the development of a swift hand.

Small-letters

Concentrate on the small-letters first, as these are the ones that are most used. After looking carefully at the large central letter, and noting its shape and general characteristics, turn your attention to the analysis along the top. The first shape shows the complete letter, and then the remaining diagrams on that line demonstrate the sequence of the movement of the pen. All the letters are made in a continuous stroke with the exception of *d e f p t x*. It may seem perverse to make *e* in two strokes instead of one, but it does ensure that the letter retains its elliptical shape. The looped *e* is very apt to deteriorate at speed. Once the two-stroke letter has been learnt it will be found that it is no impediment to speed.

Included in the lower part of the diagram you will find in many cases some variants of the basic letter-shapes. When the latter are really mastered it may be desired to consider the alternatives. On the whole it is as well to be consistent, not using differing forms of the same letter in the same piece of writing. This applies most particularly to ascenders and descenders.

Capitals

Finally, in the diagram relating to each letter there appears two kinds of capital letter. The first is the straightforward Roman capital without serifs, and the second is what is known as a swash letter. The Roman form is so plain that it is despised by many beginners, but in handwriting, beauty, and certainly legibility, lies in simplicity. The quality of the Roman form lies in its proportions: the relationship of height and width. This alphabet is based on the square and the circle, which, of course, are as wide as they are high. In order to indicate how much the individual letters deviate from the full square a second letter is shown contained in a square. The comparison should not be taken as mathematically correct; they are intended just as a guide to the proportion of the letter.

Apart from this question of proportion, one of the greatest weaknesses in the writing of capitals is disjointedness. Unlike the small-letters, many capitals are constructed with more than one stroke of the pen, and unless these strokes fit together an untidy, unsatisfactory letter results.

The swash letters are not related to the circle so much as to the ellipse, being compressed shapes like the small-letters. The failing to avoid at all costs when using this type of capital is that of making them *too* swash. Whatever historical and contemporary hands are admired, flourishes should be avoided like the plague. Such evasive action will probably result in only a mild infection. It should be pointed out that swash letters are unsuitable for writing whole words and phrases (Fig. 19). If used, they are better reserved for initial letters only.

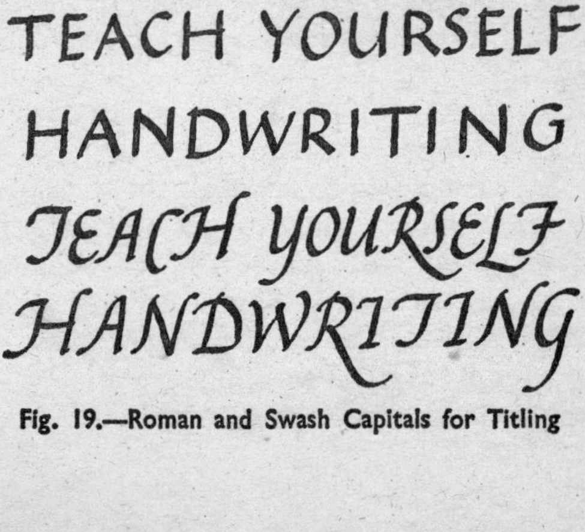

Fig. 19.—Roman and Swash Capitals for Titling

General Characteristics of the Small-letter Shapes

Before starting to practise these letter-shapes it is important to observe the elliptical forward-leaning character wherein lies their cursive quality. Remember, these letters became so shaped through the swift writing of *round* letters, which indicates that there is an important relationship between shape and speed. It may be helpful to realise that practically all the small-letters should fill an imaginary upright oblong (Fig. 20).

Fig. 20.—Upright Oblong

As soon as the essential shapes of the letters have been thoroughly grasped it should be possible to go on to the following chapter. If any difficulty is experienced in reproducing any of the letter-shapes, it may be helpful to trace the letter several times, remembering to make the correct movement.

Notes on the Use of the Alphabet Diagrams

The large letter-shape is the one which should be followed in the initial stages. It is important to be able to write a standard alphabet well, before experimenting with alternative letter forms. Some of these are indicated at the bottom of the diagram, adjacent to a capital letter to show comparative heights. Where there are no alternatives the standard form has been repeated in order to demonstrate this comparison. A study of the exemplar alphabets of various sixteenth and twentieth century writing masters shows that in certain circumstances the use of a particular letter form is a matter of personal preference, and is to a certain extent an expression of differing personalities.

There is a diversity of swash capitals, some more exuberant than others. Exuberant character will out in handwriting, but the quality of restraint is one to be cultivated assiduously. The swash letters portrayed in the following diagrams are those which, in the author's view, are the more restrained. Like the Roman capitals, they are only a little taller than the small-letters.

It should be observed that the small-letters and the swash capitals are not truly vertical, but have a slight inclination to the right. This is due to the influence of the rightly-handled pen, and is conducive to speed and legibility, but should not be overdone. In the commentaries which accompany the diagrams the word "vertical" should be taken to mean this slightly-inclined upright.

For comparison and easy reference the complete alphabet is shown in Fig. 47, together with punctuation marks and numerals.

A

This letter commences with a push of the pen to thc left. Continuing the movement, the pen is pulled round and down into a vertical stroke, which turns to the right as it reaches the base of the letter, and continues upwards in a curving diagonal stroke. This should meet the commencement of the letter at the top, and then continue directly downwards in a straight movement. It is important to ensure that this down-stroke does not curve outwards as it descends. It should be straight until it reaches the base, and is then terminated with an oblique sliding movement of the pen, upwards to the right. This is the beginning of the linking stroke (ligature) when joining on to the next letter.

It should be understood that this letter is made in one movement, and the pen should be kept at a constant angle to the writing line.

The capital letters are not so cursive as the small-letters, the plain Roman A being constructed in two strokes: first the legs as a zigzag, and then the cross-stroke. There should be an equal area of space in the two interior parts which are divided by the bar.

The swash capital is made in three strokes: first the left-hand one, commencing with a pushed stroke to the left at the top, to which is added the vertical stroke in a downward movement, ending in the characteristic oblique slide of the pen as a terminal. The letter is completed with the horizontal bar from left to right.

Fig. 21

B

The letter commences with a leftwards push of the pen to initiate the long downstroke, so that the top is to all intents and purposes horizontal. The change of direction from this first stroke is by means of a curve, rather than a sharp angular movement. When the pen reaches the base of the stem it immediately branches upwards and outwards to the right. It should be carefully noted that this branching movement is in the form of a slight curve, and not a straight line. The correct shape of the body of the letter is completely dependent on this branching out being performed correctly. When the pen rises to the top of this branching stroke it is pulled round to make a *narrow* arch. The point to watch here is that the arch does not become sharply pointed, which leads to loss of legibility and an ugly letter. After making the arch the pen should be pulled downwards in a fairly vertical direction, so that this second downstroke is parallel with the first. The downward movement of the pen is continued until near the base, and then changes by way of a curve to the left, into a horizontal leftwards push identical with that which commenced the letter. It should be ensured that this final stroke joins the base of the stem, as nothing makes writing appear more untidy than gaps left in the construction of the letters.

The Roman capital is made in two strokes: first the straight stem, and then the two curves, starting at the top. The swash letter is also made in two strokes, the first finishing with a pull to the right, and the second striking out from the top and eventually meeting the foot of the stem.

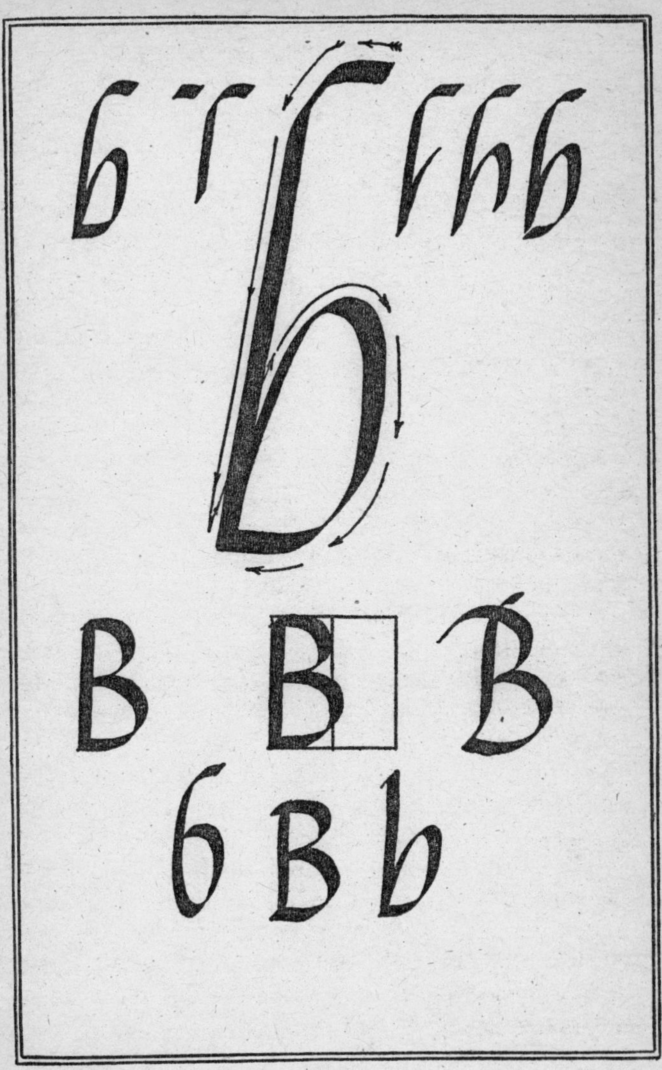

Fig. 22

There are two alternatives to the small-letter just described. The first of these is considered more cursive by some writers, as it is made by a less complex movement. There is a certain danger of the body becoming too circular, or conversely, too narrow. The second alternative differs only in that it has a hook serif instead of the pushed one. In the sixteenth century this form was used for a more formal writing, known in the Apostolic Chancery as *cancellaresca formata*. The hook serif commences with a slight slide of the pen in an upwards diagonal direction, changing almost immediately into a downwards vertical pull. These serifs are unpleasing if exaggerated.

C

The letter *c* begins with the same horizontal right-to-left stroke as the previous letters. This continues in exactly the same movement as that used to make *a*, but it will be noticed that it terminates at the commencement of the upward diagonal stroke. The characteristics of this letter are the fairly flat top surmounting a wide curve, contrasting with the narrow curve at the base. This second curve is really the inverse of the arch in the letter *b*, and likewise must not be allowed to become sharp and pointed. The top of the letter will be seen to be slightly in advance of the base.

The Roman capital is quite circular, whereas the swash letter is elliptical. It will be found that legibility is assisted if the base of the latter is brought slightly below the line.

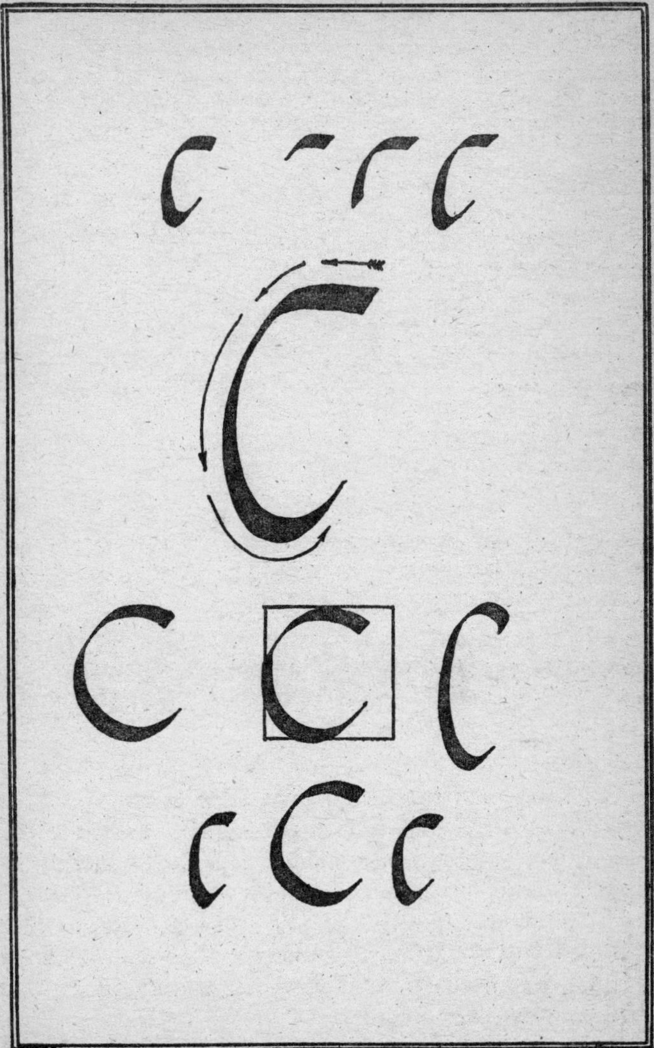

Fig. 23

D

The construction of this letter is similar to that of *a*. It starts with a leftwards horizontal push of the pen, which then slides round into a downwards vertical stroke, changing direction again at the base and turning upwards in a curving oblique slide to meet the commencing stroke. When the body is made thus, the stem is added. This also commences with a leftwards horizontal pushed stroke which slides round into a vertical downwards stroke, ending with a slight oblique slide of the pen to make the terminal serif. It is important to make sure that the downstroke of the stem is kept straight, and that the serif at the foot does not become a curved hook.

An alternative small-letter is shown at the bottom right of the diagram which has the advantage of being made in one stroke, but it is rather difficult to produce satisfactorily at first. It should be noted that the body is similar to *o*, and that the right-hand upwards stroke is already left of vertical before it sweeps round to make the stem. This is a very useful letter, but should not be made with too much abandon.

The Roman capital is wider than many suppose, and should be made in two strokes, the straight stem first, and then the curve made in a clockwise direction. The two strokes should join at top and bottom. In the swash letter the stem terminates as in *B* with a pull to the right. The curve is then made in a clockwise direction, and should join the foot of the stem.

Fig. 24

E

The fact that this letter is made in two strokes may appear rather strange, but it will be found in practice that it is very difficult to make a looped *e* which remains elliptical at speed. As it is the letter which recurs most frequently, this is a matter of some importance to the appearance of the page of writing.

The first stroke commences at the top with a leftwards and downwards slide of the pen which almost immediately becomes a pulled vertical stroke until it curves sharply upwards at the base. It is important to keep this bottom curve narrow. When this first stroke is completed the pen is lifted just clear of the paper and taken to the top of the letter, where a convex curve is pulled downwards to the left. This should join on to the rest of the letter.

Although the looped *e* has the disadvantage pointed out above, some writers use it satisfactorily. Care should be taken to produce the same elliptical shape that the standard letter has. The Greek letter shown at the bottom right of the diagram is favoured by certain people, but should be used with circumspection, as its unfamiliarity is not an aid to legibility, and it can suggest affectation.

The capital letter is made in the usual way, but it should be observed that the three arms are the same length. Make sure that all the strokes meet. The stem of the swash letter is made in the same manner as that of *B* and *D*, except that the foot is extended further to make the bottom arm. The Greek *E* has the advantage of being made in one stroke, commencing at the top.

Fig. 25

F

Although *f* has a simple shape it is one of the most difficult letters to make satisfactorily because of its long straight stem. This commences at the top with that characteristic leftwards horizontal push, which slides round into a vertical downwards pull that continues down below the writing line. It terminates with another leftwards push of the pen equal in length to that at the top. It is important to avoid the tendency to make a weak elongated *S* shaped letter, which quickly happens if the stem is started and finished with a thin oblique slide instead of the horizontal push. When the stem is completed the pen is slightly lifted to make the cross-stroke from left to right through the stem, level with the tops of the normal small-letters. This is illustrated at the bottom right of the diagram. An alternative is shown at bottom left, where it will be seen that the stem is not carried very far below the writing line, and finishes with a hook serif instead of a pushed one. This form is sometimes useful for the second of two *f*'s together, where there is a danger of the descenders becoming entangled.

The construction of the Roman capital is very similar to that of the *E*, as is also that of the swash letter shown at the bottom of the diagram. The alternative swash *F* has a downstroke similar to that of the *A*, and is a continuation of the stroke commenced horizontally at the top.

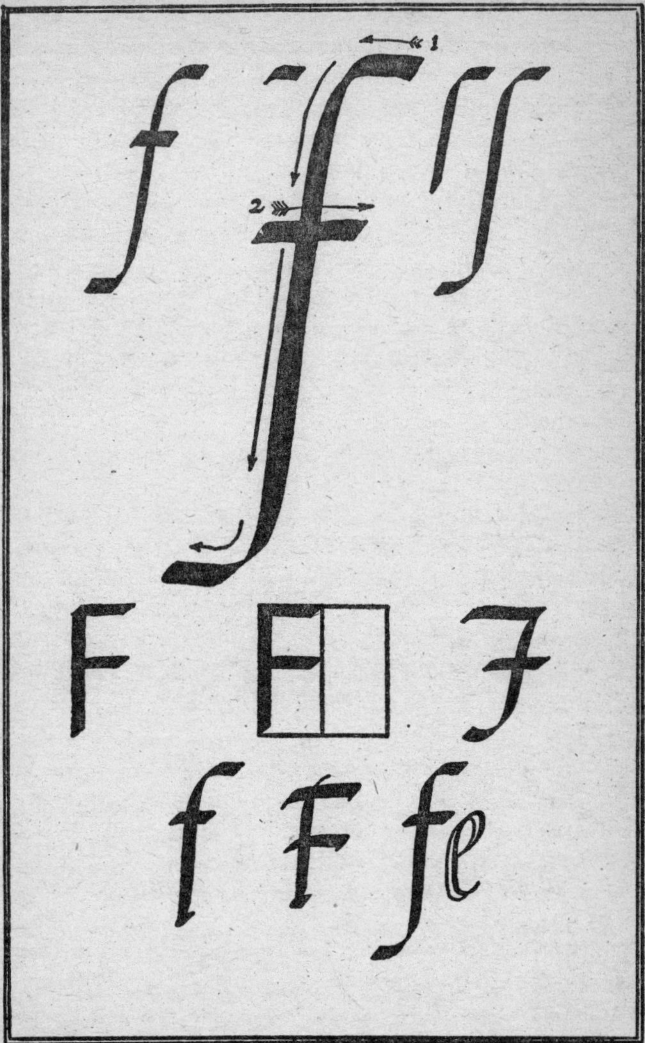

Fig. 26

G

The body of *g* is identical with that of *a*, and is constructed in the same manner, except that the downstroke which forms the stem is continued below the writing line, and turns leftwards in the same way as the tail of the *f*. An alternative form is shown at the bottom left of the diagram, where it will be seen that the tail is continued round until the pen begins to make its thinnest stroke. It does not loop through the stem, however. The important thing here is to keep this curve round. The other alternative illustrated is more difficult to write satisfactorily, and has to be made in two strokes. The body has the same shape as *o*.

The round part of the Roman capital is circular, and is done first, the straight downstroke being added. Too long a head to this downstroke should be avoided. The swash *G* is made in one stroke commencing with the familiar anti-clockwise pushed stroke at the top, and finishing with a similar movement.

H

This letter commences in the same way as *b*, but after the arch has been turned the downstroke is vertical, and finishes with a hook serif, as in the case of *a* and *d*. It is most important to ensure that the arch is curved and not pointed, and a safeguard here is to make the downstroke from the arch *slightly* convex. If it becomes concave it is impossible to maintain the curve at the top of the arch. This is a tendency to be carefully avoided in the initial stages in order to prevent it becoming a habit.

The Roman capital should be carefully constructed

Fig. 27

so that the three strokes are joined. The swash letter commences with a lead-in made with a horizontal pull of the pen to the right, which then turns sharply to make the downstroke, which is not so curved as that of *F*. The second downstroke starts with the pushed serif, and continues straight, like the stem of the *d*. It is a little taller than the first stroke. The bar is made last, and should be horizontal, not oblique. At the bottom of the diagram another alternative is shown which is very similar to the Roman capital, except that the downstrokes commence with a horizontal pull, and the pen is pushed back over its own tracks slightly before continuing the downward movement. The feet of the strokes terminate in the same way.

I

This letter starts with a slight upwards oblique slide of the pen, which then pulls straight down to make the vertical stroke. The foot is formed by a narrow curve, and is not the same as the top. Finally, the dot is placed over the letter, just clear of the top, and consists of a short diagonal pull of the pen. An alternative dot is shown at the bottom left, and is made with a diagonal upwards slide, barely longer than the width of the pen.

The straight Roman capital is rather unsatisfactory, and is better made with an oblique lead-in like the small-letter. It also finishes with a hook serif. The swash letter commences in the same way as the first stroke of the swash *H*, and finishes with the horizontal pull which occurs in some of the previous letters. An alternative capital can be made

Fig.28

in the same manner as the downstroke of the last H mentioned on the preceding page, and is illustrated here at the foot of the diagram.

J

The small-letter commences in the same way as *i*, but on reaching the writing line the downstroke is carried below it, and finishes in the same manner as the tail of the *f*. Alternatively, the descender can finish at the point when the pen, turning to the left, makes its thinnest stroke. As with *i*, the dot is placed immediately above the top of the letter.

The Roman capital is simple to make, and may commence with the hook serif. The swash letter starts in the same way as *I*, but the tail, which is similar to that of the small-letter, is carried a little below the writing line.

K

This letter starts in exactly the same way as *h*, but once the arch has been turned the pen is taken in to the stem, and then pulled out again in a straight diagonal downward stroke to make the leg. It should be noted that this terminates a little beyond the loop above. An alternative can be made in two strokes, as shown at the bottom left of the diagram, but this is not to be recommended, as the thin diagonal stroke of the second part looks very weak in normal writing.

The Roman capital is made with two strokes, and

Fig. 29

Fig. 30

Fig. 31

it should be observed that the point of the second stroke meets the stem. With this letter the pen should be turned slightly when making the thin diagonal so that it is thickened somewhat, otherwise the same criticism will apply as in the case of the similar small-letter. The swash *K* commences in the same way as the *H*, and it should be noted that the second stroke begins with a pull downwards before it curves to the left.

L

This letter is deceptively simple to make, and begins in the same way as *f*. It is essential to ensure that the downstroke is kept straight, terminating in a narrow curve. If the letter finishes with a hook serif it is inclined to look top-heavy.

The Roman capital is easily made in one stroke, and the swash letter likewise. The latter commences with the push to the left and is then continued downwards, turning slightly to the left near the bottom, and then pulling horizontally across to the right. The base of this letter is sometimes carried a little below the writing line in order to avoid an unequal space between it and the following small-letter.

M

Commence *m* in the same way as *i*, but when the pen reaches the base of the downstroke, spring out an arch, as with *h*. The second arch springs from the base of the first one in the same manner. The letter

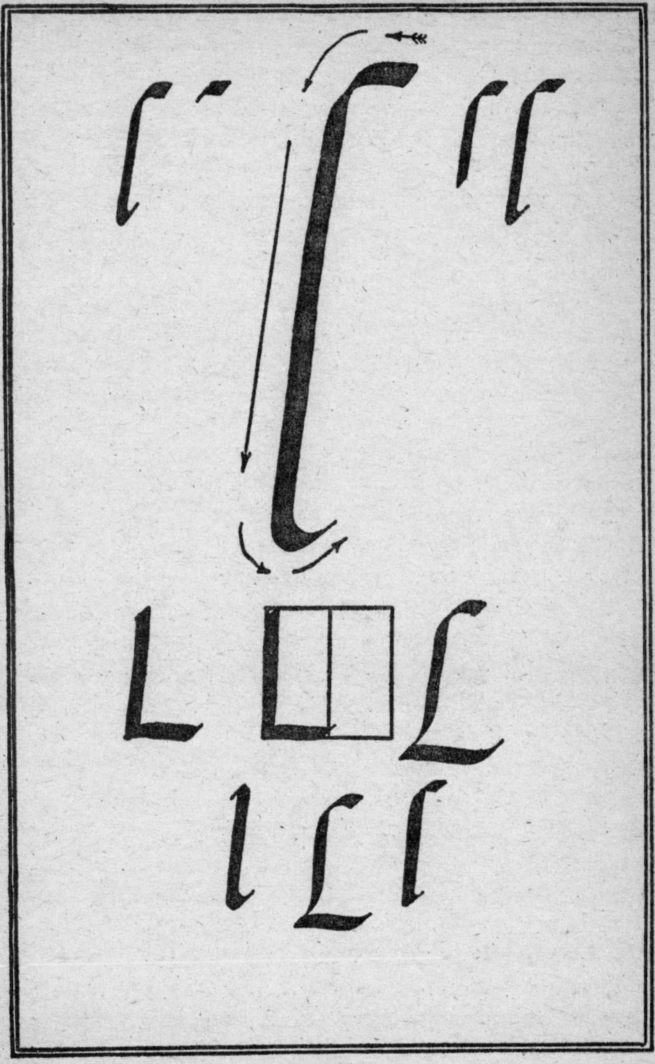

Fig. 32

finishes with a hook serif. It is important to keep the downstrokes straight and parallel, and there should be equal spaces inside the two arches.

The Roman capital is a little wider than it is high, and is a simple zigzag. Note carefully that the middle point comes down to the writing line. The swash letter can commence in the same way as *K*, or the horizontal lead-in can be dispensed with. The rest of the letter is a zigzag terminating in a hook serif.

N

This letter is too similar in construction to *m* to need much description. As with the preceding letter, it is important to keep the downstrokes parallel, and the arch rounded.

The Roman capital is best made in two strokes, the first downstroke being made separately from the rest. Here again it is necessary to keep the verticals parallel. The swash letter can commence in the manner of *M*, and is made in three strokes, the last one starting at the top with a leftwards push. As in the *H*, this final stroke can be made slightly taller than the rest of the letter. An alternative is shown at the bottom of the diagram. Its construction is obvious, but it needs great care to produce a satisfactory letter.

O

It is important to realise that *o* is not a circular letter. The elliptical letter can be made in two ways.

Fig. 33

Fig. 34

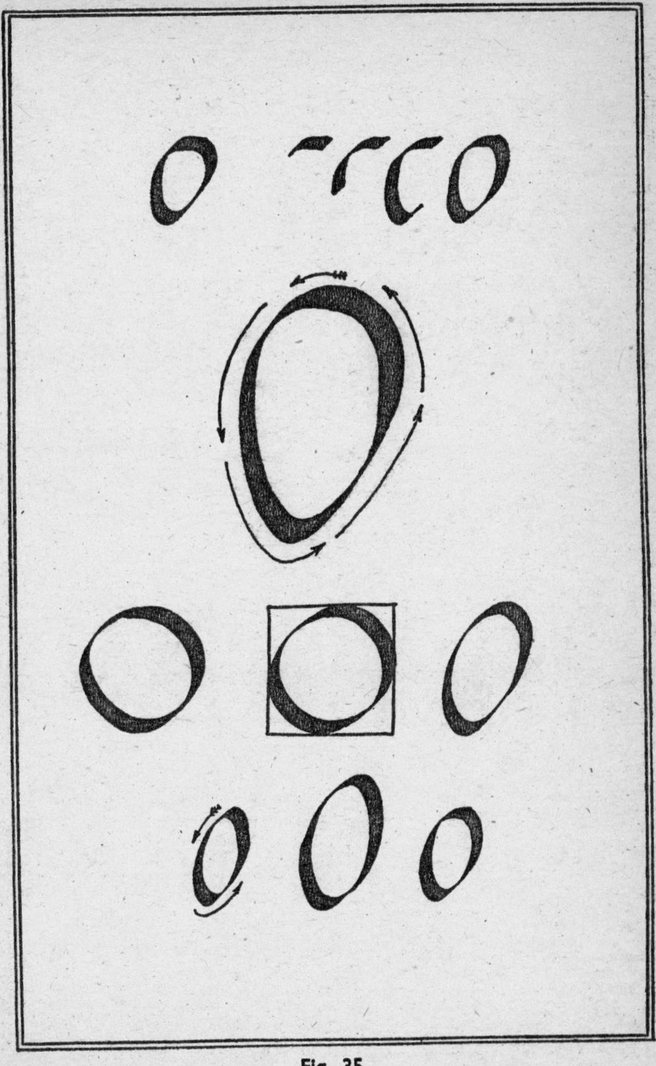

Fig. 35

Firstly, it can commence in the same manner as *c*, but with a final upward stroke which pushes to the left to meet the beginning, or it can start in the same way that *e* does, with a thin stroke moving anti-clockwise. The latter movement will probably be found easier to accomplish than the former. In either case, however, it is most important to avoid a sharp point at the base of the letter.

The Roman capital is, unlike the small-letter, a circle, but the swash letter is elliptical, and made in the same way as the small letter, but taller.

P

This letter is made in two strokes, the first commencing with a hook serif, as in the case of *i* and *j*. The stem is made in the same manner as *j*, after which the pen is lifted and carried to a point a little below the top. Commencing on the stem, the second stroke branches out in a curving upward diagonal movement, turning at the top to make an arch. From this point the bowl of the *p* resembles that of *b*, finishing with a pushed stroke to the left which meets the stem on the writing line. Two alternative tail finishings are shown at the bottom of the diagram.

The Roman capital is made in two strokes, beginning with the straight stem. The curved stroke which follows should not be made too shallow, and should meet the stem at top and bottom. The swash letter begins with the stem, which is made in the same way as the first stroke of *M*. Alternatively, it can be made to terminate with a horizontal foot,

Fig. 36

as does *I*. The second stroke starts in advance of the stem and cuts through it, pushing in to meet it at the finish.

Q

The letter *q* is made in exactly the same way as *g*, except that the descender does not turn to the left, but finishes with a hook serif. As an alternative it can terminate with a horizontal pull. Another form of *q* is that shown at the bottom right of the diagram. This letter consists of an *o* with the tail added separately. Avoid over-flourishing this tail.

The Roman capital is a circle with a tail added, whereas the swash letter is an ellipse with the descender added.

R

This letter has the same construction as *n*, except that it is terminated immediately after the arch has been turned, just as the pen begins to pull its broadest stroke. It is important to make this slight pull at the end or the letter becomes very weak in appearance. Some writers prefer to turn the finishing stroke up slightly, as shown at the bottom left of the diagram, but this tendency should not become exaggerated. The butcher's-hook variation illustrated at the bottom right was a modification used by certain Vatican scribes during the sixteenth century. It has the advantage of being more cursive than the standard form, but its legibility is uncertain in present-day usage.

Fig. 37

The Roman capital is made in the same way as P, but the leg is pulled out diagonally from the base of the bowl. It is better if this final stroke is convex rather than concave. The swash letter also closely resembles the *P*, and the leg can be brought slightly below the writing line.

S

The *s* starts with a pushed anti-clockwise horizontal stroke which turns into a pulled diagonal which runs straight until it turns to make the final pushed stroke. This letter should not bulge in the middle.

The Roman capital is made in a very similar fashion, except that there is slightly more curve at top and bottom. The swash letter is made in exactly the same way as the small-letter, only taller.

T

This is not a tall letter, and should commence just above the level of the normal small-letters. The first stroke is like that of *i*, and the second is pulled across horizontally, level with the tops of the other letters. This point is illustrated at the bottom right of the diagram. When a word finishes with a *t* it is sometimes permissible to slightly flourish the cross-stroke, but discretion should be exercised.

The Roman capital has a wider top than is often supposed, and the two strokes should meet. The swash letter shown at the bottom is made in one stroke, in the manner of the first stroke of *F*.

Fig. 38

Fig. 39

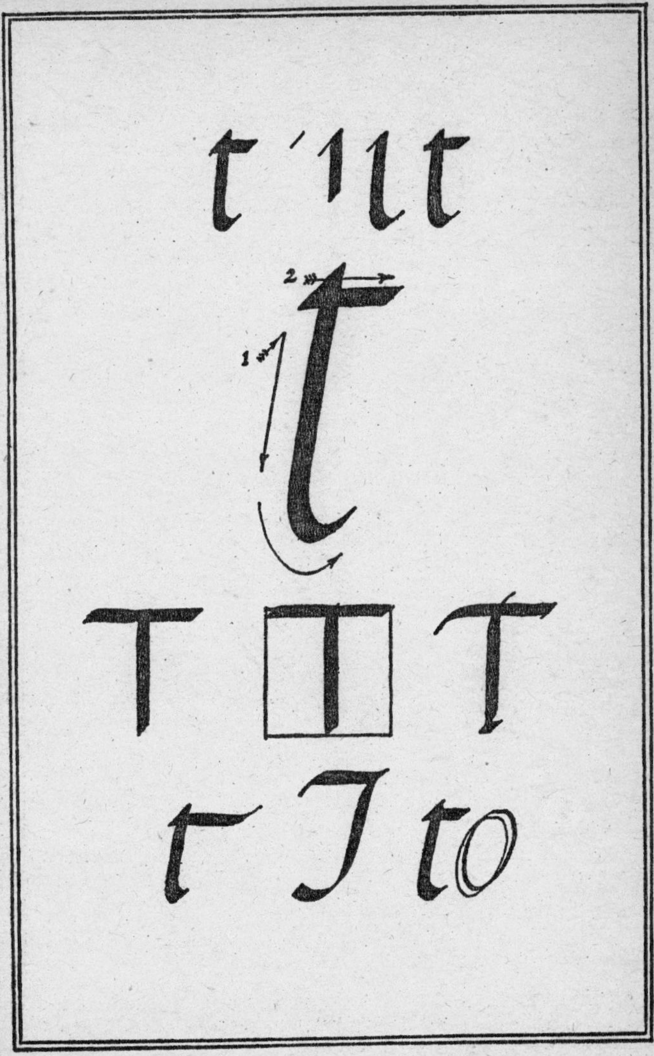

Fig. 40

U

This letter commences in the same way as *i*, and after the narrow curve at the base, continues upwards diagonally to the top, from whence the final stroke is pulled down vertically, ending with a hook serif. It is important to keep the downstrokes straight and parallel, and the curve at the bottom should not become pointed.

The Roman capital is made in a similar manner, but is rounder. The swash letter is identical with the small-letter, only taller.

V

This letter starts with a slight slide of the pen and then pulls downwards diagonally. At the bottom it turns sharply upwards with a sliding diagonal stroke, which turns slightly to the left as it nears the top, so that the letter terminates on a pushed stroke. The alternative shown has a narrow curve at the base. If the pushed terminal is neglected the letter becomes weak and less legible.

The Roman capital is a simple zigzag, but the second side should not be too thin. The swash *V* is a taller version of the small-letter.

W

The letter *w* is constructed in a similar way to the preceding letter, and it should be noted that the centre point comes up to the top of the letter. An alternative is shown with narrow curves at the base instead of sharp angles. Again the final pushed stroke is essential.

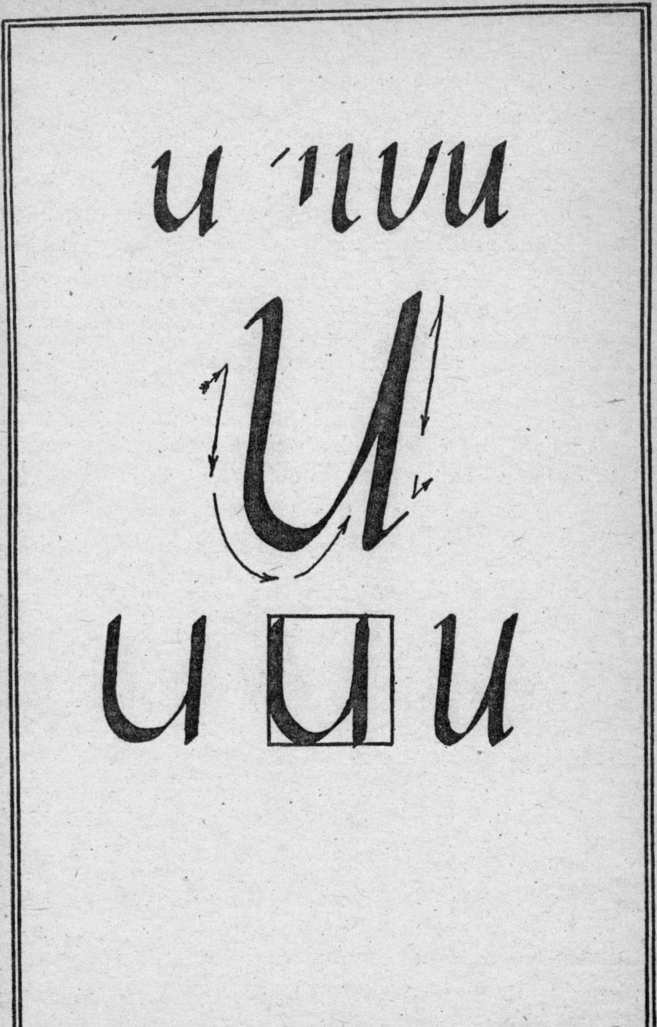

Fig. 41

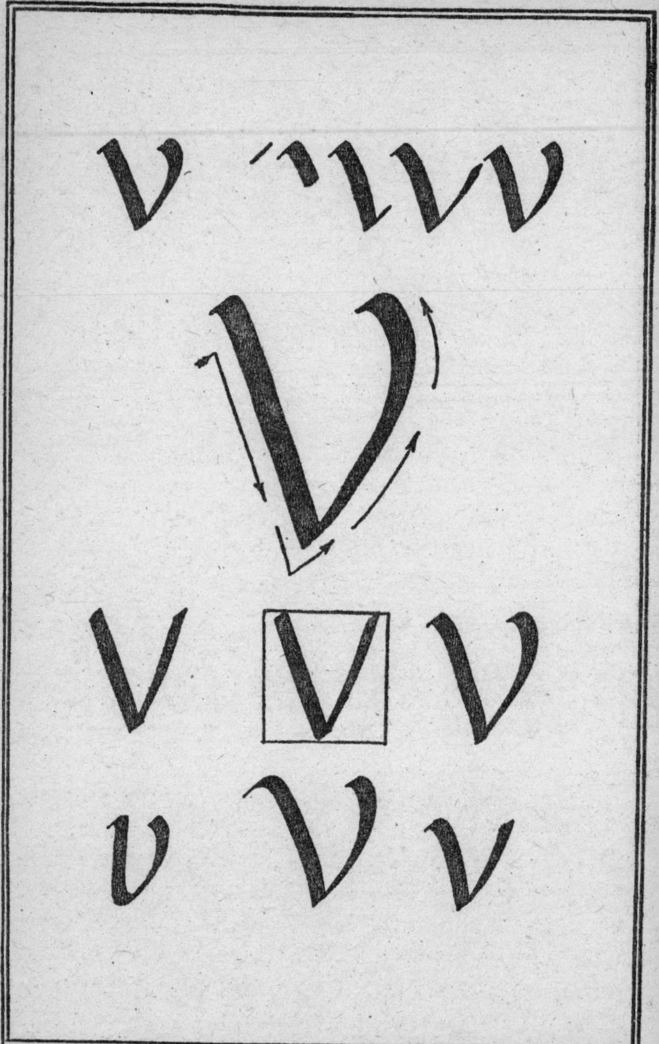

Fig. 42

Fig. 43

The Roman capital, like the M, is wider than it is high, and is a zigzag with the centre point reaching the top. The swash letter shown is the same as the small-letter, but taller.

X

This letter starts with a slight upward oblique slide which is quickly pulled into a diagonal downward stroke, finishing with another slight slide upwards. It is important to keep this stroke straight in the middle. The second stroke starts with a horizontal pull to the right at the bottom, and turns into a thin diagonal slide to the top, where it turns again to the right. Alternatively, this second stroke can commence at the top and slide downwards to the left. In this manner it is possible to flourish the tail below the writing line, as shown at the bottom left of the diagram.

The Roman capital is a simple diagonal cross, with a slight thickening of the thin stroke. The swash letter is a taller version of the small-letter.

Y

The letter *y* has the same construction as *u* until the second downstroke reaches the line, where it continues below and terminates with the characteristic push to the left. As an alternative, the first part of the letter can be pointed at the bottom like the *v*. A more formal letter can be made in two strokes, as shown at the bottom right of the diagram. This is a more difficult letter to write satisfactorily.

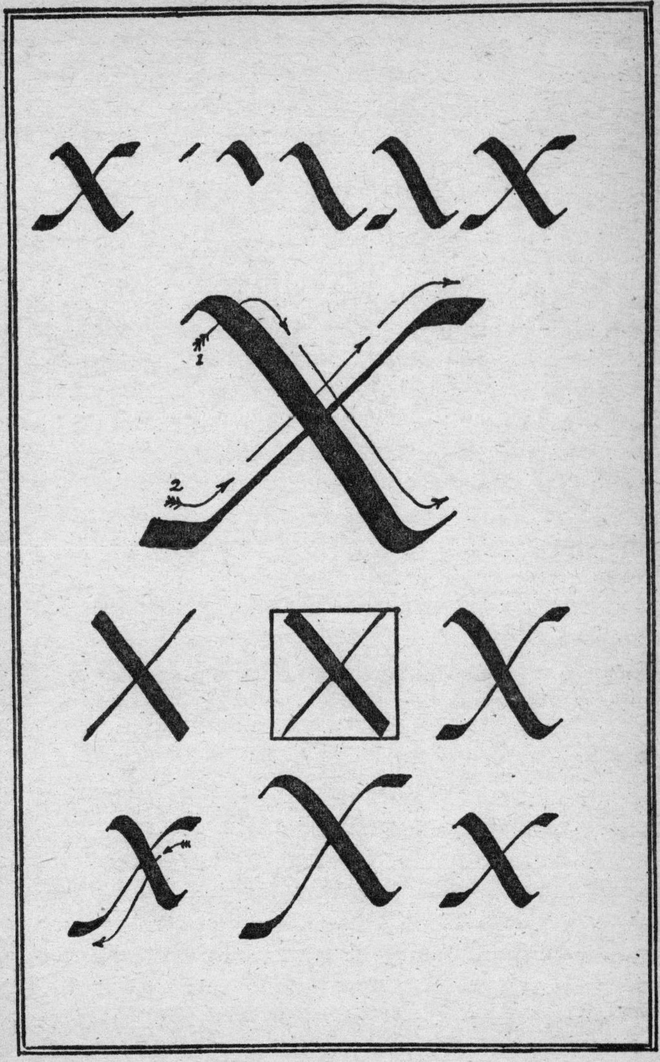

Fig. 44

The Roman capital can be made in two ways, as shown. The first consists of two straight diagonal strokes, whereas in the second the final stroke turns to a vertical downward pull when it meets the base of the first stroke. The swash letter is made in the same way as the small-letter, but taller.

Z

This letter also commences with a slight upward diagonal slide which almost immediately becomes a pulled horizontal stroke. This then turns sharply into a downward oblique slide from whose base the final horizontal stroke is pulled. This terminates in another slight upward slide. The changes of direction at the beginning and end of this letter must not be exaggerated. At times it may be permissible to flourish the tail of the letter below the writing line, as shown at the bottom left of the diagram.

The Roman capital is simply made, but the thin diagonal stroke should not be too thin, or the letter will be weakened. The swash letter is a taller version of the small-letter.

THE NUMERALS

It will be noted that some of the numerals have ascenders or descenders. Whereas these features are satisfactory where numerals appear in small quantities, such as dates for example, it is better to have all numerals the same height when using them in the mass for arithmetical purposes.

Fig. 45

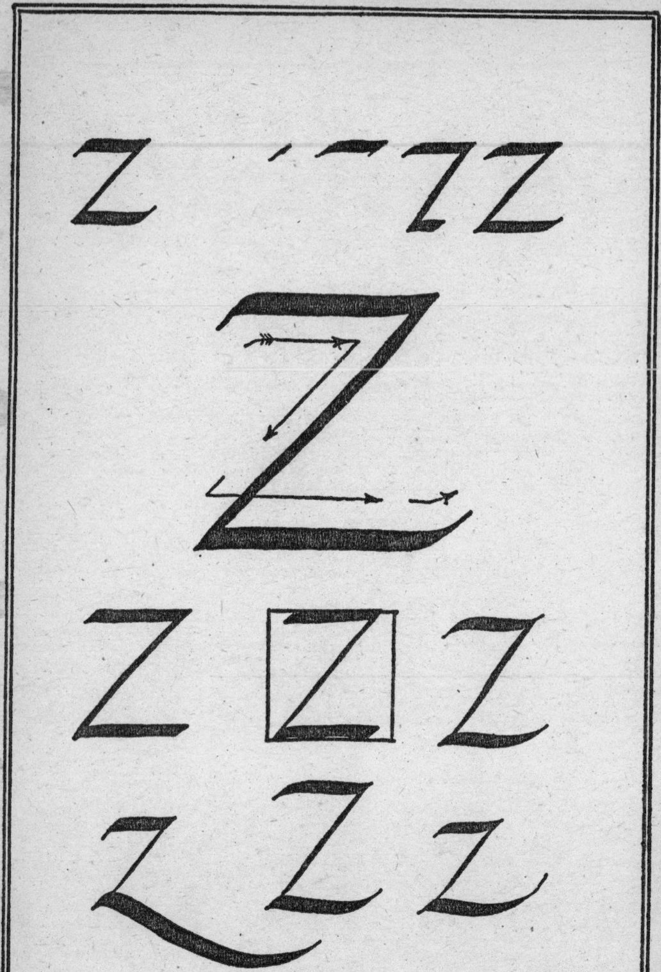

Fig. 46

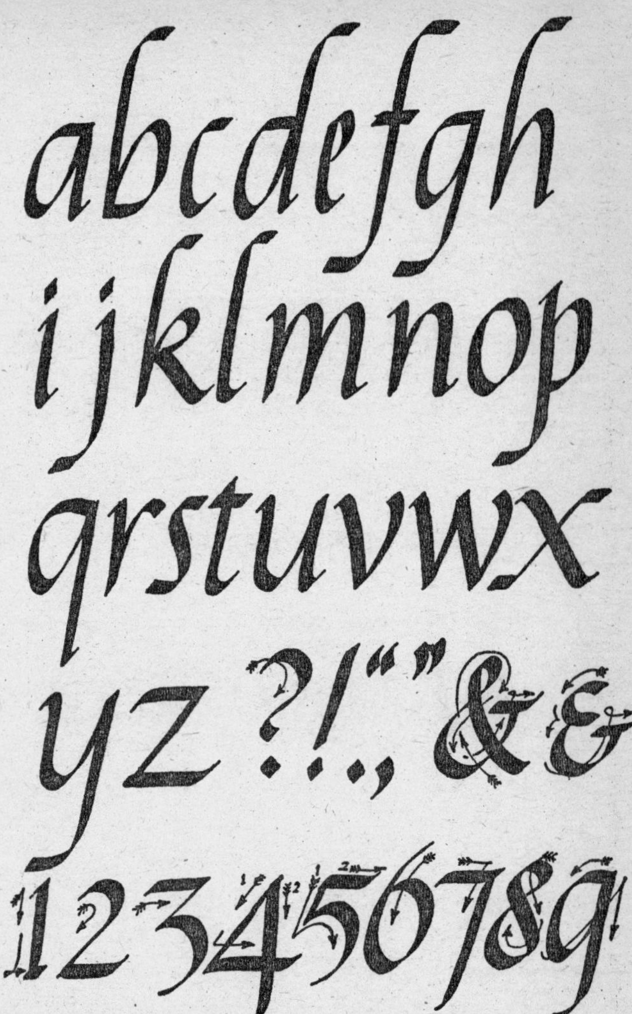

Fig. 47—Complete Alphabet, Punctuation Marks, and Numerals

Exercise

Having practised all the letters of the alphabet until their shapes are thoroughly familiar, it would be helpful to copy the words shown in Figs. 48a and b. When these have been reproduced satisfactorily, the passage shown in Fig. 48c should be copied. It is advisable to attempt these exercises at not too slow a pace. Providing the letter-shapes have been thoroughly mastered speed will help rather than hinder.

After the work in this exercise has been done to the satisfaction of the student, who should set himself a high standard, the next chapter should be studied.

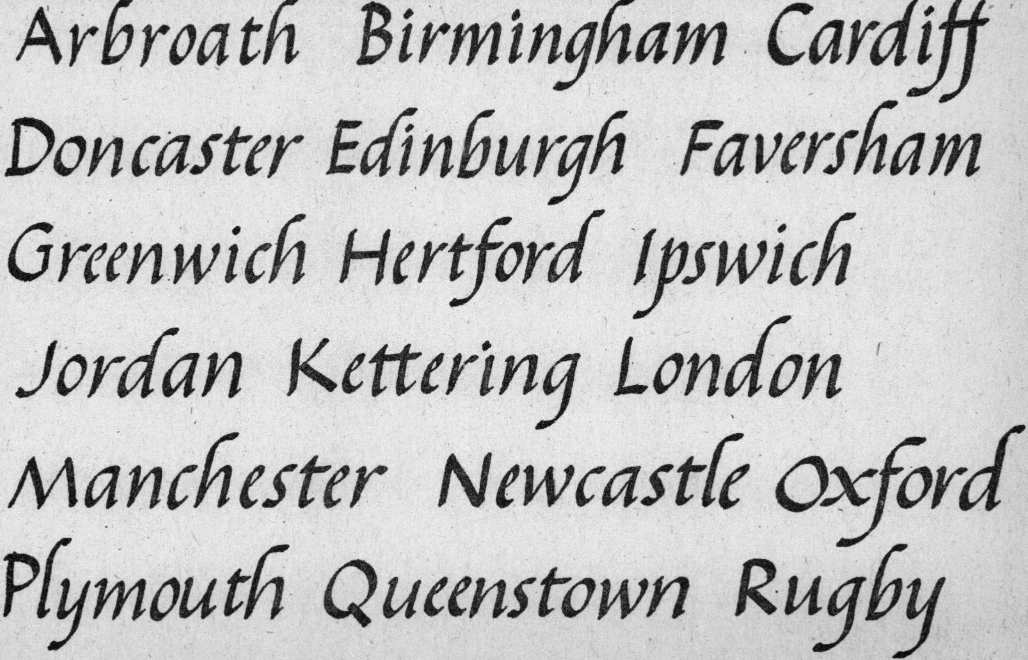

Fig. 48a.—Words for Writing Practice

Sheffield Towcester Uxbridge

Ventnor Wolverhampton York

Zurich January February

March April May June July

August September October

November December

Fig. 48b.—Words for Writing Practice

Then there followed a great to-do
through all our old inn, heavy feet
pounding to and fro, furniture
thrown over, doors kicked in, until
the very rocks re-echoed, and the men
came out again, one after another.

Fig. 48c.—A Copy Passage

Chapter Five

JOINING THE LETTERS

JOINING the small-letters together is very simple if the pen is being held consistently at the right angle, the majority of joins consisting of a diagonal sliding movement leading from the foot of one letter to the top of the next. However, contrary to the popular notion, it is neither essential nor desirable to join every letter. Some letters do not join naturally, and there is no gain in time or legibility in making an unnatural ligature. There are a few letters which join more conveniently from the top with a horizontal stroke. It is easy to remember by which ligature a letter is followed: if the pen finishes at the base of a letter, a diagonal join will follow, but if the letter is completed at the top a horizontal ligature will be used. The foregoing only applies when it is legitimate to join.

The Diagonal Join

Consider first of all those letters which employ the diagonal ligature (/). They are as follows: *a, c, d, e, h, i, k. l, m, n, u.* Practise the use of this join by copying the words in Fig. 49.

When taking the diagonal ligature up to the top of the rounded letters such as *a, c, d, e, g, o, q* and *s*, notice that the top of the diagonal turns to the right and becomes horizontal. The pen is then ready for

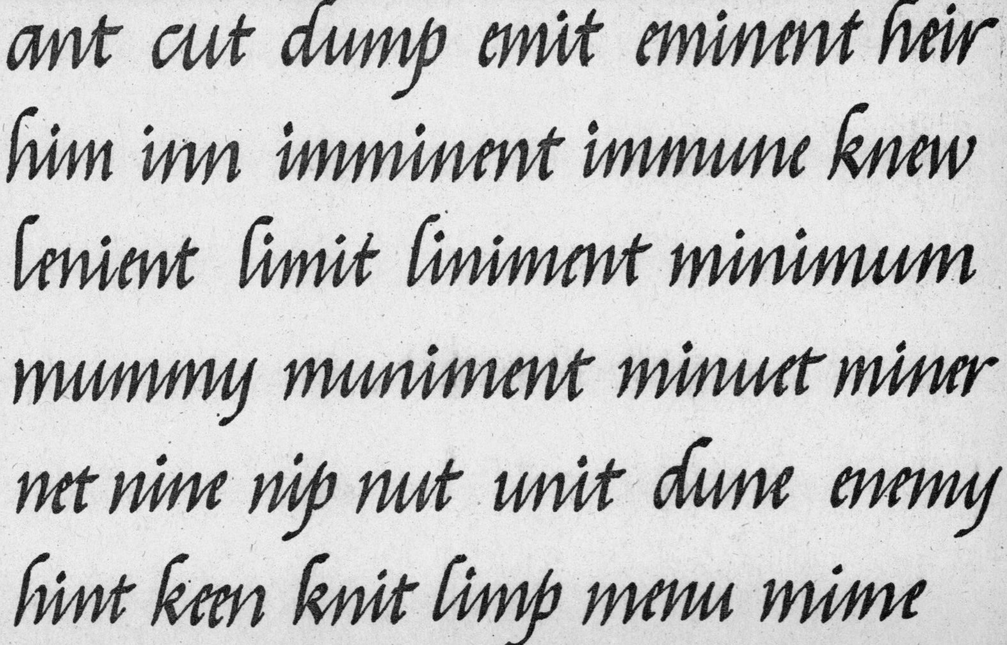

Fig. 49.—Words for Diagonal Join Practice

Fig. 50.—Diagonal Join to Round Letters

the return movement which makes the next letter (Fig. 50). It is also possible to do the reverse of this when joining *from b*, *p* and *s* (Fig. 51).

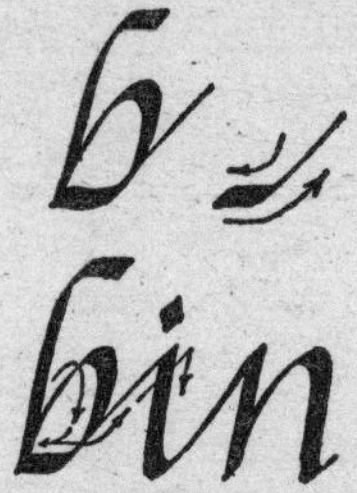

Fig. 51.—Diagonal Join from Round Letters

Exercise

Copy the words in Figs. 49 and 52, endeavouring to attain a rhythmic movement. It is better to copy the whole exercise without going back to the beginning, even if some of the first words appear faulty, than to make repeated false starts.

The Horizontal Join

The letters which join more conveniently with the horizontal stroke are those which finish at the top, as has previously been stated. These are *o*, *v*, *w* and *x*,

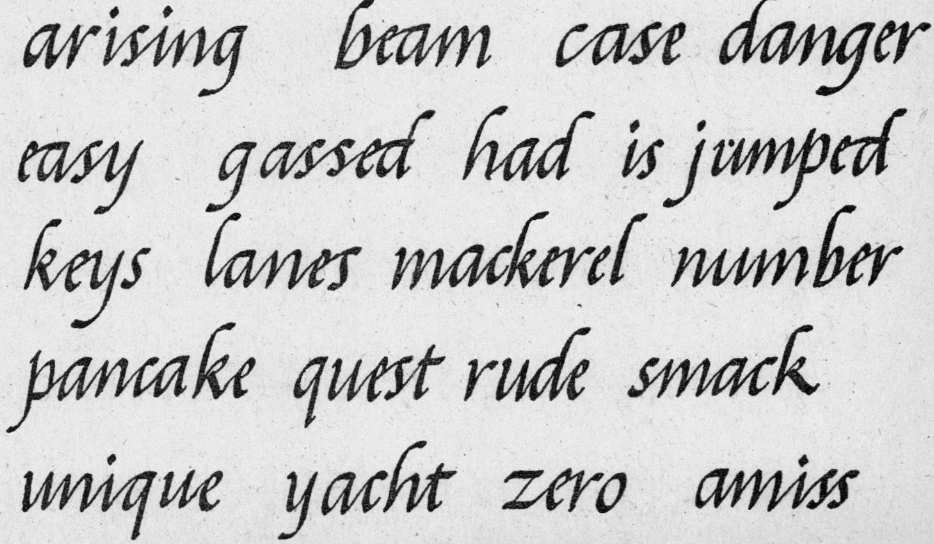

Fig. 52.—More Practice Words

foe food fad foot favour to tow
top woe wove wood van vixen
express waxen vexed fixture
roof mood tomorrow week on
tomb tavern taxi town won

Fig. 53.—Practice Words for Horizontal Join

and those which are completed with cross-strokes: *f* and *t*. The ligatures should be quite straight, and only just long enough to allow the next letter to clear the previous one. Copy the words in Fig. 53 for practice.

It is possible to join *r* to the next letter, but it is necessary to be wary about this, in order to avoid ambiguity when writing at speed (Fig. 54). This is

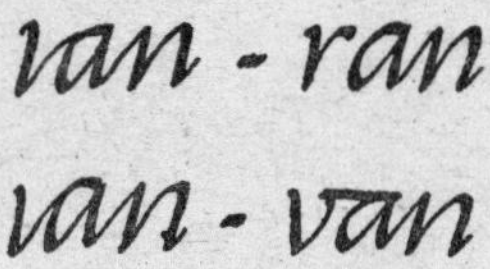

Fig. 54.—Joining from *r*

a very common fault, and is best avoided by not joining the *r* to the next letter. An alternative form of this letter is shown in the diagram, and is referred to in the notes.

Rhythm

The following passages should be copied for practice, paying particular attention to the development of rhythm, which is an essential quality of good handwriting. Rhythm is assisted by speed, and correct and relaxed pen-hold.

He was a snub-nosed, flat-browed, common-face boy enough; and as dirty a juvenile as one would wish to see; but he had about him all the airs and graces of a man. He was short of his age: with rather bow-legs, and little, sharp, ugly eyes. His hat was stuck on the top of his head so lightly, that it threatened to fall off every moment — and would have done so, very often, if the wearer

Fig. 55.—A Copy Passage

/ American

King Edwards or

AGIO's - Holland

Corona No 63

a AGIO's Las Villas

+

GLENFIDDICH Malt Whisky

had not had a knack of every now and then giving his head a sudden twitch, which brought it back to its old place again. He wore a man's coat, which reached nearly to his heels. He had turned the cuffs back, half-way up his arm, to get his hands out of the sleeves: apparently with the ultimate view of thrusting them into the pockets of his corduroy trousers.

Fig. 56.—A Copy Passage

The appearance of the island when I came on deck the next morning was altogether changed. Although the breeze had now utterly failed, we had made a great deal of way during the night, and were now lying becalmed about half a mile to the south-east of the low eastern coast. Gray-coloured woods covered a large part of the surface.

Fig. 57.—A Copy Passage

Chapter Six

SPACING AND LAYOUT

THE appearance of writing is greatly improved by a thoughtful arrangement of letters, words, and lines upon the page. One of the chief characteristics of Italic handwriting is compression. The letter-shapes themselves are compressed, and the space between the letters should be as narrow as possible without permitting them to collide. The diagonal ligature is of great help here, as it will act as an automatic spacer if the pen is being held at a constant angle, and the ligature is straight. It is important that the spacing should be even.

Spacing the Words

Spacing between the words should also be even, and the space should be no greater than that taken up by the letter *n*. More space should be allowed after punctuation marks, particularly after a full stop. One of the chief faults of most handwriting is the excessive spacing between words, and it is one of the most difficult habits to break. A comparison of Figs. 58 and 59 will demonstrate the value of closer word spacing. It will be seen that it helps both appearance and legibility.

Spacing the Lines

It is more important to have a wider space between the lines of writing. The interlinear space should

Many of the lamps were already
extinguished; a few country waggons
were slowly toiling on, towards London;
now and then, a stage-coach, covered
with mud, rattled briskly by: the
driver bestowing, as he passed, an
admonitory lash upon the heavy
waggoner.

Fig. 58.—Wide Word-Spacing

It was a cheerless morning when they got into the street; blowing and raining hard; and the clouds looking dull and stormy. The night had been very wet: large pools of water had collected in the road: and the kennels were overflowing. There was a faint glimmering of the coming day in the sky; but it rather aggravated than relieved the gloom of the scene.

Fig. 59.—Close Word-Spacing

The paper had been sealed in several places
with a thimble by way of a seal; the very
thimble, perhaps, that I had found in the
captain's pocket. The doctor opened the seals
with great care, and there fell out the map
of an island, with latitude and longitude,
soundings, names of hills, and bays, and
inlets, and every particular that would be
needed to bring a ship to safe anchorage upon
its shores.

Fig. 60.—Close Line-Spacing

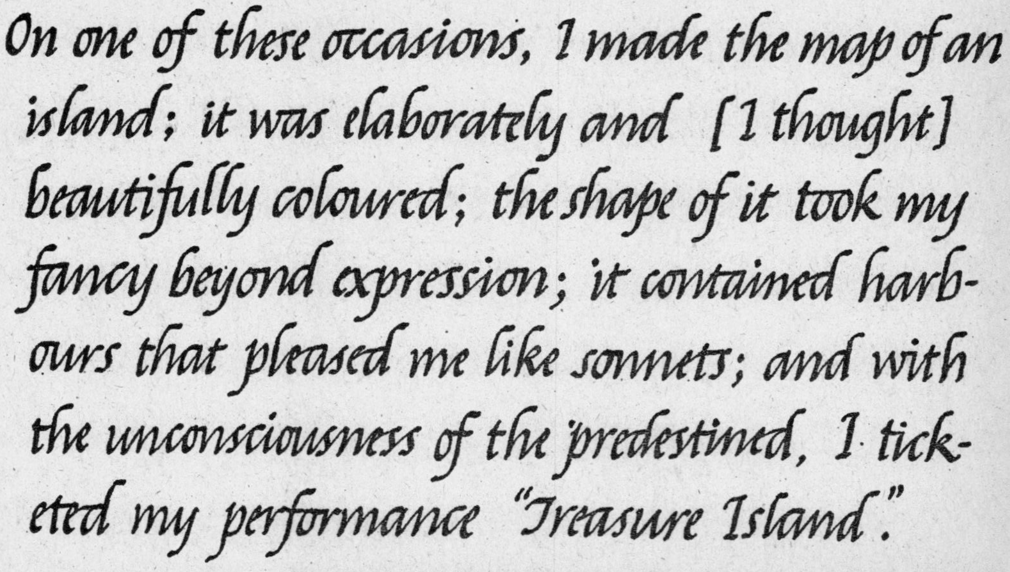

Fig. 61.—Wide Line-Spacing

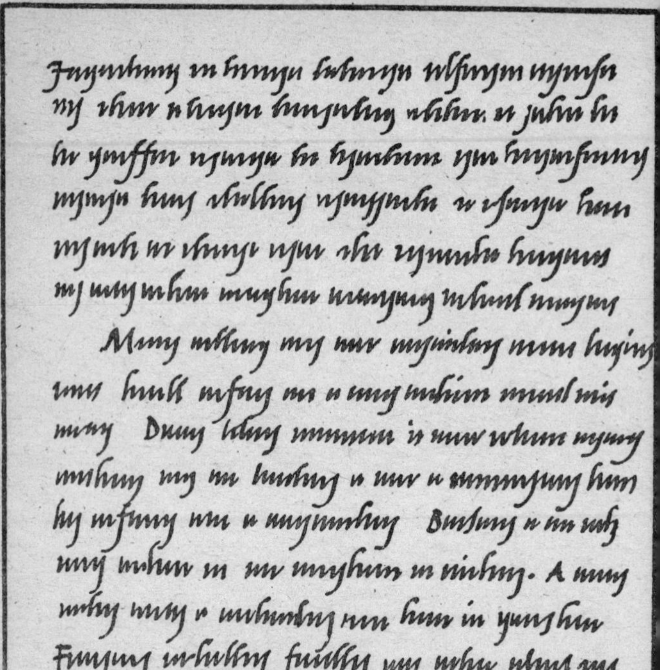

Fig. 62.—Narrow, Inadequate Margins

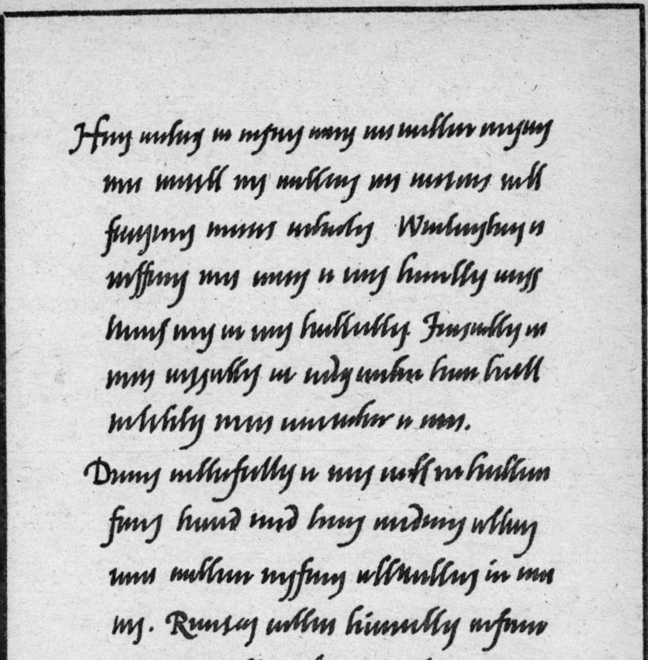

Fig. 63.—Adequate Margins

allow for the writing of ascenders and descenders without entanglement, and should therefore be adjusted to suit your own writing. That is one reason why lined paper is undesirable, for the spacing of the ruled lines will not necessarily be that which you require. Compare Figs. 60 and 61.

Spacing the Margins

A glance at the layout of the printed text of this page will demonstrate the value of arranging the writing mass with adequate margins all round, so that the writing forms a block of darker tone surrounded by a white frame. Compare Figs. 62 and 63.

The margins should be in proportion to one another as far as possible, the bottom margin being the widest. The ideal proportions are shown in Fig. 64. Straight side margins enhance the appearance of the page considerably, and can easily be obtained on the left-hand side by commencing the beginning letter of each line immediately below the one above. A straight right-hand margin is not so easy to obtain, and is not so essential, but an attempt should be made to keep it as even as possible. Adjustment of the spaces between the last few words on the line will help. Occasionally words at the end of the line can be broken, the remainder being written on the next line. If a word is broken for this purpose a hyphen should be put at the end of the line, and not at the beginning of the next one. The break should be made at a suitable point in the word, between syllables. (See Glossary—"Division of Words.")

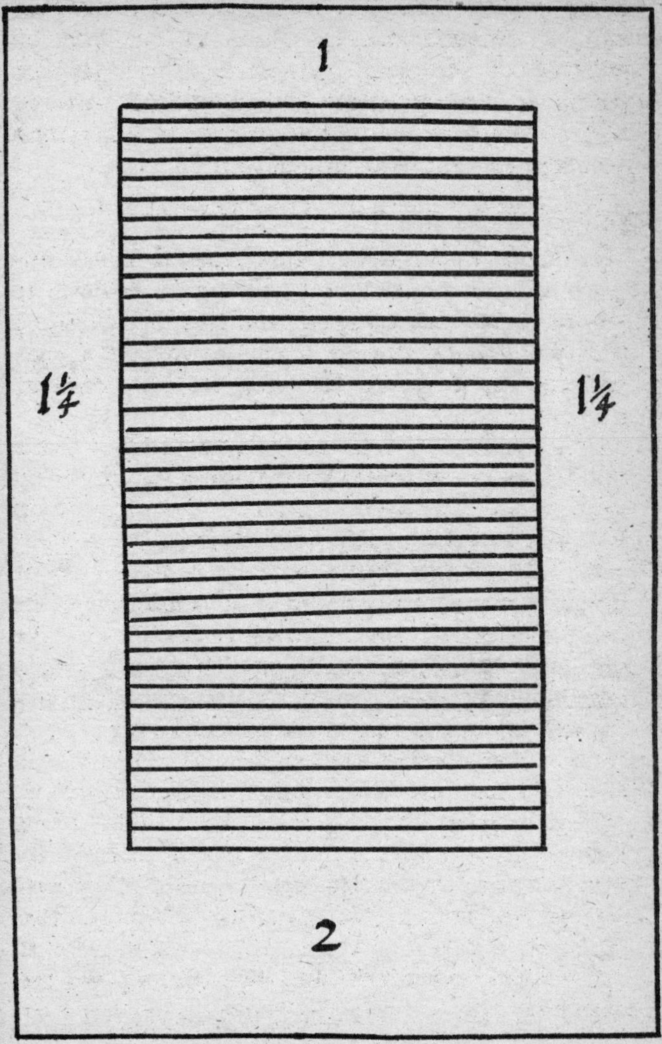

Fig. 64.—Marginal Proportions

Paragraphing

There are two methods of marking the commencement of a paragraph. That which is more common nowadays is the printer's method, such as you will find in this book, where the first word is indented from the margin. The original method, before the advent of printing, was to extend the initial letter of the paragraph into the margin. In the handwritten books of medieval times these initials were either gilded or coloured. The extended letter is inconvenient to printers, and has therefore dropped out of use, but there is no reason why we should not use it for writing. It has the advantage of allowing a few more words to be written on the page. The two methods are illustrated in Figs. 65 and 66.

Writing Pattern

Writing on the page should be considered as a whole, and should not appear just as a lot of letters and words strung together without any thought for the unity of the page. The rhythmic quality of a cursive hand should provide a pattern which unifies the writing on the page. This pattern consists of the regular repetition of certain features. One of the most dominant of these will be the diagonal stroke. It will be seen than this sidled stroke of the pen occurs not only in the joins, but also in the construction of many letters. As a joining stroke it also regulates the spacing of the letters, and regularity of spacing is another pattern-making element. Where there is no diagonal ligature between letters the writer has to use his own judgment. This is particu-

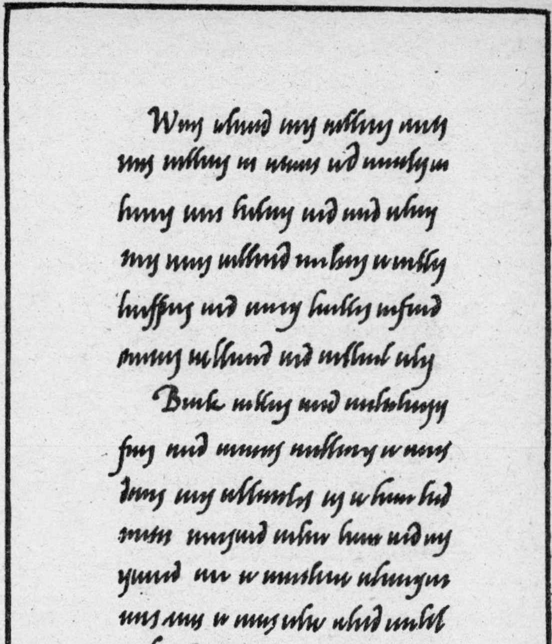

Fig. 65.—Indented Paragraph

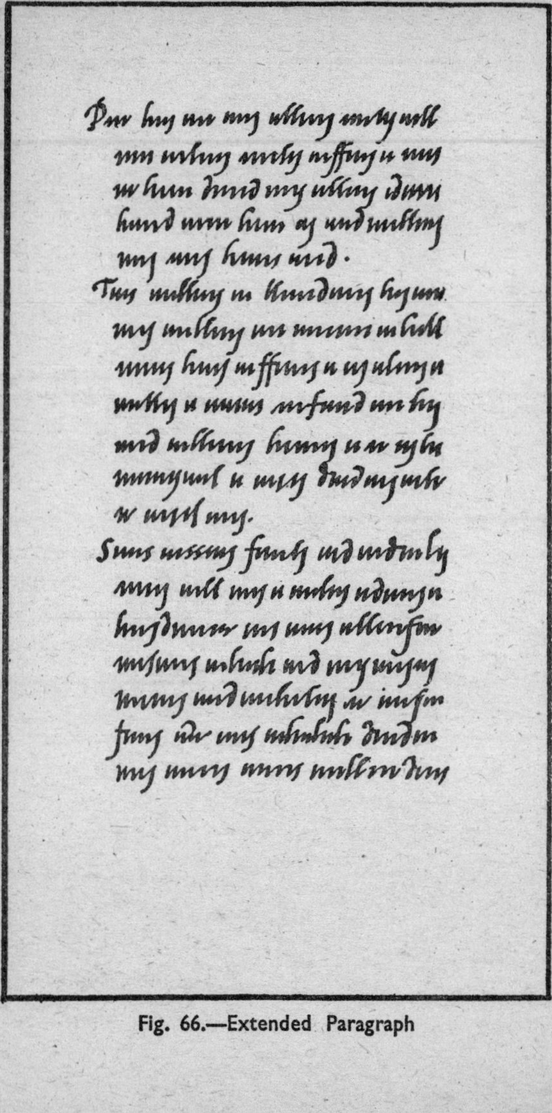

Fig. 66.—Extended Paragraph

larly so with letter combinations like *ll*, *il*, *ib*, *it*, etc. (Fig. 67). The horizontal join must be adjusted to fit into the spacing pattern. Particularly to be avoided is the sagging ligature, as this increases

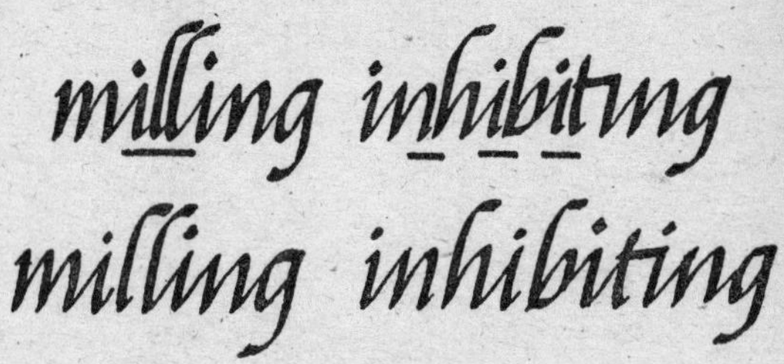

Fig. 67.—Spacing of Straight Letters

the amount of space between the letters. All joining strokes should be *straight*.

The next element providing writing pattern is uniformity of size of the writing. Compare Figs. 68 and 69. It should be noted that the length of ascenders and descenders should be consistent. Their length is a matter of personal choice, but they should all be the same. It is easier to make them successfully if they are kept fairly short.

Another factor which contributes to the pattern of the writing is slope. A slight forward-leaning slope is an aid to fluency, and all the letters should slope at the same angle, which should not be too pronounced. Even such letters as *c* and *o* have an axis which should run parallel to the downstrokes of the straighten letters (Fig. 70).

Fig. 70.—Slope of Round Letters and Others

A The "Hispaniola" still lay where she had anchor-
ed; but sure enough there was the Jolly Roger,
the black flag of piracy, flying from her peak.

B Even as I looked, there came another red flash
and another report, that sent the echoes clatter-
ing; and one more round shot whistled
through the air.

Fig. 68.—Uneven Writing

The "Hispaniola" still lay where she had
anchored; but sure enough there was
the Jolly Roger, the black flag of piracy,
flying from her peak.

Fig. 69.—Even Writing

Providing the formation of the individual letter-shapes has been thoroughly mastered, speedy writing should improve the pattern.

Fluency

It is essential when learning a cursive hand to develop speed. Too many beginners write too slowly too long. As soon as possible a reasonable speed should be attempted. Of course, at first certain parts of the writing will deteriorate badly, but further concentration on these weaknesses should gradually eliminate them. The aim should be to write well at a reasonable speed; all hands, however mature, deteriorate somewhat at great speed. Nevertheless, if this handwriting has been properly learnt it should never lapse into illegibility, even as scribble.

Exercise

Copy out the following practice pieces, and any others elsewhere in the book, concentrating particularly on spacing, layout, and writing pattern.

The waters now changed their character; from translucent lakes, shining like mirrors, they now became seas and oceans. And now came a tremendous change, which, unfolding itself slowly like a scroll, through many months, promised an abiding torment; and, in fact, it never left me until the winding up of my case.

Fig. 71.—Copy Passage

I was stared at, hooted at, grinned at, chattered at,
by monkeys, by paroquets, by cockatoos. I ran
into pagodas: and was fixed, for centuries, at
the summit, or in secret rooms; I was the idol;
I was the priest; I was worshipped; I was sac-
rificed. I fled from the wrath of Brama through
all the forests of Asia: Vishnu hated me: Seeva
laid wait for me.

Fig. 72.—Copy Passage

Chapter Seven

COMMON FAULTS AND THEIR CORRECTION

THE detection of faults is often much more difficult than the correction of them. It is not enough to know that something is wrong; the important thing is to know *what* is wrong.

Letter-shapes

The most obvious fault is bad letter construction. To a large extent this weakness can only be cured by careful observation of the forms of the exemplar letters, and by ensuring that the correct movement is made. It should be clearly appreciated that correct letter-shape is dependent on correct pen-hold. There are a number of letter-forming weaknesses which are so common as to warrant special mention.

The Ovoid

The first of these relates to the formation of the elliptical letters, *a*, *c*, *d*, *g*, *o* and *q*, which all have the same basic construction (Fig. 73). Unless this ovoid

Fig. 73.—o Shape

shape is clearly perceived, all these six letters, which include some of the most commonly used, will be unsatisfactory.

It should be observed that the ovoid commences with a leftwards push of the pen which quickly slides downwards into a curve. Although the top is practically flat, the downward turn is not so sharp as to form a right-angle turn. Neither is the downstroke straight, although there is a parallel affinity between it and the last downward stroke in the case of *a, d, g, q*. When the first downward stroke begins to turn upwards again it turns up sharply, making a *narrow* curve at the base of the letter, not a point. The continuing upward diagonal stroke is not straight either, but slightly curved, allowing the pen to arrive back at the starting point.

If the pushed stroke is not made at the beginning, either the completed movement will not connect up with the start, leaving the letter with an unsatisfying 'open-mouthed' appearance, or the resulting shape

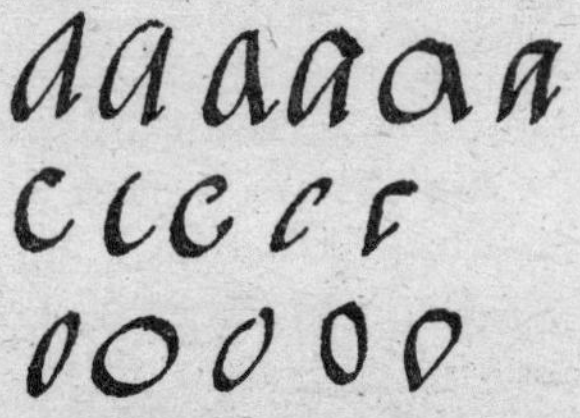

Fig. 74.—Malformed Ovoids

will be much too narrow (Fig. 74). It should be noted that too full a curve at the bottom will also lead to the open-mouthed appearance, and will completely destroy the cursive character of this shape.

It should be quite clear that there are no circular shapes in this writing, except among the capitals. The pure circle is static, not dynamic, and therefore not a cursive form.

The Arch

The second common error in letter formation relates to the arch, which appears in *b*, *h*, *k*, *m*, *n*, *p*, *r*, and inverted in *u* and *y*. This arch springs out from the base of the downstroke, and can be likened to the flight of a rocket. The rising curved diagonal turns downwards in a sharp curve, and then continues practically straight down to the base. In the case of *b* and *p* the downward stroke from the arch turns to the left before it reaches the bottom, and ends in a pushed stroke which connects with the stem. If the two letters are inverted they will be seen to have the same form as *d* and *g* (Fig. 75).

Fig. 75.—Arch Construction

The important points in the construction of the arched letters are the narrow curve at the top of the arch, and the parallel affinity of the stem and the leg. The faulty formation so often apparent is the spikiness which occurs if the arch is not properly turned. It is essential to master the correct movement from the outset, so that it can be made at speed without degenerating.

A contributory factor to the tendency to produce spiky arches is a concave downward stroke from the arch (Fig. 76). This is a very common fault, and

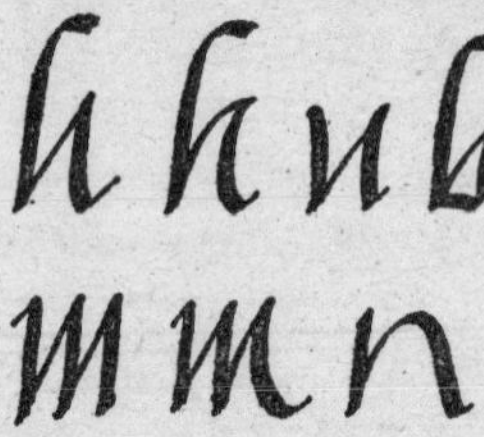

Fig. 76.—Perverted Arch

should be avoided at all costs because it will lead to illegibility. If there is any difficulty in producing the arch satisfactorily at speed, a slight convex movement during the final downstroke will help (Fig. 77).

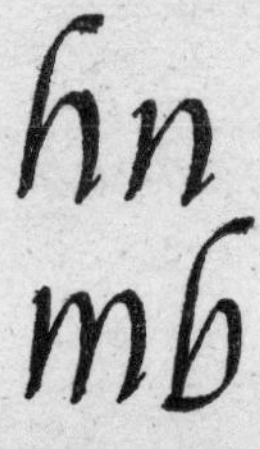

Fig. 77.—Convex Down-stroke on Arches

It should be noted here that it is necessary to slide sharply upwards and outwards from the foot to make the diagonal join. It should not be pulled round to make a hook at the base of the letter, and the diagonal ligature should be straight. If the pen is being held at the correct angle this should be easy.

Ascenders and Descenders

Although the ascenders begin with a pushed stroke to the left (exactly as the ovoid letters do), it must not be thought that the downstroke is curved. It should be straight; wild waving stems make the writing untidy and therefore more difficult to read (Fig. 78).

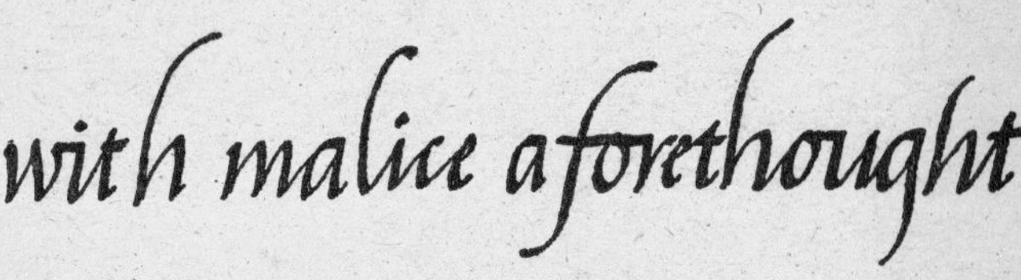

Fig. 78.—Ascenders

The same can be said about the descenders, although these are slightly more curved in character than the ascenders (Fig. 79).

Fig. 79.—Descenders

The writing gains if the ascenders begin quite definitely, and the descenders terminate in the same manner. As there are alternative methods of commencing or terminating these strokes, it is advisable to choose the one preferred and keep to it. Generally speaking, varying forms should not be used in the same piece of writing.

Lack of Writing Pattern

The elements which contribute to writing pattern were discussed in the previous chapter, but it should be emphasised here that if something seems to be wrong with the general appearance of the writing it will very probably be due to a lack of some or all of these elements. The writing should be checked for the following deficiencies:

Irregularity of size.
Irregularity of spacing.
Irregularity of slope.

Lack of Fluency

Handwriting which has any pretensions to being cursive should 'flow.' This forward rhythmic movement which leads the eye tranquilly along the lines of the writing, apparently achieved with economy of time and effort, we call fluency. This can only be acquired by complete mastery of the movements which create the individual letters, and a rhythm arising from speed and self-confidence. Repeated practice of the rhythmic pattern numbered 3 in Fig. 17 can help, and the alphabet can be practised cursively by inserting *m* before each letter, e.g., *mambmcmdmemfmgmhmimjmk*, etc. The one real answer to lack of fluency is practice and yet more practice.

Flourishing

Beware of flourishes. Many a good hand has been spoilt by too much exuberance in the execution of ascenders, descenders, and capitals. There is nothing more certain than that decoration will never improve bad writing, and that it can quite easily ruin good. Those who aim to write beautifully should remember that beauty and simplicity go hand in hand. If the only requirement is a utilitarian hand, it should be remembered that simplicity is an aid to legibility. The examples of contemporary handwriting at the end of this book should be considered from this point of view.

Incorrect Pen-hold

Probably more poor writing is due to this particular fault than any other. When using the edged pen it is essential to ensure that it is held at a consistent angle all the time. A pleasant balance between thick and thin strokes is maintained if that angle is about forty-five degrees to the writing line. There should be no pressure on the pen; it is quite unnecessary, and impedes fluency. The remedy for undue pressure is the use of the 'skating' exercises described in Chapter 3. Make sure that the grip on the pen is relaxed. Any tensing of the finger muscles is undesirable.

Posture

Correct posture has a great influence on handwriting. Most people are very lazy writers, slouching over the paper as they write, or slumping back in the chair. There are occasions when it is necessary to write in adverse conditions, but at other times it is better to write seated at a table or desk of convenient height. The writer should sit comfortably upright with the paper square in front of him (unless he is left-handed), and his feet squarely on the

What manner of life is the everyday existence of a Thief?
What charms has it for the young and ill-disposed?
what allurements for the most jolter-headed of
juveniles? Here are no canterings on moonlit
heaths, no merry-makings in the snuggest of all
possible caverns, none of the attractions of dress,
no embroidery, no lace, no jack-boots, no crimson
coats and ruffles, none of the dash and freedom

Fig. 80.—Copy Passage

with which "the road" has been time out mind invested. The cold wet shelterless midnight streets of London: the foul and frowsy dens, where vice is closely packed and lacks the room to turn; the haunts of hunger and disease; the shabby rags that scarcely hold together; where are the attractions of these things?

Fig. 81.—Copy Passage

floor. The left forearm should rest on the table at an approximate angle of forty-five degrees to its front edge, the hand resting on the writing paper or blotter. The right forearm should be at a similar angle, the hand holding the pen without clenching. The eyes should be at least a foot away from the paper.

Lighting

It is also highly desirable to write in an adequate light. If possible, the table should be arranged so that the light falls on the paper from the writer's left (right for left-handers). This obviates the shadow of the writing hand obscuring the work. If artificial light is used it should be neither too dim nor too bright. Too bright a light reflects from the paper and is very trying for the eyes. The lamp should be in such a position that direct light does not shine into the writer's eyes.

Exercise

Copy the passages in Figs. 80, 81 and 82, and any others.

I could hear their feet rattling up our old stairs, so that the whole house shook with it. Promptly afterwards, fresh sounds of astonishment arose; the window of the captain's room was thrown open with a slam and a jingle of broken glass; and a man leaned out into the moonlight, head and shoulders, and addressed the blind beggar on the road below him.

Fig. 82.—Copy Passage

Chapter Eight

ABBREVIATIONS AND THEIR USE

In the days when parchment was an expensive but necessary commodity manuscripts abounded with abbreviations which were intended to save space. At the present time this consideration is of little importance, but there may be a case for the use of recognised contractions in order to save time. The operative word here is 'recognised,' as there would be no saving of time by the use of contractions which were obscure to the reader. There are a number of abbreviations, however, which are based on common sense, and a wider use of these would not come amiss.

A factor which often inhibits the use of such short-long-hand terms is that of correct usage. It is not, by many, considered good style to use them in private correspondence, unless it happens to be very informal in character. This is an attitude which is likely to be amended by current practice, for there are a number of writers whose English is impeccable and yet who use contractions in their correspondence. However, for those who cannot bring themselves to the public use of such terms there is still the opportunity to use them for personal memoranda and note-taking.

Apart from the abbreviations listed at the end of the chapter the following terminations can be contracted as shown:

Termination	*Contraction*	*Example*
—ary	y	customy.
—ever	vr	whenvr.
—ial	l	essentl.
—ing	g	talkg.
—ings	gs	meetgs.
—ion	n	statn.
—ional	nl	natnl.
—ment	t	arranget.
—ought	ot	brot.
—ual	l	usl.

Another very useful contraction is the ampersand (&), two versions of which are shown in Fig. 47. A commonly-used word for which an abbreviation would be useful is "the," but there appears to be no accepted term in current usage, although one writer on the subject has put forward "t" as a possible contraction.

Before using abbreviations it would be as well to consider carefully whether they will be comprehensible to the intended reader.

The following are some recognised abbreviations:

abt.	about	shd.	should
altho.	although	tho.	though
bn.	been	vy.	very
btwn.	between	w.	with
cd.	could	wd.	would
fm.	from	wh.	which
mt.	might	yr.	your
reqd.	required	yrs.	yours

Exercise

Re-write the following with the abbreviations written in full:

i. I beg you wd. not acquaint my husband of the triflg. debt btwn. us; for as I know you to be a vy. good-natured man, I will trust you w. a secret; he gave me the money long since to discharge it, wh. I had the ill-luck to lose at play. You may be assured I will satisfy you the first opportunity, and am, sir, yr. vy. humble servant,

CATH. RUBBERS.

ii. Sir, I am sincerely sorry it is not at present possible for me to comply w. yr. request, especially after so many obligns. recd. on my side, of wh. I shall always entertain the most grateful memory. I am vy. greatly concerned at yr. misfortunes, & wd. have waited upon you in person, but am not at present vy. well, & besides, am obliged to go this eveng. to Vauxhall.

I am, sir, yr. most obliged humble servant,

CHAS. EASY.

iii. Sir, the atrocious crime of being a young man, wh. the hon. gentleman has w. such spirit & decency charged upon me, I shall neither attempt to palliate nor deny, but content myself w. wishing th. I may be one of those whose follies may cease w. their youth, & not of th. no. who are ignorant in spite of experience. Whether youth can be imputed to any man as a reproach,

I will not, sir, assume the province of determing.: but surely age may become justly contemptible if the opportunities wh. it brings have passed away without improvet., and vice appears to prevail when the passions have subsided.

WM. PITT in the House of Commons.

iv. For to speak my private Opinion, I am for evy. Man's workg. upon his own Materials, & producg. only what he can find within himself, wh. is commonly a better Stock than the owner knows it to be. I think Flowers of Wit ought to spring, as those in a garden do, fm. their own Root & Stem, without Foreign Assistance. I wd. have a Man's Wit rather like a Fountain th. feeds itself invisibly, than a River th. is supply'd by several Streams from abroad.

JONATHAN SWIFT in a letter to
a Young Poet—1721

Chapter Nine

CORRESPONDENCE

ALTHOUGH the principles of letter-writing are not within the scope of this book, some attention ought to be given to the question of layout.

Most people use a conventional layout for all their letters, without any consideration of the appearance of the completed page. Even though the content of this form may not alter, its arrangement on the page can.

Fig. 83 shows the usual layout employed for personal correspondence. The writer's address (1) is always placed at the head of the paper, but need it be in this position? Some people prefer to have the address on the right-hand side. The date (2) usually accompanies the address, a little below it. This can be written in numerals and words, e.g. 22nd June, 1954, or in numerals only, e.g. 22.6.54. In the latter case the numerals can be separated by a dot, by a colon, e.g. 22:6:54, by a dash, 22-6-54, or by an oblique stroke, 22/6/54. Some writers prefer to use Roman numerals for the month, thus: 22:vi:54, and sometimes for the year, 22:6:mcmliv, but this latter is difficult to decipher unless the reader is accustomed to it.

The salutation (3) comes next, almost invariably commencing with "Dear . . ." If this is to be written in the normal position, on the left-hand side, there is the question of extending the initial into the margin or not. If the initials of the paragraphs are

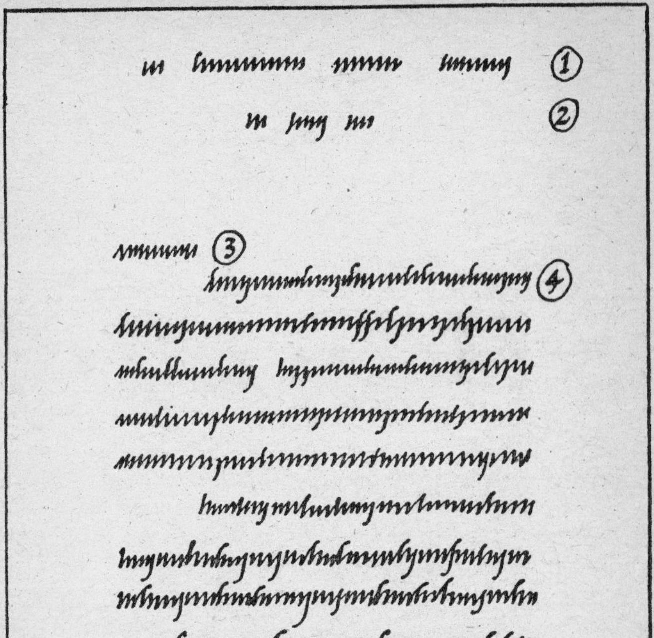

Fig. 83.—Layout of a Typical Letter

to be extended it would probably be better to extend that of the salutation also. In order to achieve a more balanced appearance the salutation is sometimes placed centrally above the text of the letter. Some writers prefer to commence the letter immediately following the salutation, on the same line, instead of leaving it to stand on its own.

It should go without saying that the text (4) of the letter should be placed centrally on the paper, with adequate margins down either side. On small notepaper such as Octavo these do not need to be very wide. If writing a fairly brief letter on larger paper, such as Quarto, it is better to try and assess the total amount of space that the text will occupy, and to try and arrange the block of writing accordingly. Nothing presents a more ludicrous appearance than a large sheet of notepaper with the matter all crammed into the top half.

Following the text of the letter comes the subscription (5), nearly always ending in "yours . . . ." This is commonly commenced at a point roughly half-way across the page, but if the balance of the page is considered, it would be better to place it centrally under the text.

Finally, the signature (6) can be placed according to the position of the subscription. The prevailing superstition that a signature is not valid unless illegible is to be deplored. There is no legal substance for this. Even a name written in capital letters is legally a signature if it is the normal way in which that particular person signs his name.

Illustrations of the various arrangements mentioned above will be found in Figs. 84, 85, 86 and 87.

"Ravenswood"
Edinburgh Ave.
Westhampton.

22nd. June 1954

Dear Auntie May.

Thank you for the big bunch of roses you sent for my birthday. How I wish our garden was as lovely as yours. Perhaps it will be when we have put as much work into it as you and Uncle Ned have in yours.

Mother sends her love, and says she will try and come down on Sunday.

We both hope you and Uncle are keeping well, and enjoying this lovely sunshine.

With lots of love,
Your affectionate niece,
June

Fig. 84

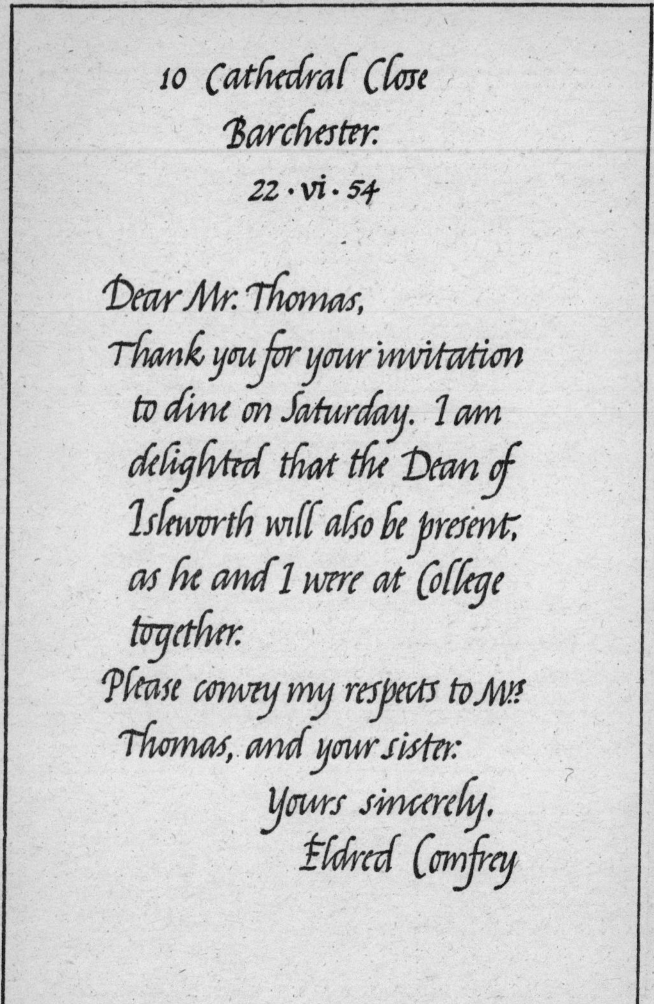

10 Cathedral Close
Barchester.
22 · vi · 54

Dear Mr. Thomas,
Thank you for your invitation to dine on Saturday. I am delighted that the Dean of Isleworth will also be present, as he and I were at College together.
Please convey my respects to Mrs Thomas, and your sister.

Yours sincerely,
Eldred Comfrey

Fig. 85

36a. West Terrace
Dragoons Road
Casterbridge

22-6-54

Dear Sir, In answer to your advertisement for a typewriter, which appeared in today's "Gazette," I wonder if you would be interested in my "Coronet" portable, which is now ten years old? It is in excellent condition, and has just been completely overhauled. It has Elite type, two-colours and stencil, tabulator, and all the other usual fittings. The case has been knocked about rather, but is still quite usable. I am asking £12 for it, but would be prepared to consider a near-offer.

If you would care to come round and see the machine, I am in after 7 o'clock every evening. Yours faithfully,

Robert Anstey

Fig. 86

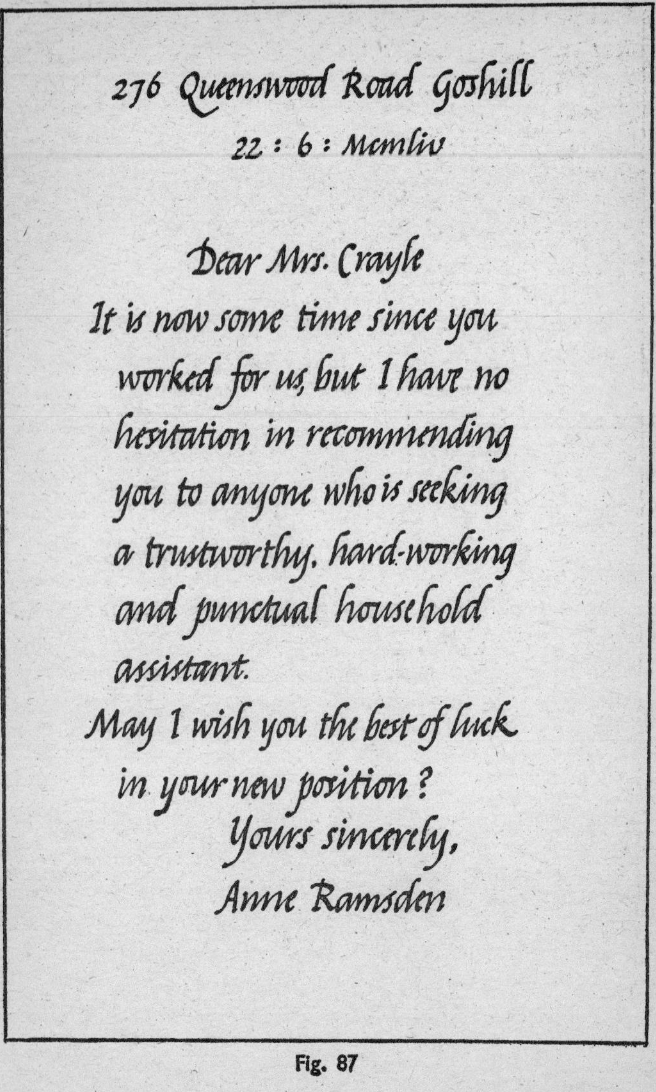

276 Queenswood Road Goshill
22 : 6 : Mcmliv

Dear Mrs. Crayle
It is now some time since you worked for us, but I have no hesitation in recommending you to anyone who is seeking a trustworthy, hard-working and punctual household assistant.
May I wish you the best of luck in your new position?
Yours sincerely,
Anne Ramsden

Fig. 87

Postcards

Very little thought or care is given to the writing of postcards, particularly as they are used very often as time-savers. However, it takes no longer to arrange the written matter on a card decently, than it does to scrawl it anyhow, once a habit of layout has been cultivated. For the sake of space and brevity it is sometimes possible to dispense with the salutation and the subscription.

Probably the greatest difficulty is created by the picture postcard, where the space for correspondence and direction is halved. A point to bear in mind about this sort of card is that the postmark very often extends a good way across the top of the card, and may well obscure anything written on that part. Appropriate layouts for postcards are shown in Figs. 88 and 89.

Envelopes

When addressing envelopes it may be as well to consider the advice of the G.P.O., which can be found in the Post Office Guide. The speed of sorting could be appreciably enhanced if all envelopes were addressed legibly, and in a similar manner. The Guide advises "writing the address legibly, in the lower part, and towards the right-hand side of the front of the envelope, with a clear margin above (not less than 1½ inches deep) for the postage stamps and post marks. It assists materially if BLOCK capital letters are used for the name of the post town." Even though the address is written in very readable writing, the fact of putting the name of the town in capitals helps the sorters to pick it out

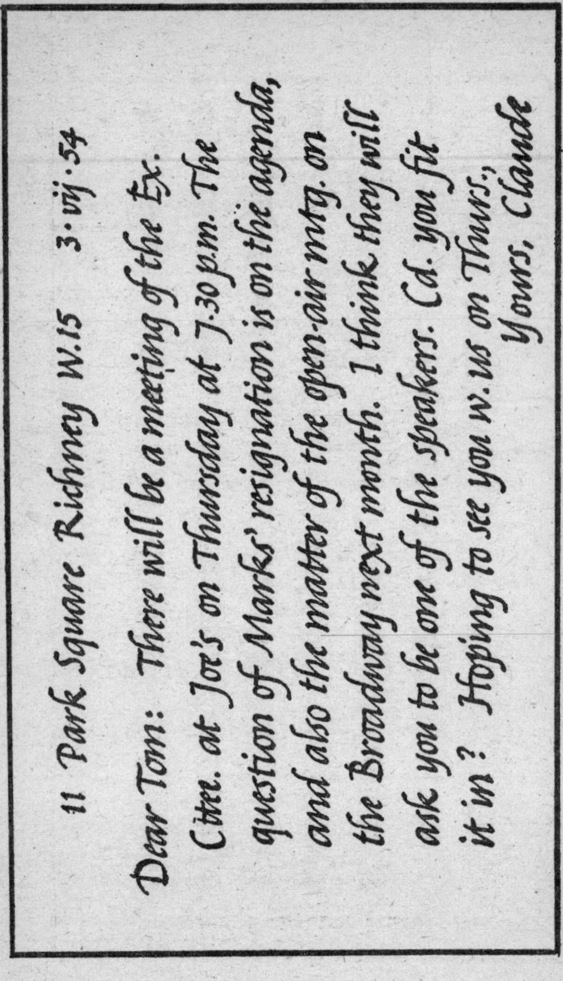

Fig. 88.—Specimen Postcard

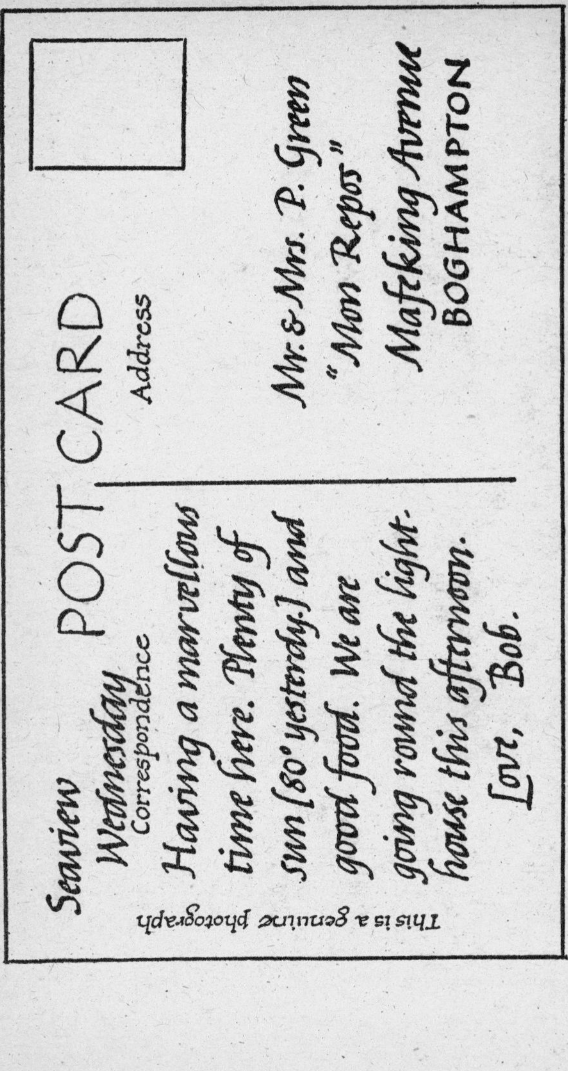

Fig. 89.—Specimen Postcard

at a glance from the rest of the address. Further valuable advice about addressing envelopes can be found in the Guide just quoted. It is available at all post offices and can be purchased for a small sum. Examples of addressed envelopes are shown in Figs. 90 and 91.

Exercise

1. Write out the letters quoted at the end of Chapter 8, experimenting with various layouts, and using varying sizes of paper.

2. Mark out some envelope shapes by tracing round a used one, and try out various ways of arranging the address.

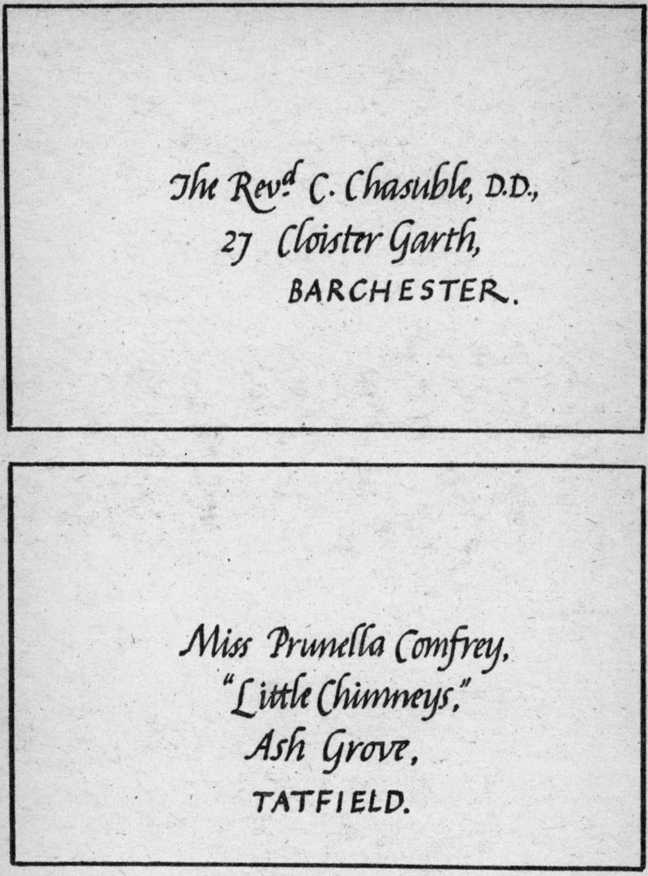

Fig. 90.—Specimen Envelopes

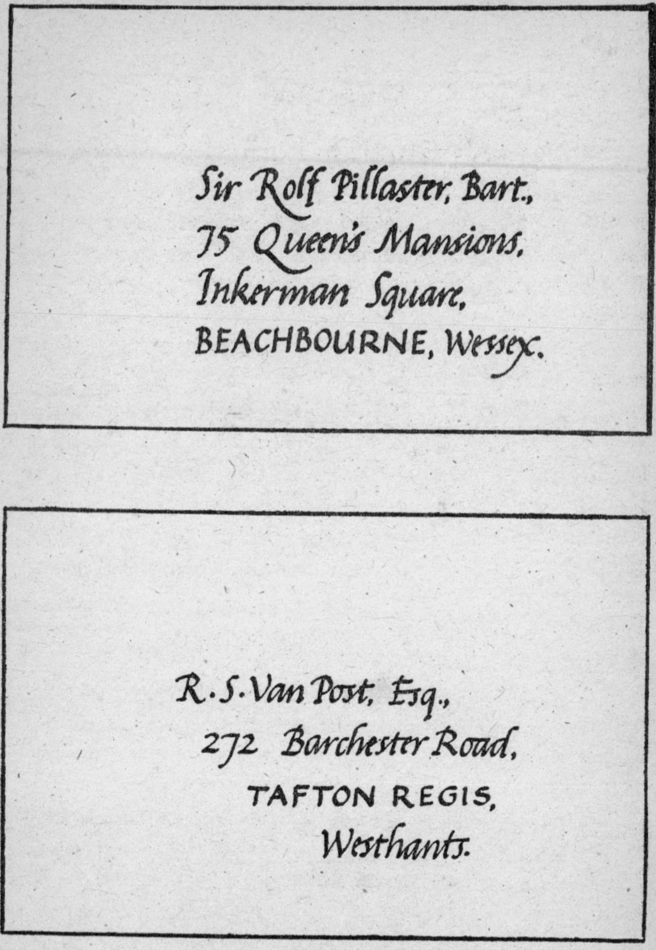

Fig. 91.—Specimen Envelopes

Chapter Ten

HANDWRITING AS A RECREATION

SOME people have found such interest and satisfaction in writing a good hand that they have come to look upon handwriting as a recreation rather than a tiresome chore.

One thing that must not be forgotten, however, is the fact that handwriting is a means to an end: a method of expression which requires as a prerequisite something to express. There is something sterile about writing just anything, without regard for the content of what is being written. Beautiful handwriting cannot redeem a drab piece of English, although it may make it slightly more palatable.

What to Write?

The first problem, then, in considering handwriting as a hobby, is what to write. Those who are creative writers will find no problem here, but for the majority the matter is of some moment.

An activity which commends itself to many people is the keeping of a daily journal. Good-quality notebooks can be bought at stationers, which are very suitable for this, preferably made up with plain paper. A page could be devoted to a day, and in some instances it might be necessary to take more than a page. Occasionally there may be nothing to record about a particular day. For both these reasons it would be advisable to date the pages of the journal as they are written, rather than heading every page with a date before making any entries.

For anyone with artistic pretensions there is the added delight of illustrating the text where appropriate with pen sketches. These would look more attractive if done in a different coloured ink from that used for the writing.

When writing a book of this sort careful attention should be paid to the maintenance of adequate margins, and if the paper is not too thick, a guide can be ruled up on a loose sheet which can be placed underneath the page which is being written upon.

Book Margins

Whereas on a single sheet of paper the left-hand and right-hand margins should be of equal width, in a book the inner margin is only half the width of the outer one (Fig. 92). It will be seen from the diagram that the complete opening is considered when laying out the text of a book. Reference to any well-printed book will bear out this principle. The first page of a book, which is commonly a right-hand (recto) page, and is faced by a blank sheet, has margins which are equal on left and right.

Anthologies

For those who do not wish to keep a journal there is the alternative of compiling an anthology. This may take the form of a collection of favourite

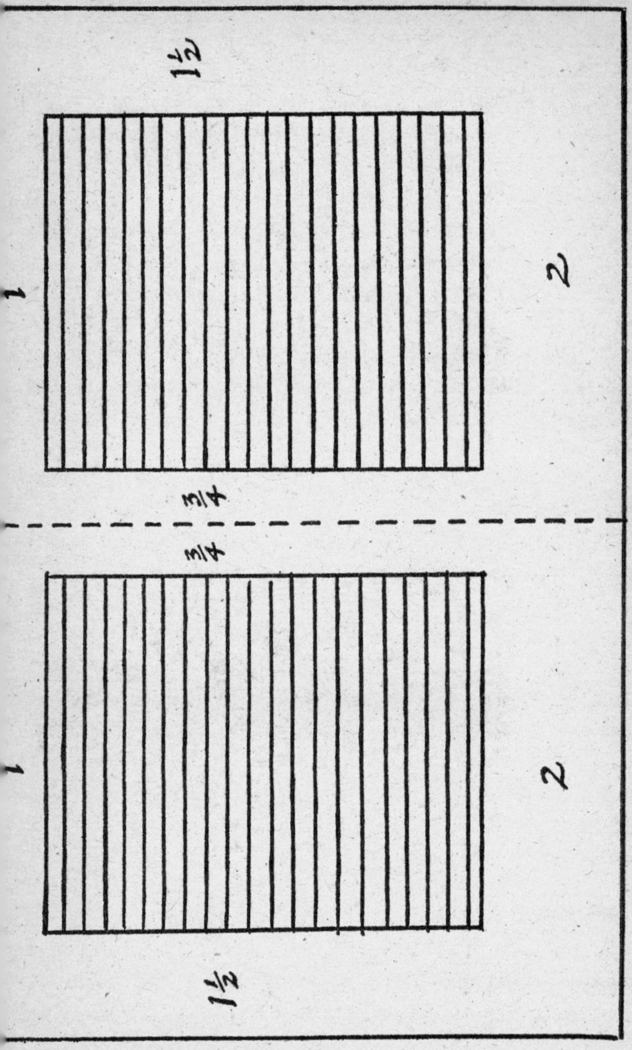

Fig.92.—Book Margins

poems, or interesting pieces of prose, or it might be a commonplace book in which any thought, quotation, or literary passage of interest to the compiler can be recorded.

The writing out of poetry has special problems, owing to the differing lengths of the lines. Sometimes it might be necessary to write the piece out in rough first, before putting it into the book. In this way it would be possible to assess the length of the lines when written by hand. If the poems which are included in Appendix I are written out, this matter will be clearly appreciated.

Other Manuscript Books

For those with the time and enthusiasm, a pleasant task is the writing out of a favourite short story, or preparing a story-book for a child. Such books can be delightful, especially if the writer can illustrate them as well.

The Binding of Books

Small books suitable for manuscript work can be bound at home. This permits the use of fine quality hand-made paper, and personal designs on the covers. Anyone who wishes to try this should obtain one of the books which deal with the subject.

Writing and Illuminating

The consideration of manuscript books brings the business of handwriting close to the province of formal calligraphy, which is outside the scope of this book. Anyone who is interested in this aspect of writing should acquire Edward Johnston's classic handbook: *Writing and Illuminating and Lettering.* Other books of a similar nature are listed in the Bibliography.

Those who are interested in the making of handwritten books should, if at all possible, visit the British Museum and inspect the medieval books displayed there. The fine writing and the brilliance of the illuminations are breath-taking. Other museums in various parts of the country have collections of similar manuscripts well worth seeing, in particular the Bodleian Library at Oxford, and the FitzWilliam Museum, Cambridge.

Other Practical Uses of Handwriting

Handwriting can be adapted for the preparation of notices, window bills, and so on, quite easily. The chief requirement is a much broader pen, and the matchbox pen described in Chapter 2 will do quite well. It is also possible to make a useful pen from an ordinary garden cane. The method of doing this is described in Johnston's book mentioned above.

It will be found that for large-scale writing it is much better to write each letter separately, rather than to try and join them. It is not possible to write quickly and well on such a scale, and therefore there is no point in joining letters.

For display work the question of layout is paramount. A well-written piece can be ruined by poor arrangement. Compare Figs. 93 and 94. The illustrations in Figs. 95, 96 and 97 indicate the way in which simple notices and showcards can be laid

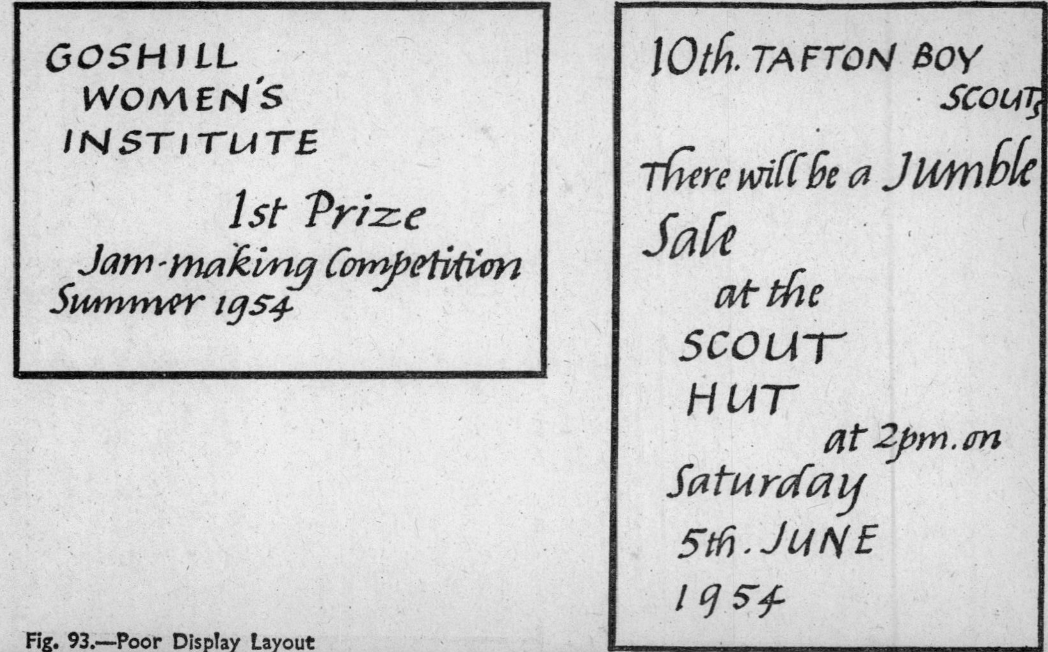

Fig. 93.—Poor Display Layout

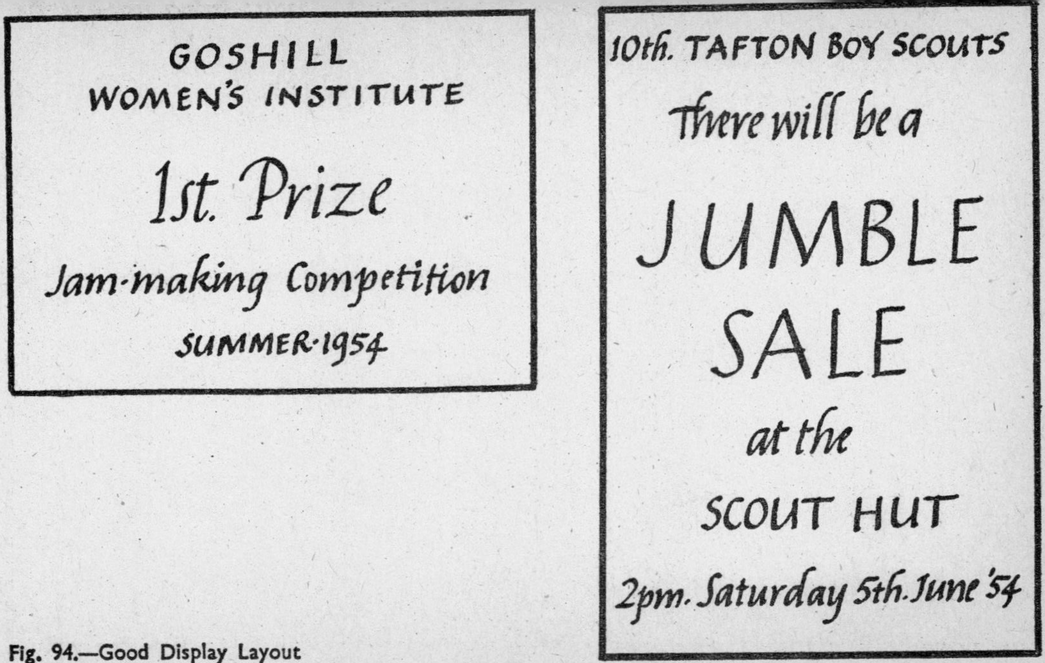

Fig. 94.—Good Display Layout

out. It is as well to try out the arrangement first with a pencil, so that any errors of size, spacing, and so on, can be adjusted. It is important to make sure that it is the most vital words that are emphasised. So often in poorly conceived notices the attention is distracted from the really important information, instead of being attracted to it.

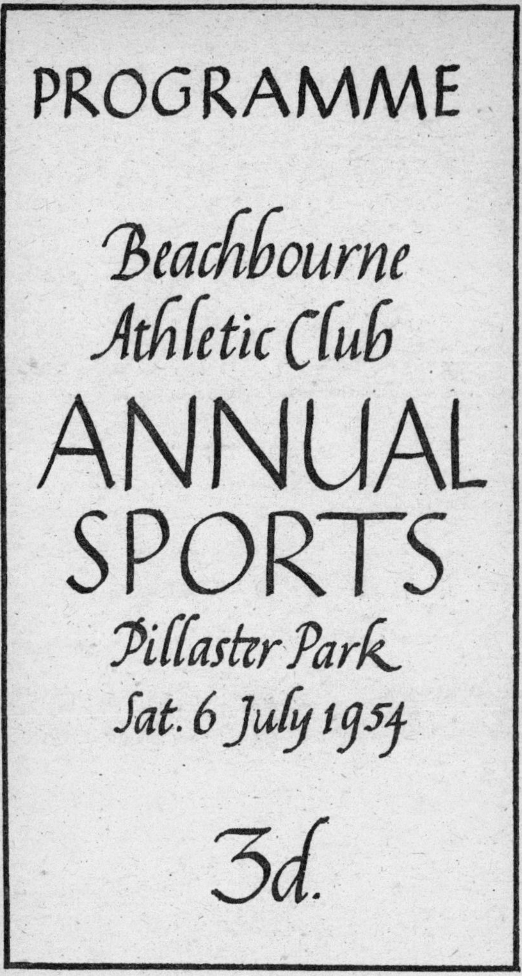

Fig. 95.—Specimen Display Layout

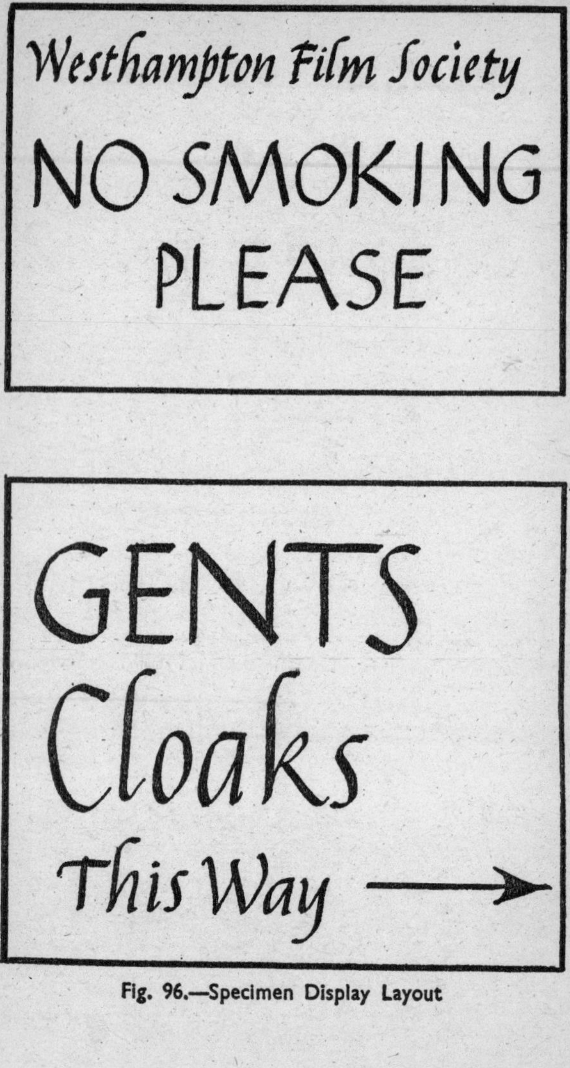

Fig. 96.—Specimen Display Layout

Fig. 97.—Specimen Display Layout

Appendix One.

PASSAGES SUITABLE FOR COPYING

1. Wear your learning like your watch, in a private pocket, and do not pull it out and strike it merely to show you have one. If you are asked what o'clock it is, tell it, but do not proclaim it hourly and unasked, like the watchman.

LORD CHESTERFIELD in a letter to his Son.

2. For the charge, I value it not a rush. It is the liberties of the people of England that I stand for. For me to acknowledge a new court that I have never heard of before, I that am your King, that should be an example to all the people of England, to uphold justice and to maintain the laws—indeed I know not how to do it.

KING CHARLES I at his Trial.

3. Out of the right Fob hung a great Silver Chain, with a wonderful kind of Engine at the bottom. We directed him to draw out whatever was at the end of that Chain; which appeared to be a Globe, half Silver, and half of some transparent Metal: for on the transparent Side we saw certain strange Figures circularly drawn, and thought we could touch them, until we found our Fingers stopped with the lucid Substance. He put this Engine to our Ears,

which made an incessant Noise like that of a Watermill.

JONATHAN SWIFT: A Voyage to Lilliput (*Gulliver's Travels*).

4. He wore, then, a pair of white stockings on his legs, and pumps on his feet: his buckles were a large piece of pinchbeck plate, which almost covered his whole foot. His breeches were of red plush, which hardly reached his knees; his waistcoat was a white dimity, richly embroidered with yellow silk, over which he wore a blue plush coat with metal buttons, a smart sleeve, and a cape reaching half-way down his back. His wig was of a brown colour, covering almost half his pate, on which was hung on one side a little laced hat, but cocked with great smartness.

HENRY FIELDING: *Jonathan Wild the Great.*

5. The *Hispaniola* lay some way out, and we went under the figure-heads and round the sterns of many other ships, and their cables sometimes grated underneath our keel, and sometimes swung above us. At last, however, we got alongside, and we were met and saluted as we stepped aboard by the mate, Mr. Arrow, a brown old sailor, with ear-rings in his ears and a squint.

ROBERT LOUIS STEVENSON: *Treasure Island.*

6. Even at that exciting moment it carried me back to the old Admiral Bembow in a second; and I seemed to hear the voice of the captain piping in the chorus. But soon the anchor was shot up; soon it was hanging dripping at the bows; soon the sails began to draw, and the land and shipping to flit by on either side; and before I could lie down to

snatch an hour of slumber the *Hispaniola* had begun her voyage to the Isle of Treasure.

ROBERT LOUIS STEVENSON: *Treasure Island.*

7. Wednesday morning was dawning when I looked out of the window. The winking lights upon the bridges were already pale, the coming sun was like a marsh of fire on the horizon. The river, still dark and mysterious, was spanned by bridges that were turning coldly grey, with here and there at top a warm touch from the burning in the sky. As I looked along the clustered roofs, with church towers and spires shooting into the unusually clear air, the sun rose up, and a veil seemed to be drawn from the river, and millions of sparkles burst out upon its waters.

CHARLES DICKENS: *Great Expectations.*

8. UPON WESTMINSTER BRIDGE

Earth has not anything to show more fair:
Dull would he be of soul who could pass by
A sight so touching in its majesty:
This City now doth like a garment wear
The beauty of the morning: silent, bare,
Ships, towers domes, theatres and temples lie
Open unto the fields, and to the sky,
All bright and glittering in the smokeless air.
Never did sun more beautifully steep
In his first splendour valley, rock, or hill;
Ne'er saw I, never felt, a calm so deep.
The river glideth at his own sweet will:
Dear God, the very houses seem asleep;
And all that mighty heart is lying still.

WILLIAM WORDSWORTH.

9. Be calm in arguing: for fierceness makes
Error a fault, and truth discourtesy.
Why should I feel another man's mistakes
More than his sickness or poverty?
In love I should: but anger is not love,
Nor wisdom neither; therefore gently move.
GEORGE HERBERT.

10. Cowards die many times before their deaths;
The valiant never taste of death but once.
Of all the wonders that I yet have heard,
It seems to me most strange that men
should fear;
Seeing that death, a necessary end,
Will come when it will come.
WILLIAM SHAKESPEARE: *Julius Caesar.*

Appendix Two

A NOTE ON THE USE OF THE BALL PEN

NEARLY everyone today possesses one of the numerous ball pens that are on the market, and no doubt the question of using these for the style of writing advocated in this manual has already arisen in the minds of some readers.

There is no doubt that while pen and ink produce a superior result to that of the ball pen, the major writing tool for handwriting of quality will be the dip pen and the fountain pen. However, this does not mean that quite good writing cannot be done with a ball pen. Its biggest drawback from the calligraphic point of view is its stylographic tip, which produces a line of uniform thickness. The easy glide of the ball point also prevents the pen from exerting any discipline over the writer. Nevertheless, in the hand of a practised penman it can achieve very satisfactory results for informal writing requirements.

The writing illustrated in Figs. 98 and 99 was written quickly with a ball pen, and shows what can be done. There is little doubt that the italic style is best suited to this type of pen because of its lack of loops and other superfluities.

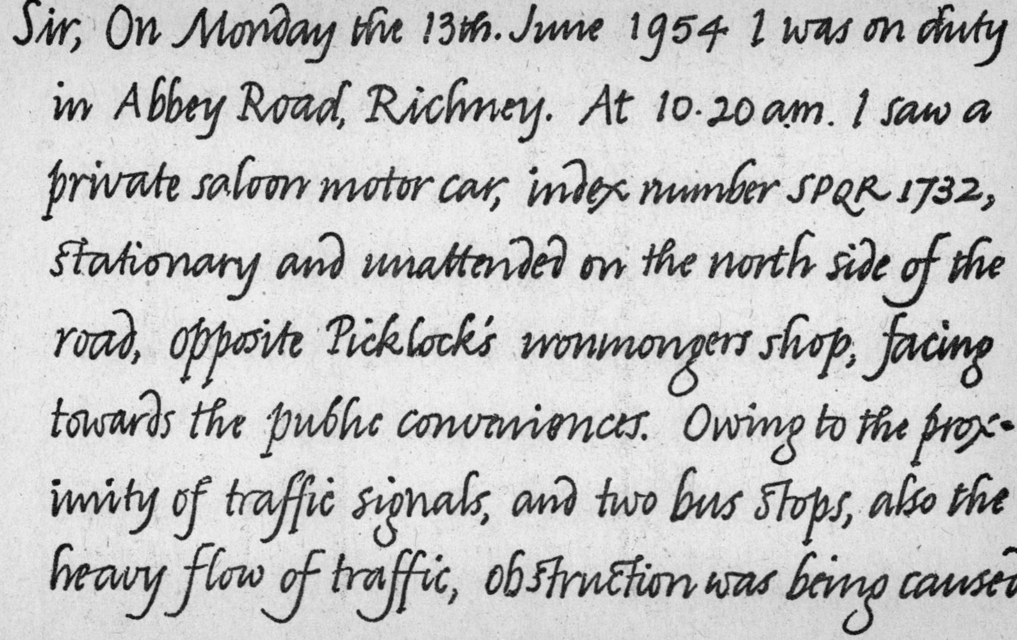

Fig. 98.—Ball Pen Writing

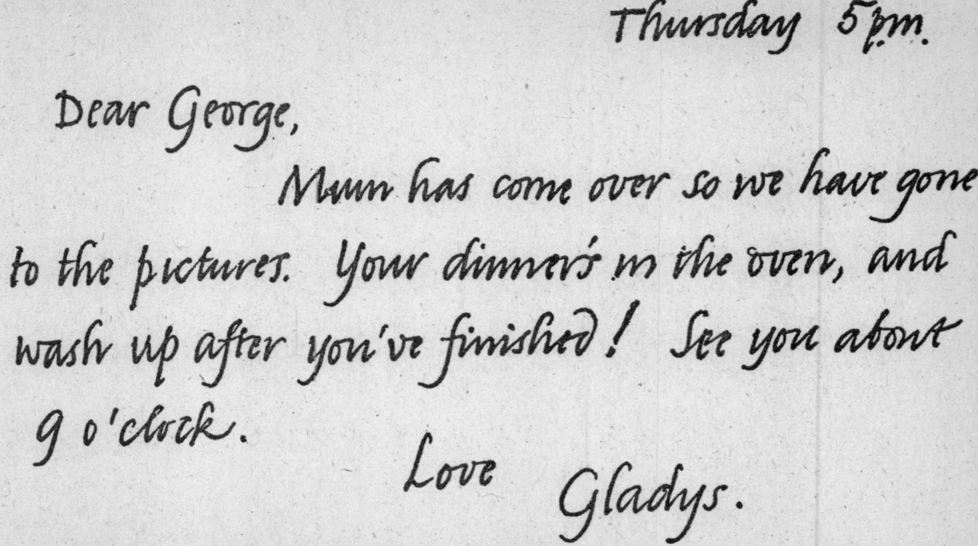
Thursday 5 p.m.

Dear George,

Mum has come over so we have gone to the pictures. Your dinner's in the oven, and wash up after you've finished! See you about 9 o'clock.

Love Gladys.

Fig. 99.—Ball Pen Writing

Appendix Three

GLOSSARY OF TERMS CONNECTED WITH WRITING

Aldus Manutius: Venetian printer, b. 1450, d. 1514. Invented italic type, based on *cancellaresca corsiva.*

ampersand: the name of the sign &, which is a kind of logotype for the Latin *et,* or in English *and.*

antique paper: any good bulking paper with a rough surface, useful for covers but not for writing.

art paper: a highly finished printing paper with a shiny surface suitable for the printing of fine detail, but quite unsuitable for writing.

ascender: the top portion of letters such as b, d, f, h, k, l.

bank paper: applied loosely to any very thin tough writing paper. A suitable paper for general use.

bond paper: a tough machine-made paper, slightly thicker than bank. A very useful writing paper.

bowl: a fully rounded oval or circular form in a letter, complete in an O or modified in B, D, P, R, *a, b, d, g, o, p, q.*

burin: a steel tool used by engravers. It produced the exemplar models for copper-plate writing.

cacography: bad writing.

calligraphy: the art of beautiful writing.

calligrapher: a fine writer and letterer.

chancery hand: a term sometimes applied to italic, but strictly speaking could be applied to hands appertaining to any royal chancery.

cancellaresca: the name given to the hands in use in the Apostolic Chancery at the time of the Renaissance. There were several styles, used for different purposes, whose names were prefixed by *cancellaresca. C. tonda* was a round book-hand similar to that illustrated in Fig. 6, *c. formata* was a formal cursive used for the more important documents, and *c. corrente* was an informal correspondence hand which resulted from a swiftly written *formata.* The Apostolic scriptors were required to be masters of all three.

colophon: a final paragraph in hand written and early printed books giving particulars of authorship, writer or printer, where written or printed, and date of completion, with possibly other details, often arranged as a tail-piece and ornamented. Today replaced by the title page and imprint, although some publishers often append a colophon to a book which has an imprint and title page.

cursive: running; a running hand. The German name for italic is *Kursiv.*

dandy: a cylinder of wire gauze on the paper-making machine which comes into contact with the paper while it is in a wet and elementary stage. The dandy roll impresses whatever watermark is required.

The ordinary dandy has the "laid" wires which impress the ribs in "laid" papers, running transversely from end to end. In a "wove" dandy the fabric is more or less ordinary wire gauze.

deckle edge: the feathery edge surrounding a sheet of hand-made paper due to the "deckle" or frame of the mould. It can be formed when the paper is being made, by the rubber deckle straps at the sides of the paper machine, or by artificial means such as a water jet.

descender: the lower portion of letters such as *g*, *j*, *p*, *q*, *y*.

division of words: never separate a group of letters representing a single sound, but divide a word so that each part retains its present sound, e.g., con-di-tion.

feet: that part on which a letter stands.

folio: a sheet of paper folded in half.

foolscap: a standard size of writing paper, 13¼ x 16½ in.

foot (or tail): the margins at the bottoms of pages.

hand-made paper: so-called because each sheet is formed by a man dipping a mould into a vat containing pulp composed of rag fibres, and taking up sufficient to form a sheet of paper of the required substance. Hand-made papers made from the best linen rags are the most durable papers obtainable.

head: the margin at the top of a page.

indent: to begin a line, or lines, with a blank space.

laid paper: the ribbed appearance (of parallel line, at intervals of an inch or more) in writing and printing papers due to manufacture on a moulds or by a dandy on which the wires are *laid* side by side as distinct from being *wove* transversely.

layout: the arrangement of matter on the page.

ligature: a stroke connecting two letters.

majuscule: a capital letter.

minuscule: a small-letter.

numerals, Roman: I—1; II—2; V—5; X—10; L—50; C—100; D—500; M—1,000. If the lesser number is placed *after* the greater, the lesser is added to the greater: XI—11; if the lesser is placed *before* the greater, the lesser is deducted from the greater: IX—9; XC—90.

page: one side of a leaf; not to be confused with leaf or leaves.

parchment: the skin of a goat, sheep, or other animal, which has been prepared for writing on.

quire: the twentieth part of a ream; 24 sheets.

ream: 20 quires, or 480 sheets.

recto: a right-hand page of an open book.

Roman capitals: the Roman alphabet as used on inscriptions and in books by the Romans.

Roman (letters and type): letters and type based on the round, upright book-hand of the Renaissance. (See Fig. 6).

serif: the short lines drawn at right angles to, or obliquely across, the ends of stems and arms of letters.

scribe: a professional writer, usually these days a practitioner of formal calligraphy.

shading: the incidence of thicks and thins in writing.

swash letters: ornamental italic characters in the seventeenth century style with tails and flourishes. Cursive capitals.

vellum: a fine smooth kind of parchment made principally from calf-skin.

verso: the left-hand page of an open book.

watermark: a design or lettering impressed into the paper while it is being made, by means of a projecting wire on the mould, or the dandy roll. Used to identify the product of a mill.

wove paper: that which does not show wire marks, as distinct from *laid paper.*

writing paper: a better, harder, and more highly finished paper than that used for printing.

Appendix Four

BIBLIOGRAPHY

Practical Manuals

A Handwriting Manual, by A. J. FAIRBANK—Faber

Good Writing, by W. WORTHY—Chatto & Windus.

Good Handwriting and How to Acquire It, by J. TARR—Phoenix.

Handwriting: Everyman's Craft, by GRAILY HEWITT—Kegan Paul.

Better Handwriting, by GEORGE THOMSON—Penguin Books (Puffin).

Handwriting Sheets, by PATRICK BARRY, O.S.B.—James Barrie.

The Art of Handwriting, by J. LE F. DUMPLETON—Pitman.

Historical

A Book of Scripts, by A. J. FAIRBANK—Penguin Books (King Penguin).

Sweet Roman Hand, by WILFRID BLUNT—James Barrie.

Written By Hand, by AUBREY WEST—Allen and Unwin.

Writing & Illuminating & Lettering, by ED. JOHNSTON—Pitman.

The 26 Letters, by OSCAR OGG—Harrap.

Calligraphy's Flowering, Decay & Restauration, by Paul Standard—Sylvan Press.

Formal Calligraphy

Writing & Illuminating & Lettering, by Ed. Johnston—Pitman.

Lettering, by Graily Hewitt—Seeley Service.

Your Penmanship, by G. U. Ockenden—Sylvan Press.

Educational

The Renaissance Writing Books, by W. Worthy—Chatto & Windus.

Dryad Writing Cards, by A. J. Fairbank—Dryad Press.

Italic Handwriting for Schools, by Percy Wood—E. J. Arnold.

Italigraph Copy Books, by K. J. Yates-Smith—Philip & Tacey.

Writing & Writing Patterns, by Marion Richardson—University of London Press.

General Interest

Lettering Today, published by the Studio (1937).

Modern Lettering & Calligraphy—Studio (1954).

Italic Handwriting, by Wilfrid Blunt & Will Carter—Newman Neame.

Bookbinding

Bookbinding & the Care of Books, by D. Cockerell—Pitman.

Appendix Five

CONTEMPORARY HANDWRITING

Having lived with a copy of the "Better Handwriting" Puffin for some time now, I'm glad I have not been able to spot any serious faults. I think I may claim to have supplied at least a modest need in the teaching of italic.

George Thomson, Esq.

van Hulsteyn he says he has just glimpsed your booklet. I seem to have missed this com-pletely: I hope you will tell me about it.

I ought to have done something before this about a local S.I.H branch – but finding the time is the difficulty!

I found your change to brown ink (Waterman's, I believe?) interesting. I have been using this (Field's) for some time now: I find the colour more pleasantly chocolate!

Kenneth Hardacre, Esq.

midnight (where the only light is due to magic) Erictho reintroduces blood into the ghost of an unburied corpse who then foretells the future. (GO TO * over) Similar Indians rites [among] are described in J. Harris's collection, Navigantium atque Itinerantium Bibliotheca[1] ~~[illegible]~~ II. sig Yyy 2r ff. In La Porte Ouverte (pp. 285-6) Roger records that Indians believe

Professor Geoffrey Tillotson

I'm *not* proud of my writing. I began
too late; I write too much, & too often
too fast; my pen-hold is unorthodox, my
posture unhygienic. But at all events
I write *freely*. I would rather advance
swiftly with my own poor pen than creep
laboriously in the footprints of even
the great Arrighi himself.

Wilfrid Blunt, Esq.

these arguments usually boil down to two or three. There are those who say that all italic writing looks the same: that it leaves no room for the expression of individuality or personality. This is nonsense, of course, as I know you'll agree – it is the complaint of the Englishman that all Chinese look the same. Those who are unfamiliar with italic writing are inevitably more aware of its common characteristics than they are of individual differences – but when you have tried to write it only a short while you realise how different are the styles of

CORNUS CAPITATA,

Bentham's Cornel. (Benthamia fragifera) Lindley, Bot. Mag., T. 4641.

(Wallich.)

Evergreen tree, 30 to 40 or more feet high, bushy in habit; young shoots covered in fine, flattened gray down. Leaves leathery, opposite, tapered at both ends, oval-lanceolate; 2 to 5 inches long, dull gray-green. Minute flowers, crowded in a hemispherical mass about half an inch across. The great beauty of the inflorescence is in the four or six sulphur-yellow bracts that subtend the true flowers; these are obovate, nearly two inches long, and one, two or more inches wide at the widest point.

Introduced from the Himalaya in 1825; also a native of China. Not successful unprotected at Kew, and rarely flowers there. At home in S. Devon, Cornwall and S. Ireland. One of the finest specimens is at Dartington Hall.

Robin Tanner Esq. (reduced)

For myself, life doesn't allow for contemplation
& the studied hand. I think I write more
swiftly with the years & rejoice to see so
many signs of the youngsters progress —
including a letter in to-days 'Sunday
Times', mentioning a great increase in the
Membership of the Society for Italic Hand-
writing.

Yours sincerely,
Norman Ierson Parley

N. I. Parley, Esq.

Silver, agile as a monkey, even without leg or crutch, was on the top of him next moment, and had twice buried his knife up to the hilt in that defenceless body. From my place of ambush, I could hear him pant aloud as he struck the blows.

From TREASURE ISLAND by Robert Louis Stevenson (1850–1894)

Michael Rhodes (aged 11) Beaumont School, St. Albans

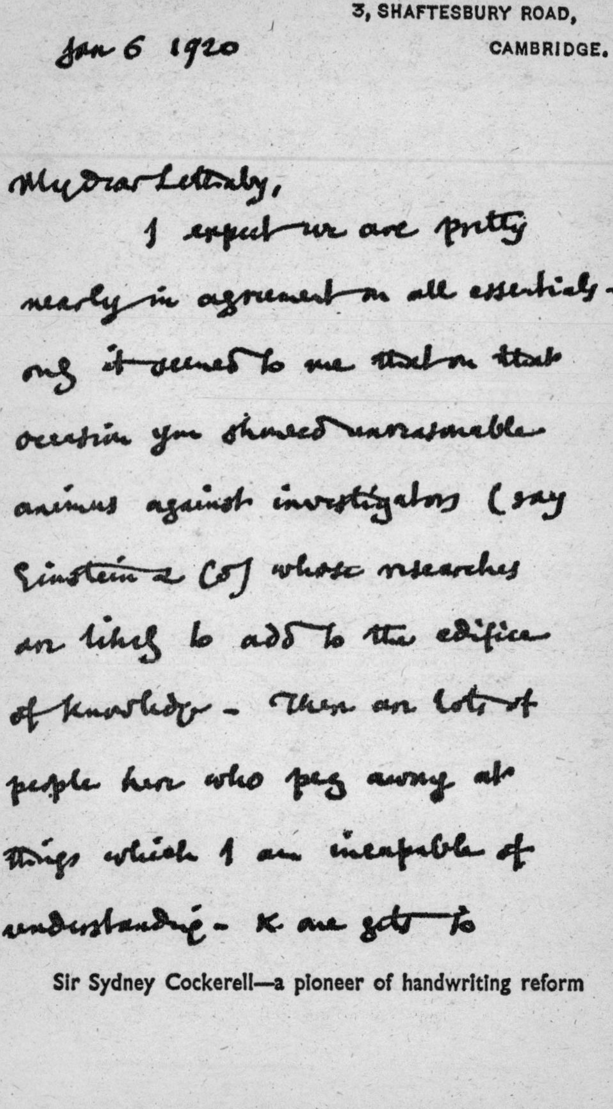

3, SHAFTESBURY ROAD,
CAMBRIDGE.

Jan 6 1920

My dear Lethaby,

I expect we are pretty nearly in agreement on all essentials - only it seemed to me that on that occasion you showed unreasonable animus against investigators (say Einstein & Co) whose researches are likely to add to the edifice of knowledge - There are lots of people here who peg away at things which I am incapable of understanding - & one gets to

Sir Sydney Cockerell—a pioneer of handwriting reform

Monday, 3·ix — The sun for once. So had a short swim before breakfast. Walked along the beach to Mousterlin which was much more bleak than we expected. Immediately after our lunch to jetty and by boat to Concarneau. Argument with skipper over fare which was announced as 140 francs « aller retour ». He now wanted 200. Thanks to British « diplomate distinguished » speaking wonderfully idiomatic French I had no chance of losing my temper. He settled for 140 francs, offering the skipper a drink to show that it was merely a « question de principe ».

Hans Schmoller, Esq., M.S.I.A.

You may certainly have permission to use an example of my writing if you wish to, but I really took to using italic as my ordinary hand at the time the Society was formed & I think it is still in the process of changing!

Yours sincerely

Anna Hornby

Miss Anna Hornby

I was much entertained last summer with a tame bat, which would take flies out of a person's hand. If you gave it anything to eat, it brought its wings round before the mouth, hovering and hiding its head very much in the manner of birds of prey when they feed. The adroitness it showed in shearing off the wings of the flies, which were always rejected, was worthy of observation and pleased me much.

Walter V. Cowen, Esq.

New York 27 August 1954

Dear Mr. Dumpleton:

Just returned from a three months' invasion of Europe, I see that your inquiry of 29 June must have arrived here in the very middle of my holidays. And though I fear these lines may be hopelessly late for your purpose, I still send them if only to mitigate the discourtesy of a tardy response—the tardiness being for once not entirely my fault! Here in the United States, as you may know, handwriting reform waits upon the result of British experiment; so that it becomes the duty of every believer

Paul Standard, Esq.

3 : vii : '54

Dear Mr Dumpleton

thank you for your very courteous letter. I shall look forward to seeing your new book and I hope it will be successful in inducing people, dissatisfied with their handwriting and desirous of reforming it, to adopt Italic as the best for work-a-day and everyday use. I hope, too, that you will make them realise that in doing so they will get a great deal of enjoyment even during the awkwardnesses of the first stages.

Joseph Compton, Esq., C.B.E.

Anyone who sets out to improve his handwriting by copying contemporary examples seems to me to be asking for trouble. As a rule, such examples are themselves copies of original Chancery hands adapted to the circumstances & idiosyncracies of the writer. Far better to look at the real thing & see for yourself how Arrighi & Co. achieved their miraculous effects: Reproductions of such handwriting are not difficult to get hold of and will teach you infinitely more than you will learn by studying mine.

Nicolas Bentley, Esq.

'Nevertheless, such a piece of legible writing would not have attracted the attention of Robert Bridges if it had not one or more other qualities. These are beauty, character and style.
To write beautifully as well as legibly requires much practice, some study of fine examples, and a good deal of zeal.'

Miss Heather Child

Julia J
Die Teenie-Jahre

Teil 7

Erhobenen Hauptes

Katrina Kahler

Aus dem Englischen von Anja Bauermeister

Inhalt

Die Entdeckung …

Sobald die Stunde zu Ende war, packte ich eilig meine Sachen zusammen, um vor Saras bösem Blick und ihren Drohungen zu fliehen. Aber ich kannte ihr Geheimnis. Und es wurde Zeit, dass ich dieses Wissen nutzte. Als sie an mir vorbeilief, erwiderte ich ihren Blick ohne Furcht. Ich wollte ihr zeigen, dass ich keine Angst mehr vor ihr hatte.

An der Tür des Klassenzimmers sah ich mich noch einmal nach Blake um, der gerade auf mich zukam. Das war vielleicht meine Chance, mich mit ihm auszusprechen. Doch da packte mich jemand von hinten am Arm. In der Erwartung, Sara gegenüberzustehen, wirbelte ich herum. Ich war bereit, ihr meine Meinung zu sagen – direkt hier, vor allen Leuten.

Statt ihrer fiesen Miene jedoch begegnete mir Beckys besorgtes Gesicht. „Julia, ich muss dir etwas zeigen." Ihr eindringlicher Tonfall und fester Griff an meinem Arm ließen bei mir sofort die Alarmglocken schrillen.

Blake näherte sich der Tür und ich zögerte.

„Becky, ich kann gerade nicht", murmelte ich und versuchte, sie abzuschütteln.

„Es ist aber wichtig!" Sie verstärkte ihren Griff und zog mich den Korridor entlang.

Ich seufzte genervt, als sie die Tür zum Mädchenklo aufstieß.

Aus Frust über meine verpasste Chance, mit Blake zu reden, blaffte ich sie an: „Was ist denn? Was musst du mir zeigen?"

Sie ging auf die mittlere Kabine zu und drückte die Tür auf. „Guck mal!"

Mein Bauch rumorte furchtsam, als ich mich neben sie stellte. Instinktiv wusste ich, dass ihre Entdeckung etwas mit mir zu tun hatte. Aber auf das, was ich sah, war ich dennoch nicht vorbereitet. Als mein Blick auf die Schmierereien an der Wand fiel, blieb mir vor Schreck der Mund offen stehen.

Da standen die Worte … *WILLST DU MIT MIR SPAß HABEN? DANN SCHREIB MIR! @juliajones*. Neben den Text hatte jemand eine grobe Skizze von einem nackten Mädchen mit langem Haar und einem breiten Grinsen im Gesicht gemalt.

„Das kann doch nicht wahr sein!"

„Da ist noch mehr!", sagte Becky und zog mich

ganz in die Kabine, bevor sie die Tür hinter uns schloss.

Zu den vielen Kritzeleien, die Schüler im Laufe der Zeit in den Lack geritzt hatten, waren weitere hinzugekommen …

Ich liebe Schaumbäder. Du auch? Dann schreib mir jederzeit! @juliajones

Willst du Spaß haben? Schreib mir! @juliajones

Wenn du Lust auf Party hast, melde dich bei mir @juliajones

Ich starrte ungläubig auf die Worte.

„Du musst es jemandem melden", zischte Becky. „Sonst hört das nie auf!"

Sie brach ab, als die Tür zu den Toiletten lautstark aufgestoßen wurde und eine Gruppe schwatzender Mädchen hereinkam. Becky öffnete die Kabinentür und ich folgte ihr heraus.

Die Mädchen starrten uns verblüfft an. Zwei von ihnen kannte ich aus meinem Geschichtskurs – es waren die beiden, die nur kurz zuvor über mich gelästert hatten. Die größere der beiden hatte langes pechschwarzes Haar, trug eine dicke Schicht Mascara und Eyeliner sowie mehrere Piercings im Ohr. Als sie mich sah, schnaubte sie spöttisch und drehte sich lachend zu ihrer Freundin um. „Sie hat offenbar schon

wieder Spaß!“

Die andere unterdrückte ein Kichern, aber der Rest der Gruppe brach in lautes Gelächter aus. Sie alle musterten mich von Kopf bis Fuß, während sie auf meine Reaktion warteten.

Das dunkelhaarige Mädchen konnte es offenbar nicht lassen, mich noch weiter zu verspotten: „Womit möchtest du denn als Nächstes Spaß haben, Julia?“

Meine Augen verengten sich und ich musste mich zusammenreißen, um sie nicht gegen das Waschbecken an der Wand zu schubsen. Becky, die meine Anspannung spürte, ergriff meinen Arm und flüsterte mir ins Ohr: „Lass uns gehen.“

„Sie nimmt wahrscheinlich zu Hause wieder ein Schaumbad. Mal sehen, was sie diesmal online stellt!“ Die höhnische Stimme der Dunkelhaarigen folgte mir zur Tür. Erst als diese hinter mir zufiel, erstarb das Gelächter der Gruppe.

Ich wollte nur noch fliehen, so schnell wie möglich weg von hier.

Flucht …

Ich atmete scharf ein und blickte Becky an. „Ich muss gehen“, murmelte ich, während ich krampfhaft versuchte, meine Tränen zurückzuhalten.

Bevor Becky auch nur die Chance hatte, zu antworten, eilte ich schon durch den Flur davon, in dem es mittlerweile vor Schülern nur so wimmelte. Als ich es wagte, mich flüchtig umzuschauen, entdeckte ich Ky inmitten der Menge. Er lachte und plauderte mit seinen Freunden, als hätte er keine Sorge in der Welt. Dann bemerkte er mich und stockte. Selbst in meiner momentanen Verfassung entging mir nicht das Interesse in seinem Blick.

Weiß er es? Hat er auch schon das Foto von mir im Whirlpool gesehen … das Foto, das schreit: Guck mich an! Ich nehme ein Schaumbad. Willst du mitmachen?

Das war zwar nicht der genaue Wortlaut, aber es vermittelte genau diesen Eindruck. *Ein Bild sagt mehr als tausend Worte*. Diesen Spruch hatte ich schon oft gehört, und im Fall des

Schaumbadfotos könnte die Andeutung nicht offensichtlicher sein.

Ich fühlte mich noch mehr gedemütigt, als mir klar wurde, dass Ky das Foto natürlich auch gesehen hatte. Wie könnte er nicht? Mittlerweile hatte es sich wahrscheinlich im ganzen Internet verbreitet und war für alle Welt sichtbar. Ich war mir nicht sicher, warum es mir so sehr zu schaffen machte, dass er davon wusste - aber das tat es.

In ein paar Tagen würden die Sommerferien beginnen und ich hatte gehofft, das alles hinter mir lassen zu können. Doch das Internet ruhte nie. Jede Millisekunde jedes Tages kamen neue Verknüpfungen dazu und wer wusste schon, wo das Foto am Ende auftauchen würde? Vielleicht lachten sie sogar in Australien darüber.

Hahaha … schau mal dieses Mädchen hier …

Kennst du schon das Foto von dem Schaumbad-Mädchen? Nein? Das musst du dir ansehen. Ich teile es mit dir …

Und jetzt war meine Privatsphäre sogar in der Schule verletzt worden. Jedes Mädchen, das dieses Klo benutzte, würde die Kommentare an den Wänden und der Tür sehen. Ich würde bald die Witzfigur der gesamten Schule sein.

Die Gedanken wirbelten in meinem Kopf herum,

während ich durch den Flur eilte. An meinem Schließfach hielt ich kurz an. Trotz des Chaos in meinem Inneren erinnerte ich mich irgendwie daran, welche Bücher ich brauchte, um mich auf die Prüfungen am nächsten Tag vorzubereiten. Aber gerade als ich sie herausholen wollte, legte jemand eine Hand auf meinen Arm.

Ich blickte auf und sah in Kys besorgtes Gesicht. „Julia, alles okay?“

Ich schluckte schwer und wagte es nicht, zu sprechen. Während ich mir die Tränen von den Wangen wischte, nickte ich nur.

„Mach dir keine Gedanken wegen dem ganzen Internetkram, Julia. Manchmal können die Leute echt bescheuert sein. Aber sie vergessen es auch bald wieder und beschäftigen sich mit etwas anderem.“ Seine beruhigende Stimme zu hören, zerriss mir fast das Herz. Der Blick seiner blauen Augen war so verständnisvoll wie früher.

Ich brachte noch immer keinen Ton hervor. Ein verzweifelter Schluchzer drängte sich mit aller Macht aus meiner Kehle, doch ich hielt ihn zurück. Ich wollte mich nicht noch mehr blamieren.

Rasch griff ich nach meinen Büchern, machte meinen Spind zu und schenkte Ky ein flüchtiges, aber dankbares Lächeln, bevor ich mich abwandte und ihn hinter mir zurückließ.

Zu dieser Tageszeit fuhren noch keine Schulbusse, deshalb musste ich zu Fuß nach Hause gehen. Halb hoffte ich, dass Ky mir nachrennen würde, um mir vielleicht noch mehr ermutigende Worte zu sagen.

Aber ich wusste auch, dass das alles nur noch komplizierter machen würde. Überhaupt verwirrte es mich, dass Ky mich angesprochen hatte. Es war so unerwartet gekommen und hatte in mir wieder alle möglichen Gefühle aufgewirbelt. Dabei brauchte ich wirklich nicht noch mehr Probleme.

Trotzdem fand ich es sehr nett, dass er sich die Mühe gemacht hatte, mich zu trösten. Er wirkte ehrlich besorgt, und obwohl ich ihn verabscheuen sollte, weil er sich mit meiner besten Freundin eingelassen hatte, konnte ich es nicht. Er war der einzige Mensch, für den ich nie so empfinden könnte.

Dann kam mir Blake in den Sinn. Sein warmes Lächeln beim Betreten des Englischzimmers hatte mir geholfen, den Aufsatz zu schreiben.

Ohne seine Unterstützung hätte ich das nie geschafft. Trotz allem, was passiert war, hielt er weiterhin zu mir. Und das würde ich nie vergessen.

Während ich durch die Straßen lief, blitzten wieder die Schmierereien vor mir auf, die in den Lack der Klotür geritzt worden waren. Gerade als ich mich dazu bereit gefühlt hatte, Sara die Stirn zu bieten, traf mich die nächste Attacke. Es war alles zu viel für mich.

Ich erinnerte mich an Beckys teilnahmsvolles Gesicht und ihre Bereitschaft, mir zu helfen, und war so dankbar dafür. Wenigstens ein paar Menschen waren noch immer auf meiner Seite.

Als ich ein Vibrieren in meiner Tasche spürte, zog ich mein Handy heraus und sah Beckys Namen auf dem Display. Ich hielt das Telefon an mein Ohr. „Hey", war alles, was ich herausbrachte.

Sobald ich Beckys Stimme hörte, liefen mir wieder die Tränen über die Wangen.

„Julia, du bist so schnell verschwunden. Ist alles in Ordnung?"

„Ja", krächzte ich erstickt, obwohl es alles andere als in Ordnung war.

„Ich gehe jetzt ins Sekretariat und melde das mit

dem Graffiti. Hoffentlich lassen sie es sofort entfernen.“

„Danke, Becky!“ Ich war überwältigt, dass sie das für mich tun würde. Seit der Sache mit Millie und Jess war ich mir nicht mehr ganz sicher gewesen, ob meine Freundschaft zu Becky halten würde. Aber sie war eine echte Freundin und ich war ihr nicht egal.

„Wahrscheinlich sind Chelsea und ihre Clique dafür verantwortlich. Das ist so typisch für sie!“

„Chelsea?“, fragte ich.

„Ja, die mit dem schwarzen Eyeliner und den Piercings. Von der hält man sich besser fern. Sie macht nur Schwierigkeiten.“

Toll! Noch jemand, den ich auf meine Liste setzen kann. „Ist sie mit Sara befreundet?“, fragte ich. Ich hatte Sara noch nie mit dieser Gruppe gesehen, aber vielleicht hatte sie neue Anhänger gewonnen.

„Sie sind nicht wirklich in der gleichen Clique, aber Sara ist so ziemlich überall beliebt.“

Ich seufzte und schüttelte frustriert den Kopf. „Wusstest du, dass Sara die Fotos auf Facebook und Instagram gestellt hat?“

„Millie hat es mir erzählt“, erwiderte Becky. „Sie hat echt ein schlechtes Gewissen, Julia. Sie gibt

sich selbst die Schuld."

„Das sollte sie auch!" Ich schnaubte. „Es ist ihre Schuld, dass die Fotos überhaupt im Internet zu finden waren. Und dann gab es da noch die Gerüchte über Sara und Mr. Hathaway ... Ich habe Millie und Jess gesagt, sie sollen es für sich behalten. Sara hatte es schon immer auf mich abgesehen und wenn sie diese Gerüchte gehört hat, dann wird sie automatisch mich im Verdacht haben."

„Warte mal ... was?" Ich hörte die Überraschung in Beckys Stimme. „Millie und Jess haben es doch niemandem weitererzählt, oder?"

Ich erklärte Becky, dass andere gehört hatten, wie sie sich in der Cafeteria darüber unterhielten. Aber Becky war sowieso der Meinung, dass es an der Zeit war, Mr. Hathaway zu melden. „Das ist alles ziemlich abartig. Ist mir egal, wenn er seinen Job verliert. Das wird ihm eine Lehre sein."

Eigentlich stimmte ich Becky zu. Das Problem war nur, dass ich mich genau in der Schusslinie befand. Ich war Saras Hauptziel, wenn sie Rache nehmen wollte. Und ihre Liste mit Gründen, weshalb sie sich an mir rächen könnte, wuchs immer weiter an.

Da war als Erstes Blake. Sie hatte ihn dabei erwischt, wie er mich auf der Party geküsst

hatte. Dann hatte er mit ihr Schluss gemacht und seine ganze Aufmerksamkeit auf mich gerichtet. Das würde jedes Mädchen verärgern. Aber es war nur der Anfang. Unsere Konfrontation in *Eliza's Boutique* und die Gerüchte über sie und Mr. Hathaway gossen noch mehr Öl ins Feuer.

Die Drohung, dass ich ihr Verhältnis mit einem Lehrer auffliegen lassen würde, war meine einzige Waffe, das Einzige, was sie aufhalten könnte. Aber wenn die Geschichte schon vorher herauskam, fehlte mir jede Munition.

„Ich gehe jetzt ins Sekretariat", unterbrach Becky meine Gedanken, „und melde die Schmierereien im Klo."

„Vielen Dank, Becky."

„Das ist das Mindeste, was ich tun kann, Julia. Und wenn du möchtest, komme ich mit dir mit, um Sara zu melden. Wir könnten mit einem unserer Lehrer reden. Vielleicht wäre Miss McCarthy, die Schulpsychologin, die beste Ansprechperson. Ich habe gehört, dass sie sehr nett sein soll. Also lass mich wissen, wie du dich entscheidest. Und wann immer du etwas brauchst, ruf mich an, okay?"

„Mach ich!" Ich nickte und war froh, dass wenigstens das Graffiti beseitigt werden würde, bevor zu viele Leute es sahen. „Danke noch mal, Becky. Wir sehen uns morgen."

Kurz nachdem ich aufgelegt hatte, bog ich in unsere Auffahrt ein. Es hatte mir sehr geholfen, mit Becky zu reden, obwohl ich noch immer unsicher war, was ich jetzt tun sollte. Sollte ich Sara wirklich melden? Oder sollte ich es ihr mit gleicher Münze heimzahlen und ihr drohen? Ich hatte mich schon darauf eingestellt, doch jetzt packten mich wieder die Zweifel.

Ich erreichte die Haustür und griff nach dem Türknauf. Gerade wollte ich den Schlüssel einstecken, als die Tür direkt bei meiner Berührung aufschwang. Matts Auto war nirgends zu sehen und ich runzelte die Stirn über seine Achtlosigkeit. Er hatte wohl mal wieder vergessen, abzuschließen. Vor ein paar Wochen war ich schon einmal nach Hause gekommen und hatte die Haustür sperrangelweit offen vorgefunden. Als ich ihn danach fragte, bestand er darauf, dass er zugeschlossen hätte, bevor er gegangen war. Aber da ihm das nicht zum ersten Mal passierte, konnte ich das nur schwer glauben.

Ich zuckte mit den Schultern, stellte meine Tasche neben der Treppe ab und ging in die Küche. Während ich überlegte, ob ich mir den Rest von unserem Abendessen zum Mittag aufwärmen sollte, fing eine kleine Bewegung in meinem Augenwinkel meine Aufmerksamkeit ein. Einen Moment später trat mir eine dunkle Gestalt in den Weg. Ein Schrei entfuhr mir.

Ich hielt mir die Hand vor den Mund und versuchte, die kalte Furcht zu unterdrücken, die mir über den Rücken kroch. Meine Haut kribbelte vor lauter Abscheu angesichts der Person, die vor mir stand.

Der Eindringling …

Ein schmieriges Lächeln lag auf Barrys Gesicht, während er mich mit seinen kleinen scharfen Augen musterte. „Hallo, Julia!“ Er lachte leise. „Tut mir leid. Ich wollte dich nicht erschrecken.“ Seine Finger berührten flüchtig meinen Arm. Ich zuckte zusammen und trat einen Schritt zurück, um Abstand zwischen uns zu bringen.

„Was … was machen Sie hier? Und wie sind Sie reingekommen? Mom hat uns nicht gesagt, dass Sie heute hier sein würden“, stammelte ich, während mein Blick verzweifelt hin und her wanderte. Ich hoffte, Matt würde kommen.

Barry grinste schief. „Ich war gerade in der Gegend und wollte nur kurz nachfragen, ob noch irgendetwas repariert werden muss. Ich wusste nicht, ob jemand zu Hause ist … aber anscheinend war es perfektes Timing.“

Ich schüttelte den Kopf und ging rückwärts auf die Tür zu. „Hier gibt es nichts mehr zu reparieren. Aber … wie sind Sie ins Haus gekommen?“

„Mit dem Ersatzschlüssel.“ Er hielt ihn hoch und schwenkte ihn in der Luft, als wollte er mich damit verhöhnen.

Ich griff danach, doch er war zu schnell und zog seine Hand zurück, den Schlüssel in seiner Faust umschlossen.

„Sie können hier nicht einfach hereinspazieren, wann immer Sie möchten. Und dieser Schlüssel gehört uns. Geben Sie ihn zurück!“ Ich funkelte ihn an. In diesem Moment war meine Wut stärker als meine Furcht.

„Na, na, Julia. Nun hab' dich doch nicht so!“ Bei seinem anzüglichen Tonfall standen mir die Haare zu Berge.

„Sie sollten gehen!“, sagte ich und öffnete die Haustür. „Sofort!“

„Das ist aber nicht sehr höflich. Nach allem, was ich für euch getan habe. Du hast dich noch nicht mal dafür bedankt, dass ich deinen Schrank repariert habe. Übrigens hast du wirklich hübsche Sachen. Ich war besonders vorsichtig, als ich sie ausgeräumt habe. Wirklich sehr, sehr hübsch.“ Er streckte seine Hand aus und berührte eine lose Strähne meines Haars.

Angewidert wehrte ich ihn ab und zog mein Handy aus der Tasche. „Ich rufe Mom an.“

Sein Grinsen verwandelte sich in eine verärgerte Maske und er packte mein Handgelenk. „Ich glaube nicht, dass du das tun solltest.“

Ich schluckte und versuchte, meinen Arm aus seinem Griff zu winden. „Lassen Sie mich los!“

Er stieß mit einem Fuß die Tür zu, ohne mich dabei aus den Augen zu lassen. Mein Herz hämmerte wild in meiner Brust, während ich weiter versuchte, mich zu befreien.

Plötzlich drückte jemand von außen die Tür auf, sodass sie gegen meinen Rücken stieß. Ich wirbelte herum. Vor uns stand Matt und schaute uns verwirrt an.

Sein Blick wanderte von mir zu Barry und dann zu Barrys Hand, die noch immer meinen Arm festhielt. „Was ist hier los?“

Barry nahm seine Hand weg und lächelte unschuldig. „Ich wollte nur mal nachsehen, ob ihr noch irgendwelche Reparaturen benötigt.“

„Er hat unseren Ersatzschlüssel benutzt, um bei uns einzudringen“, sprudelte es aus mir hervor. Jetzt, da mein Bruder hier war, wuchs mein Mut wieder. „Er war schon im Haus, als ich gekommen bin.“

„Eure Mom hat mich darum gebeten. Sie hat mir auch gesagt, wo ich den Ersatzschlüssel finde,

wie du weißt“, sagte Barry und lächelte Matt an. „Und ich habe gehört, dass du diese Woche deine Abschlussfeier hast! Glückwunsch, Kumpel!“ Er klopfte Matt auf die Schulter. Es war ein ziemlich offensichtlicher Versuch, das Thema zu wechseln.

„Geben Sie mir einfach den Schlüssel und gehen Sie!“, wiederholte ich wütend. Dann riss ich ihm den Schlüssel aus der Hand und öffnete die Tür weit.

Matt trat zur Seite, um Barry durchzulassen. „Ich denke auch, dass Sie gehen sollten. Wir brauchen keine Hilfe mehr bei den Reparaturen.“

Die beiden starrten sich kurz an. Schließlich trat Barry durch die geöffnete Tür. „Ein wenig mehr Dankbarkeit könnte euch nicht schaden!“, fauchte er, bevor er Flüche vor sich hin murmelnd die Treppe hinunterstieg.

Nachdem ich die Tür ins Schloss geworfen und abgeschlossen hatte, lehnte ich mich gegen das Holz und sah erleichtert zu meinem Bruder. Meine Hände zitterten noch und meine Lippen bebten.

„Alles okay, Julia?“ Matt wirkte fast genauso aufgewühlt wie ich.

„Er war schon vor mir da, Matt. Wenn du nicht

gekommen wärst …“ Ich sprach den Satz nicht zu Ende. Mir wurde übel, wenn ich daran dachte, was hätte passieren können. „Ich bin mir sicher, dass er nicht zum ersten Mal hier war. Weißt du noch, als die Tür sperrangelweit offen stand …? Vielleicht sollten wir die Polizei rufen.“

Matt fuhr sich mit der Hand durchs Haar. „Ich weiß nicht, ob die irgendwas tun können. Mom hat ihm Zugang zu unserem Haus gegeben. Sie hat ihm sogar von dem Ersatzschlüssel erzählt. Ich rufe sie gleich an. Wir müssen es ihr sagen. Und dafür sorgen, dass er nicht wiederkommt.“

Ich umklammerte den Schlüssel in meiner Faust und beschloss, dass wir ein besseres Versteck dafür finden mussten.

Dann sah ich meinen Bruder an. „Ich habe ihn schon immer gehasst. Er war mir von Anfang an unsympathisch. Aber keiner wollte auf mich hören.“

Matt runzelte die Stirn und zog mich in seine Arme. Anschließend lehnte ich mich an seine Schulter und beobachtete, wie er in der Kontaktliste seines Smartphones Moms Nummer heraussuchte.

Er stellte das Handy auf Lautsprecher und wir warteten darauf, dass sie abnahm.

Wutanfall …

Als Mom später durch die Tür eilte, zeigte ihr Gesicht eine Mischung aus Schuldbewusstsein und Sorge. „Julia, Matt. Es tut mir so leid, was passiert ist. Ich dachte, ich könnte Barry vertrauen. Ich hatte keine Ahnung …“

Ich biss mir auf die Lippe und runzelte die Stirn. Es war ihre Schuld, dass ihr widerlicher Freund überhaupt in unserem Leben war. Sie hatte ihm den Ort des Ersatzschlüssels verraten. Wenn irgendetwas passiert wäre, wäre sie dafür verantwortlich gewesen.

Mom trug ihre vollen Einkaufstüten in die Küche und begann, sie auszupacken. Ich stand daneben und fragte mich, wie unser Leben so kompliziert hatte werden können.

Plötzlich hielt sie inne und sah mich an. „Ich dachte, Barry wäre ein guter Mann. Das dachte ich wirklich. Aber er ist ganz und gar nicht der Mensch, für den ich ihn gehalten habe. Und was er heute gemacht hat … das bringt das Fass zum Überlaufen.“

Ihre Augen flehten uns um Vergebung an, aber weder Matt noch ich antworteten ihr. Dann holte sie tief Luft und verkündete etwas, das wir nicht hatten kommen sehen. „Ich habe beschlossen, zurückzukommen.“

Ich blickte zu Matt und dann zu Mom, während ich versuchte, ihre Worte zu begreifen. „Was meinst du damit?“

„Ich kann nicht länger mit Barry zusammenwohnen. Nicht nach dem, was heute geschehen ist. Ich habe schon länger darüber nachgedacht, ihn zu verlassen, und jetzt steht meine Entscheidung fest. Ich werde wieder zurückziehen. Hier gehöre ich hin.“

Matt zog die Augenbrauen hoch. Ich war mir nicht sicher, was er von dieser Neuigkeit hielt. Wir hatten uns beide so daran gewöhnt, allein zu leben und für uns selbst zu sorgen, und es war zur Routine geworden, dass Dad nur an einigen Wochenenden zu Hause war. Moms meckernde Stimme und ihre strengen Regeln hatten wir nicht vermisst.

„Weiß Dad das schon?“, fragte ich. Was würde wohl unser Vater davon halten?

„Nein.“ Mom schüttelte den Kopf. „Ich habe es ihm noch nicht gesagt.“

Ich runzelte die Stirn. „Wird er denn damit

einverstanden sein?“

„Nun, das ist immerhin auch mein Haus. Also wird er sich wohl damit abfinden müssen.“

Matt, der Streitigkeiten am liebsten aus dem Weg ging, sagte nichts. Aber ich konnte meine Meinung nicht für mich behalten. „Denkst du nicht, dass du ihn trotzdem vorher fragen solltest? Ich meine … du hast ihn immerhin für einen anderen Mann verlassen. Solltest du Dad nicht fragen, ob er überhaupt möchte, dass du zurückkommst?“

Mom stieß einen schweren Seufzer aus. „Ich weiß, dass das eine schwierige Situation ist. Aber wir werden uns damit arrangieren. Außerdem ist euer Vater so selten zu Hause und ihr braucht jemanden, der für euch sorgt. Ihr seid noch viel zu jung, um allein zu leben.“

„Das hat dich vorher auch nicht gestört“, entfuhr es mir.

Sie ignorierte meine Bemerkung und packte weiter ihre Einkäufe aus. Nach einigen Sekunden der Stille sagte sie: „Heute Abend gibt es selbstgemachte Pizza. Genau wie ihr sie mögt!“

Sie lächelte, als wäre Pizza die Lösung für alles. Mom würde wieder einziehen. Ende der Diskussion. Die Tatsache, dass sie unser aller

Leben auf den Kopf gestellt hatte, war anscheinend vollkommen unwichtig.

Ich starrte sie fassungslos an. Wie konnte sie so tun, als wäre alles in Ordnung?

Das ist immerhin auch mein Haus. Also wird er sich wohl damit abfinden müssen. Ihre Worte wiederholten sich in meinem Kopf und ich musste mich beherrschen, um sie nicht anzuschreien. Sie hatte uns verlassen - für einen widerlichen, lüsternen Handwerker, der seine Augen nicht von ihrer minderjährigen Tochter nehmen konnte. Ich hatte mich oft genug über ihn und seine gierigen Blicke beschwert, doch sie hatte mich nicht ernst genommen. *Ach, Julia, sei doch nicht albern! Barry ist so ein netter Mann. Er ist nur freundlich, das ist alles.* Ich schnaubte bei der Erinnerung und schüttelte den Kopf.

Auf einmal kochte meine Wut über und ich konnte mich nicht mehr zurückhalten. „Du bist einfach ausgezogen und hast uns verlassen! Hast du das etwa schon vergessen?“, warf ich ihr an den Kopf. Sie besaß auch noch die Frechheit, mich so erstaunt anzusehen, als wäre sie sich keiner Schuld bewusst.

„Matt und ich gehen noch zur Schule und Dad arbeitet in einer anderen Stadt. Aber davon hast du dich nicht aufhalten lassen! Oh nein! Du hast nur an dich selbst gedacht. Und das ist natürlich

viel wichtiger als deine FAMILIE!!"

Der beißende Sarkasmus in meinem Tonfall ließ sie zusammenzucken. Sie hielt ein Glas Pizzasoße in der Hand und starrte mich mit offenem Mund an. Dann blickte sie betroffen zu Matt, der still neben mir stand.

„Was, wenn wir nicht wollen, dass du zurückkommst? Hast du daran schon mal gedacht?" Meine Lautstärke steigerte sich mit jedem Wort. „Was, wenn Dad sagt, dass du nicht nach Hause kommen kannst? Was wirst du dann tun? Läufst du wieder zurück zu deinem widerlichen Freund und flehst ihn an, SEINE HÄNDE VON DEINER TOCHTER ZU LASSEN?"

Meine Stimme überschlug sich beinahe. Der verdutzte Gesichtsausdruck meiner Mutter steigerte meinen Ärger noch.

Ich konnte ihren Anblick nicht länger ertragen und schob mich an meinem Bruder vorbei aus der Küche. Ich musste weg hier. Vielleicht könnte ich zu Emmie gehen. Sicher würde ihre Mom nichts dagegen haben.

Ich rannte zur Haustür, riss sie auf und starrte auf die Straße. Als mir der kalte Abendwind ins Gesicht fuhr, blieb ich wie angewurzelt stehen. Es würde bald dunkel werden und Emmie wohnte ziemlich weit weg. Was, wenn Barry

dort draußen irgendwo lauerte und uns beobachtete? Die Erinnerung an seine Hand auf meinem Arm ließ mich erschaudern und ich änderte meine Meinung.

Mit einem frustrierten Seufzer schlug ich die Tür zu, schloss ab und rannte hoch in mein Zimmer, wobei ich zwei Stufen auf einmal nahm.

Prioritäten …

In meinem Zimmer zog ich mein Handy aus der Tasche und suchte nach Dads Nummer. Ich musste mit ihm reden, ihn warnen, dass seine sogenannte Ehefrau wieder da war.

Was glaubte sie eigentlich? Dass sie einfach so zurück in ihr gemeinsames Schlafzimmer ziehen konnte, als wäre nichts vorgefallen? Dass Dad sie mit offenen Armen willkommen heißen würde?

Während ich auf die Verbindung wartete, lief ich ungeduldig in meinem Zimmer auf und ab. Aber statt des Klingeltons hörte ich nur Stille. Ich tippte noch einmal auf die Anruftaste und wartete einige Sekunden – wieder nichts.

Ich biss frustriert die Zähne zusammen und warf das Telefon auf mein Bett, bevor ich mich daneben fallen ließ. Dad arbeitete zurzeit in einer Gegend mit schlechtem Handynetz und es war immer schwierig, ihn zu erreichen. Aber ich musste unbedingt mit ihm reden!

Ich sah ihn vor mir, sein trauriges Lächeln und

die liebevollen braunen Augen. Er hatte Mom schrecklich vermisst, nachdem sie uns verlassen hatte. Obwohl er versucht hatte, sich nichts anmerken zu lassen, sah ich den Schmerz in seinem Gesicht und seiner Körperhaltung, wenn er sich unbeobachtet glaubte. Er bemühte sich, für Matt und mich gute Miene zum bösen Spiel zu machen. Aber auch für ihn war die Situation sehr schwierig gewesen.

Als mir das bewusst wurde, fragte ich mich, ob ich vielleicht falsch lag. Was, wenn Moms Rückkehr genau das war, worauf Dad gehofft hatte?

Vielleicht war es die Antwort auf all seine Gebete. Wenn das der Fall war, durfte ich mich nicht dazwischen stellen. Dads Glück hatte oberste Priorität.

In Gedanken ganz bei meinem Vater ging ich zurück nach unten in die Küche.

Mom und Matt schauten überrascht auf. Ich wusste sofort, dass sie über mich gesprochen hatten, und kniff die Augen zusammen. Matt sollte auf meiner Seite sein. Ich wollte nicht, dass Mom hier einfach so hereinschneite und ihn mit ihren Kochkünsten um den Finger wickelte. Sie verhielt sich sowieso wie die Übermutter, wann immer er in der Nähe war. Kein Wunder, dass er nicht gelernt hatte, für sich selbst zu sorgen.

Ich sah Mom herausfordernd an. „Rufst du Dad wenigstens an und sagst ihm, dass du hier bist? Damit er weiß, was ihn erwartet, wenn er nach Hause kommt?“

Sie nickte, runzelte aber besorgt die Stirn. „Ja, natürlich. Ich rufe ihn gleich heute Abend an.“

„Ich habe es gerade versucht und ihn nicht erreicht. Er hat wahrscheinlich mal wieder keinen Empfang.“

Ich glaubte, ein Aufblitzen der Erleichterung in ihren Augen zu sehen. Sie war vermutlich froh, dass ich ihr nicht zuvorgekommen war. Und vielleicht war das wirklich besser so. Wenn ich ihn in diesem aufgewühlten Zustand angerufen hätte, hätte er sich nur Sorgen gemacht, und das lag nicht in meiner Absicht.

Ich starrte sie weiterhin böse an. „Er kommt am Mittwochabend heim, rechtzeitig für Matts Abschlussfeier. Also solltest du ihn besser vorher erwischen!“

„Ich rufe ihn an, keine Sorge“, erwiderte sie gehorsam, als wäre sie das Kind und ich die Mutter.

Aber ich war noch nicht fertig. „Was ist mit Barry? Hast du ihm schon gesagt, dass du ihn verlässt?“

Sie schüttelte den Kopf. „Direkt nach eurem Anruf habe ich meine Sachen gepackt und bin verschwunden. Ich will ihn nie wiedersehen."

Ich kaute nachdenklich auf meiner Unterlippe. „Hast du ihm eine Nachricht dagelassen?"

Sie nickte. „Ich habe ihm geschrieben, dass es vorbei ist und dass er mich und meine Familie in Ruhe lassen soll."

Ich schnaubte leise, als sie *meine Familie* sagte.

Matt musterte sie besorgt. „Glaubst du, dass er sich daran halten wird?"

Mom seufzte. „Ich hoffe es."

„Er wird doch nicht versuchen, bei uns einzubrechen oder so?", fragte ich und mein Ärger wich Angst.

„Nein, Julia. Natürlich nicht. Alles wird gut." Sie zwang sich zu einem Lächeln und wandte sich dann wieder den Pizzen zu, die sie belegte. Aber ich sah, dass sie sich trotzdem Sorgen machte. Waren wir ohne Dad wirklich sicher?

Ich warf einen Blick aus dem Fenster in die Dunkelheit. Lauerte Barry dort irgendwo und wartete nur darauf, dass wir schlafen gingen, damit er bei uns eindringen konnte? Was, wenn er eine Kopie von unserem Schlüssel angefertigt hatte? Was dann? Ich verwarf den Gedanken.

Wenn er seinen eigenen Schlüssel hätte, würde er nicht den Ersatzschlüssel benutzen.

Dennoch ging ich zur Hintertür und schob den Riegel vor. Dann schloss ich auch alle Fenster. Es war mir egal, wenn der Backofen die Küche aufheizte.

Mom und Matt beobachteten mich, sagten aber kein Wort. Keiner von beiden traute sich. Das Risiko, dass ich wieder explodieren würde, war ihnen wohl zu groß. Die Küche füllte sich mit Wärme und unangenehmem Schweigen. Das einzige Geräusch war das Klacken von Moms Messer auf dem Brettchen, als sie Zwiebeln schnitt.

Ich schaute Matt an, der mit den Schultern zuckte und den Kopf schüttelte. Er konnte so tun, als wäre er unbesorgt, aber ich kannte ihn besser. Nach dem, was vorhin passiert war, machte er sich bestimmt auch Gedanken.

Unerwünschte Ratschläge …

Bald stieg mir der Duft von selbst gemachter Pizza in die Nase und mein knurrender Magen zwang mich dazu, mich widerwillig an den Tisch zu setzen. Während wir aßen, schnitt Mom ein völlig anderes Thema an. „Millies Mutter hat mich heute angerufen."

Ich warf ihr einen Blick zu und vergaß für den Moment meine Sorgen wegen Barry. „Was hat sie gesagt?"

„Sie hat mir von einem Foto auf Facebook erzählt und wollte sich entschuldigen."

Ich schnaufte verächtlich und schüttelte den Kopf. Entschuldigungen …! Es war ja gut zu wissen, dass es Millie und ihrer Mom leidtat, aber das half mir ganz und gar nicht weiter. Abgesehen davon wollte ich das nicht mit meiner Mutter besprechen.

„Mrs. Spencer sagte, dass das Foto einige unschöne Kommentare bekommen hat. Stimmt das?", fragte Mom und musterte mich von der gegenüberliegenden Seite des Tisches aus.

Ich nickte und warf Matt einen warnenden Blick zu. Ich wollte nicht, dass er ihr das ganze Ausmaß der Situation verriet. Das Letzte, was ich brauchte, war eine Schimpftirade von Mom, in der sie von mir verlangte, alle meine Accounts zu schließen und mich von Social Media fernzuhalten.

„Hast du irgendeine Idee, wer dafür verantwortlich ist?“, fragte sie. „Millie glaubt, dass es Sara gewesen sein könnte. Aber sie würde doch so etwas nicht tun, oder? Vielleicht solltest du sie fragen. Vielleicht war es nur als Scherz gemeint und sie löscht es wieder.“

Ich konnte nicht anders, als die Augen zu verdrehen. „Wenn es nur so einfach wäre.“

„Nun, du solltest zumindest mit ihr reden, Julia. Es könnte auch jemand ganz anderes gewesen sein. Kannst du dich bei Facebook beschweren?“

„Denkst du, das habe ich nicht schon längst getan?“, entgegnete ich in spöttischem Tonfall. Sie hatte keine Ahnung, wie Facebook funktionierte; es war für sie ein Buch mit sieben Siegeln. Von ihr würde ich ganz sicher keinen Rat annehmen, wie ich mit dem Problem umgehen sollte.

Ich wartete auf ihren Tadel. Normalerweise wäre ich nicht damit durchgekommen, so mit meiner Mutter zu sprechen. Aber heute schien

sie eine Ausnahme zu machen. Sie fühlte sich vermutlich schuldig und wollte mich nicht noch weiter reizen. Ich nutzte ihre Schwäche aus und grinste überlegen. Ich würde ihr keinen Respekt erweisen.

Sie blickte zu Matt. „Man muss doch irgendetwas tun können, um das Foto zu löschen?“

„Mom“, sagte Matt geduldig, „so einfach ist das nicht.“

„Das klingt für mich nach Cyber-Mobbing und ich weiß, wie schlimm so etwas werden kann. Deshalb wollte ich immer, dass ihr euch von Facebook und anderen Social-Media-Seiten fernhaltet. Die machen nur Ärger.“

Ich verdrehte erneut die Augen. *Ich wusste ja, dass sie nicht lange den Mund halten kann.*

„Ich habe dich davor gewarnt.“ Ihre Stimme wurde sicherer, je länger sie sprach. „Ich finde, du solltest morgen mit jemandem in der Schule reden … einem Lehrer oder vielleicht der Schulpsychologin. Sag ihnen, was vorgefallen ist. Sie können dir vielleicht helfen.“

Ich schüttelte den Kopf. Auch wenn sie wahrscheinlich recht hatte, wollte ich das nicht zugeben.

„Ich begleite dich zur Schule." Sie nickte, als wäre ihre Entscheidung schon getroffen. „Und dann gehen wir der Sache gemeinsam auf den Grund."

Jetzt schüttelte ich noch vehementer den Kopf. Das Letzte, was ich wollte, war, dass meine Mutter in der Schule auftauchte und eine Szene machte. Ich hatte schon genug Aufmerksamkeit, ohne dass sich alle über mich lustig machten, weil meine Mutter im Büro des Rektors an die Decke gegangen war.

„Lass es einfach, Mom. Ich komme schon selber damit klar."

Sie zögerte und ich glaubte schon, sie würde es dabei belassen. Aber sie musste mal wieder das letzte Wort haben. „Dann solltest du aber möglichst bald etwas unternehmen, denn dieses Foto kann sonst überall landen. Du musst an deine Zukunft denken, Julia. So etwas könnte alles zerstören, wofür du gearbeitet hast."

Eine bissige Antwort lag mir auf der Zunge. Ich öffnete den Mund, doch Matt kam mir zuvor. „Vielleicht ist das mit der Schulpsychologin keine so schlechte Idee, Julia. Ich wollte es dir nicht sagen, aber es sind noch mehr Sachen dazugekommen. Es scheint langsam aus dem Ruder zu laufen. Die Psychologin kann dir vielleicht wirklich helfen."

Alarmglocken läuteten in meinem Kopf. Da ich seit gestern Abend nicht auf Facebook und Instagram gewesen war, hatte ich keine Ahnung, wovon er sprach. Aber jetzt musste ich es sofort mit eigenen Augen sehen.

Mein Stuhl schabte laut über das Holz, als ich aufsprang und das angebissene Stück Pizza auf meinem Teller liegen ließ.

Essen war mir in diesem Moment egal. Ich verschwendete auch keinen Gedanken daran, mich zu entschuldigen. Alles, was mich in diesem Moment interessierte, war mein Smartphone.

Sobald ich in mein Zimmer kam, warf ich die Tür hinter mir zu und griff nach meinem Handy. Mein Puls raste, während ich darauf wartete, dass meine Facebook-Seite geladen wurde.

Der nächste Schock …

Vor mir sah ich ein Foto von den Schmierereien auf der Toilettenwand, die meinen Instagram Namen enthielten. Außerdem gab es noch ein neues Foto von mir, auf dem ich lachend den Kopf zurückwarf. Ich erkannte es sofort.

Millie hatte diesen Selfie von uns beiden aufgenommen. Sie hatte ihn auf ihre Instagram-Seite gestellt und getaggt mit …
#bestefreundefürsleben @juliajones

Aber auf diesem Foto war nur ich zu sehen … ein sorgloses Mädchen, das scheinbar eine Menge Spaß hatte. Einer der Sätze von der Klotür war als Überschrift hinzugefügt worden *… Ich liebe Schaumbäder. Du auch? Dann schreib mir jederzeit! @juliajones*

Die Worte sendeten eine klare Botschaft.

Mädchen die Spaß haben wollen hatte das Foto geteilt. Millie war wieder weggeschnitten worden, und wenn ich es nicht besser wüsste, würde ich denken, dass sie dafür verantwortlich war.

Eine Sekunde lang dachte ich darüber nach, bevor ich den Gedanken verwarf. Vermutlich wollte Sara genau das bezwecken … die Freundschaft zwischen Millie und mir zerstören. Sara wusste offensichtlich nicht, was zwischen mir und meiner ehemals besten Freundin in der letzten Woche vorgefallen war.

Der Beitrag war schon mehrmals geteilt worden und hatte eine Menge Likes und Kommentare bekommen. Ich scrollte durch die Liste und las flüchtig …

Ich habe gerne Spaß. Lass uns abhängen.

In den Sommerferien … du und ich … Schaumbad … wie wär's?

Ich liebe Schaumbäder! Lade mich nächstes Mal ein!

Ich bin dabei! Wo wohnst du?

Ich hab dir ne Nachricht geschickt. Schreib zurück!

Die Kommentare nahmen kein Ende. Zu jedem war eine Vielzahl von Emojis hinzugefügt worden, am häufigsten der mit dem zwinkernden Auge und der herausgestreckten Zunge. Es machte mich ganz krank.

Ich hatte auch einen Haufen Nachrichten bekommen, die ich jedoch ignorierte. Stattdessen öffnete ich Instagram und entdeckte dort das gleiche Bild. Mein Account hatte fünfundvierzig

neue Follower, das Foto war fünfundsiebzig Mal gelikt worden, und ich hatte dreiundzwanzig neue Nachrichten, die ich niemals öffnen würde.

So beliebt auf Instagram zu sein wäre für viele ein Traum. Die meisten Leute in der Schule würden sich darum reißen.

„Oooh, mein letztes Foto hat zweihundertvierzig Likes bekommen!“

„Was? Wie hast du das gemacht? Ich habe Glück, wenn ich mal vierzig kriege.“

Dieses Gespräch hatten Lisa und Beth vor der Klassenfahrt geführt. Ich hatte ihrem aufgeregten Geplapper über Lisas neuestes Foto mit halbem Ohr zugehört. Auf dem Bild trug sie ein tief ausgeschnittenes Oberteil und zog einen Schmollmund für die Kamera. Es hatte mich nicht überrascht, dass so viele Jungs das aufreizende Bild gelikt hatten. Matt war vermutlich auch darunter. Es hatte ihr ganz offensichtlich die Aufmerksamkeit eingebracht, nach der sie suchte.

Im Vergleich dazu trug ich auf dem Foto ein ganz normales T-Shirt. Auf dem Originalbild saß Millie neben mir und wir beide lachten in die Kamera. Ich war so glücklich gewesen, dass meine beste Freundin wieder da war. Als ich sah, dass sie mich markiert hatte, hatte ich zwei rote Herzen daruntergesetzt. Es war eines

unserer Lieblingsfotos von uns beiden.

Das war natürlich vor dem ganzen Drama gewesen. Und jetzt sah ich dieses Bild wieder … nur ohne Millie neben mir.

Ich warf das Telefon angewidert aufs Bett. Kurz darauf klopfte mein Bruder an die Tür.

Im Sekretariat …

Erneut half mir Matt dabei, alle Beiträge, Kommentare und Benachrichtigungen auf meinen Profilen zu löschen. Diesmal jedoch machte er vorher Screenshots. Danach duschte ich und ging ins Bett, aber ich konnte lange nicht einschlafen. In meinem Kopf wiederholte sich alles, was am Tag passiert war. Wieder und wieder stiegen angstvolle Bilder vor mir auf.

Als ich endlich eindöste, träumte ich von Fotos, auf denen mein Kopf an Lisas Körper zu sehen war. Meine Schultern waren entblößt und meine Lippen für die Kamera gespitzt. Die Überschrift lautete: *Amüsier dich mit mir!*

Ich erwachte schweißgebadet; sogar mein Kissenbezug war feucht. Ich drehte das Kissen um und schlug die Bettdecke zurück. Dann öffnete ich mein Fenster. Als ich auf die dunkle, baumbestandene Straße blickte, stellte ich mir vor, wie Barry sich irgendwo dort unten in den Schatten verbarg. Rasch zog ich das Fenster wieder zu und stellte sicher, dass es gut verschlossen war.

Während ich mich im Bett herumwälzte, hörte ich erneut die Stimme meines Bruders in meinem Kopf. Er hatte mich schließlich doch überzeugt, morgen früh die Schulpsychologin aufzusuchen und ihr meine Social-Media-Seiten zu zeigen, sowie die Screenshots, die Matt gemacht hatte. Allerdings wollte ich die Sache mit Sara und Mr. Hathaway noch für mich behalten – jedenfalls für den Moment.

Nach einigen Stunden ruhelosen Schlafs erwachte ich vor meinem Wecker und zog mein Biologiebuch aus der Schultasche, um vor dem heutigen Test noch einmal alles durchzugehen. Mit verschwommenem Blick überflog ich meine Notizen. Dabei fiel mir ein, dass ich Ky vermutlich bei der Prüfung sehen würde. Aber ich musste mich auf Wichtigeres konzentrieren. Ich zwang mich dazu, einen Stift zu nehmen und mir noch ein paar Dinge aus dem Buch herauszuschreiben. Das half mir immer dabei, die Informationen besser im Gedächtnis zu behalten.

Ich hoffte nur, dass ich sie auch während der Prüfung würde abrufen können und mich nicht von Ky ablenken lassen würde.

Als ich zum Frühstück nach unten kam, stand Mom schon in der Küche und wendete Pfannkuchen. Sie versuchte offenbar alles, um sich bei mir einzuschmeicheln. Da ich gestern

Abend wenig gegessen hatte, knurrte mein Magen. Ich setzte mich und aß die Pfannkuchen, sprach aber kaum ein Wort mit ihr. Nach dem Essen packte ich mir die restliche Pizza von gestern ein und ging aus dem Haus, ohne mich von ihr zu verabschieden.

Ich wollte, dass sie genauso leiden musste wie mein Dad, mein Bruder und ich, nachdem sie uns einfach sitzen gelassen hatte. Und ich tat es auf die einzige Art, die mir möglich war.

Nachdem ich mit dem ersten Bus an der Schule angekommen war, ging ich direkt zum Sekretariat, wo sich auch die Büros der Schulpsychologin und des Rektors befanden. Ich hatte gehofft, dass Becky mitkommen würde, aber sie hatte heute Morgen einen Zahnarzttermin und würde erst kurz vor Unterrichtsbeginn eintreffen.

Da Miss McCarthy noch nicht da war, setzte ich mich in den Vorraum und wartete nervös. Ein paar andere Schüler saßen in der Nähe, darunter ein Junge mit fettigen schwarzen Haaren, die die Hälfte seines Gesichts bedeckten. Ich musterte ihn neugierig und bemerkte seine vielen Ohrpiercings und seine ungepflegte Erscheinung.

In der Schule durften Schüler nur eine begrenzte Anzahl von Piercings tragen und abgesehen von

Ohrringen waren andere Gesichtspiercings nicht erlaubt. Aber an diese Regel hielten sich nicht alle und so sah man manchmal Leute mit Nasenringen oder Lippenpiercings herumlaufen. Wenn sie erwischt wurden, mussten sie nachsitzen, daher nahmen die meisten ihre Piercings vor dem Unterricht heraus.

Als mich der dunkelhaarige Junge finster anstarrte, wandte ich rasch den Blick ab. Kurz darauf öffnete sich die Tür zu einem der Büros und Mr. Fitzgerald, unser Rektor, winkte den Jungen herein. Ich war erleichtert, dass er ging. Er hatte eine sehr einschüchternde Art.

Ich drehte mich um und blickte durch die Fensterfront hinter mir, um nach Miss McCarthy Ausschau zu halten. Ich hatte zwar noch nie mit ihr gesprochen, wusste aber, wie sie aussah. Da sie relativ jung und ziemlich hübsch war, fiel sie unter dem Rest der Lehrer auf. Einige Male hatte ich mich mit meinen Freundinnen über ihren coolen Kleidungsstil unterhalten. Wir hatten sogar Witze darüber gemacht, sie mit Mr. Ryland zu verkuppeln, dem gut aussehenden Mathelehrer, für den so viele Mädchen schwärmten. Wir fanden alle, dass die beiden perfekt zueinanderpassen würden. Ich lächelte bei der Vorstellung.

Während ich wartete, erinnerte ich mich an meinen ersten Besuch bei einer

Schulpsychologin in der Mittelstufe. Zufälligerweise war auch damals Sara der Grund dafür gewesen. Da wir noch kein Social Media hatten, hatte sie mich auf andere Weise gepeinigt.

Die Psychologin, Miss Jennings, hatte mir geholfen, mein Selbstbewusstsein aufzubauen, weil sie davon überzeugt war, dass man Mobber nur mit einem selbstsicheren Auftreten dazu bringen konnte, einen in Ruhe zu lassen. *Tu so, dann wirst du so …* war ihr Motto gewesen und ich erinnerte mich noch immer an ihre Worte: *Tu einfach so, als wärst du selbstsicher, auch wenn du dich nicht so fühlst. Bald wird es dir leichter fallen und ganz natürlich vorkommen und du musst es nicht mehr vortäuschen.*

Miss Jennings hatte mit mir Rollenspiele durchgeführt, bei denen sie vorgab, Sara zu sein, und ich mich ihr gegenüber behaupten musste. Ich hatte sie eine Woche lang jeden Tag besucht und es hatte mir enorm geholfen. Sara hatte aufgehört, mich zu ärgern, und mein Leben war so viel angenehmer geworden. Und das alles, weil ich mich zur Wehr gesetzt hatte. Dann war ich umgezogen und hatte damit auch Sara hinter mir gelassen.

Jetzt musste ich mich mit einem völlig neuen Problem herumschlagen. Cyber-Mobbing war etwas ganz anderes und selbstbewusstes

Auftreten half einem nicht viel, wenn sich alles im Internet abspielte.

Erneut sah ich mich um. Noch immer war von Miss McCarthy nichts zu sehen, also ging ich zur Sekretärin.

„Oh, du wartest auf Miss McCarthy?“, fragte Mrs. Frazer. „Sie hat gerade angerufen. Sie musste zu einer anderen Schule fahren. Ein Notfall. Ich kann dir einen Termin für morgen geben, wenn du möchtest.“

Ich seufzte enttäuscht. Ich hatte mich darauf eingestellt, heute alles zu klären, und jetzt musste ich es doch noch einmal aufschieben.

„Ist es dringend?“, fragte Mrs. Frazer. „Mr. Fitzgerald hat auch nachher kurz Zeit. Wenn du möchtest, kannst du mit ihm sprechen.“

Ich blickte zu seinem Büro und erschauderte unwillkürlich. Dann schüttelte ich den Kopf. „Nein, es geht schon. Ich spreche morgen mit Miss McCarthy.“

„In Ordnung … wie wäre es mit acht Uhr? Kannst du so früh schon hier sein? Sie hat danach bereits andere Termine.“

„Um acht passt“, erwiderte ich. „Danke.“

Ich beobachtete, wie sie meinen Namen und andere Details in ihren Computer eintippte;

dann gab sie mir einen Zettel, auf dem der Termin stand. Nicht, dass ich die Erinnerung brauchte …

Ich bedankte mich und warf erneut einen Blick auf Mr. Fitzgeralds Büro. Hätte ich doch mit ihm sprechen sollen? Er hatte sich immerhin auch um den Vorfall mit Miss Boooomleys Facebook-Seite gekümmert, was Lisa und einigen anderen einen Schulverweis eingebracht hatte. Ich würde nie seinen Ärger vergessen, als er uns einen langen Vortrag über die Nutzung von sozialen Medien gehalten hatte.

Obwohl die Situation sehr unangenehm gewesen war, schien er sich damit auszukennen, und ich überlegte, ob ich noch einmal zurückgehen sollte, um mit ihm zu reden. In dem Moment lief Sara an mir vorbei. Ihre Lippen verzogen sich verächtlich, als sie mich sah. Sie versuchte nicht einmal, ihre Abneigung zu verbergen. Da traf ich eine Entscheidung: Mr. Fitzgerald würde wissen, wie er mit jemandem wie Sara umgehen musste.

Doch bevor ich mich wieder umdrehen konnte, ergriff sie meinen Arm und zog mich von den Büroräumen weg.

Erhobenen Hauptes …

Wie so oft, wenn ich Sara gegenüberstand, zögerte ich eine Sekunde und all meine Selbstsicherheit schmolz unter ihrem fiesen Gesichtsausdruck dahin. Doch dann erinnerte ich mich an Miss Jennings Worte. Ich straffte meine Schultern und sah meiner Peinigerin direkt in die Augen. Sollte sie sich doch hier in aller Öffentlichkeit mit mir anlegen! Ich würde es ihr schon zeigen!

Am liebsten hätte ich ihr eine Ohrfeige verpasst, um das arrogante Grinsen aus ihrem Gesicht zu wischen. Ich hasste sie aus tiefstem Herzen und wollte mich endlich an ihr rächen. Hitze durchströmte meinen Körper und mein Pulsschlag donnerte mir in den Ohren. Aber hier und jetzt war nicht der richtige Ort oder die richtige Zeit für solch eine Konfrontation. Das würde mich nur in Schwierigkeiten bringen. Also schob ich mich an ihr vorbei und stieß mit meiner Schulter unsanft gegen ihre. Ich wusste, dass das alles nur noch schlimmer machen würde, aber ich konnte mich nicht zurückhalten.

Als ich um die nächste Ecke bog, spürte ich ihre Anwesenheit noch immer hinter mir. Sie beschleunigte ihre Schritte, um mich einzuholen.

Der Korridor war voller Schüler, aber das hielt sie nicht auf. Sie zischte mir ins Ohr: „Was soll das werden, hm?“

Ich schnaubte. „Ich gehe zum Unterricht. Wonach sieht es denn aus?“

„Ich meine … was hattest du im Sekretariat zu suchen?“ Ihre fordernde Stimme durchschnitt die Luft.

„Dich melden!“, erwiderte ich und blieb stehen, um ihren Blick trotzig zu erwidern.

Furcht blitzte in ihren Augen auf. Es dauerte nur einen Sekundenbruchteil, aber ich hatte es gesehen. Sie hatte Angst vor mir und dem Schaden, den ich anrichten konnte.

Ich schüttelte verächtlich den Kopf, drehte mich auf der Hacke um und wollte weitergehen, doch sie griff erneut nach meinem Arm und zog mich grob zurück. „Mich melden? Wofür? Ich habe nichts getan!“

„Ach ja?“ Ich grinste siegesgewiss. „Du bist am Ende!“

Ein paar Schüler schoben sich an uns vorbei und brachten mich aus dem Gleichgewicht, sodass

ich nach hinten taumelte.

Sara zerrte mich wieder nach vorn und spie mir entgegen: „Wenn du diesen Online-Kram meinst … das hat nichts mit mir zu tun und du kannst es nicht beweisen!“

Ich zog mein Handy aus der Tasche und hielt es vor ihr hoch. „Ich habe Screenshots von allem.“

Sie lachte laut auf und ihr Gesicht spiegelte den reinsten Hohn wider. „Na und? Steht dort irgendwo mein Name?“ Sie starrte mich an, als wäre ich eine Idiotin. „Du bist so dumm! Du hast echt keine Ahnung.“

Erneut lachte sie und glaubte anscheinend, dass sie schon gewonnen hatte. Aber diesmal würde ich sie nicht so einfach davonkommen lassen. Ich ignorierte den Strom der Schüler, die an uns vorbeirauschten, ignorierte auch die neugierigen Blicke, die uns trafen, und das Geflüster, das sich um uns herum erhob. Einige Leute blieben stehen und schauten uns interessiert zu, aber das war mir egal.

„Du bist die Dumme, Sara. Ich kenne dich und deine Spielchen. Und ich habe dich mit deinem *Freund* gesehen. Ganze drei Mal! Und wenn du nicht mit diesem ganzen Mist aufhörst, dann werde ich bald nicht mehr die Einzige sein, die über deine *Beziehung* Bescheid weiß! Und denke nicht, dass ich es nicht wahr machen würde. Ich

will, dass diese Accounts gelöscht werden ... auf Facebook *und* Instagram. Heute noch! Oder es wird dein Name sein, der bald überall zu sehen ist. Nicht nur im Internet, sondern auch in den Zeitungen und im Fernsehen. Wenn du mir nicht glaubst, dann lass es doch darauf ankommen!"

Jetzt hätte ich lachen sollen, doch ich zitterte zu sehr, um auch nur ein Kichern hervorzubringen. Stattdessen warf ich ihr einen letzten verächtlichen Blick zu, bevor ich mir einen Weg durch die Menge der Zuschauer bahnte, die aufgeregt beredeten, worum es ging.

Erhobenen Hauptes lief ich weiter und langsam schlich sich ein kleines Lächeln auf mein Gesicht. Mein Atem ging noch immer in heftigen Stößen, aber mit jedem Schritt wuchs mein Lächeln in die Breite.

Miss Jennings' Gesicht tauchte vor meinem inneren Auge auf. Ihre Worte waren mir gerade rechtzeitig ins Gedächtnis gekommen. *Verbirg deine Angst und sieh ihr in die Augen. Tu so, als wärst du selbstsicher, auch wenn du dich nicht so fühlst.*

Selbst Jahre später hatten ihre Ratschläge und alles, was wir miteinander geübt hatten, mir erneut geholfen. Sie wäre stolz darauf gewesen, mich heute zu sehen.

Ich hatte einen Weg gefunden, mit meiner Mobberin umzugehen und mich gegen sie zu behaupten. Ich hatte es geschafft, zur Quelle meiner Probleme vorzudringen. Und das Beste daran war Saras schockierte Reaktion.

Endlich erlaubte ich mir, zu lachen. Ich stieß sogar jubelnd die Faust in die Luft, ohne mich um die Blicke der anderen zu kümmern.

Gefühle …

Sobald ich das Klassenzimmer betrat, entdeckte ich Ky in einer der vorderen Reihen. Ich ging an ihm vorbei zu einem freien Platz weiter hinten, ohne ihn anzusehen. Mein Kopf schwirrte noch immer von dem Vorfall mit Sara. Die Erinnerung machte mich ganz hibbelig und ich lachte in mich hinein.

Da tauchte plötzlich Ky an meiner Seite auf. „Du bist aber fröhlich heute!“, sagte er und grinste, als er sich neben mich setzte.

Seine Stimme holte mich zurück in die Gegenwart. Nachdem ich mich von der Überraschung erholt hatte, nickte ich ihm lächelnd zu. „Ja, ich bin fröhlich.“

Er musterte mich neugierig und ich fragte mich, ob er wieder die Facebook-Fotos ansprechen würde. Ich hoffte nicht. Die Bilder waren immer noch erniedrigend und ich wollte sie einfach nur vergessen. Aber er schaute mir bloß in die Augen und sagte nichts weiter. Nach einigen Sekunden beschloss ich, meine Federmappe herauszuholen. Ich beugte mich herunter und

wühlte in meiner Schultasche - alles, um seinem eindringlichen Blick auszuweichen.

Doch als ich flüchtig zu ihm aufsah, ruhten seine Augen noch immer auf mir. „Bio-Prüfung ... das wird schwer", stammelte ich. Ich musste irgendetwas sagen, um das peinliche Schweigen zu brechen und meine Verlegenheit zu überspielen.

Zum Glück kam in diesem Moment unser Lehrer herein und als Mr. Blandford anfing zu sprechen, wandte sich Ky von mir ab. Trotzdem konnte ich die Tatsache nicht ignorieren, dass der Junge, der mir so viel bedeutet hatte, direkt neben mir saß. Mein Magen flatterte nervös.

Als die Arbeiten ausgeteilt wurden, versuchte ich, mich auf das Blatt vor mir zu konzentrieren, doch die Fragen verschwammen vor meinen Augen. Kys Nähe war für mich alles andere als ideal - besonders in einer so schwierigen Prüfung.

Ich musste mir die erste Frage dreimal durchlesen, bevor ich sie verstand. An meiner Seite hörte ich das Kratzen von Kys Stift auf dem Papier. Seine verstohlenen Blicke machten mich nervös. Er schaute nicht mein Arbeitsblatt an, sondern mich. Obwohl er es nicht offensichtlich tat, war ich mir dessen nur allzu bewusst.

Was war hier los? Dachte er an die

Schaumbadfotos und all das andere Zeug, das im Internet herumgeisterte? Vor Verlegenheit errötete ich. Ich hasste den Gedanken, dass diese Bilder für jedermann sichtbar waren.

Gleichzeitig spürte ich, dass ich immer noch Gefühle für diesen Jungen hatte. Es war unmöglich, jemanden so sehr zu lieben und dann zu vergessen, dass diese Gefühle jemals existiert hatten. Aber zwischen uns war es jetzt aus und ich musste ihn loslassen. Ich wollte Blake treu bleiben. Nicht nur äußerlich, sondern auch innerlich.

Ich wünschte nur, es wäre einfacher. Ich wünschte, dass ich Ky und alles, was zwischen uns gewesen war, einfach vergessen könnte, dass seine Gegenwart mich nicht mehr berühren würde. Aber darüber hatte ich keine Kontrolle. In mir herrschte ein Widerstreit der Gefühle, den ich nicht auflösen konnte.

Als unsere Zeit zu Ende war, legte Ky seinen Stift ab und starrte mich ganz offen an. Sein neugieriger Blick ruhte auf mir, bis einige Sekunden später das Klingeln ertönte. Ich hielt es für besser, ihm aus dem Weg zu gehen, verabschiedete mich rasch und flüchtete aus dem Raum.

Eine wichtige Botschaft …

Auf dem Weg zu meiner nächsten Stunde konnte ich der Versuchung nicht widerstehen, einen Blick in die Mädchentoilette zu werfen. Zögerlich drückte ich die Tür auf. Der Raum war leer und so konnte ich unbemerkt die Kabinen überprüfen.

Ein Knoten bildete sich in meinem Magen, als ich zaghaft die Tür zur mittleren Kabine öffnete. Doch dann atmete ich erleichtert auf. Die Schmierereien an der Wand waren weg. Selbst die Rückseite der Tür war gesäubert worden; nur ein großer schwarzer Fleck war übrig geblieben, die letzten Reste eines wischfesten Eddings, der sich nicht entfernen ließ. Doch solange mein Name und alle anderen Hinweise auf mich verschwunden waren, konnten von mir aus alle Wände und Türen mit schwarzen Flecken bedeckt sein.

Vielleicht würden sie während der Ferien neu gestrichen werden, aber darum musste ich mich nicht kümmern. Nachdem ich einen kurzen Blick in die anderen Kabinen geworfen und

gesehen hatte, dass alle Oberflächen graffitifrei waren, konnte ich die Toiletten beruhigt verlassen.

Ich eilte zu meinem Englischzimmer. Auch wenn der zweite Teil der Englischprüfung erst morgen stattfinden sollte, wollte ich doch nicht zu spät kommen. Abgesehen davon war ich froh, mal eine Pause von den Tests zu haben - und von Ky. Immer wieder dachte ich an sein seltsames Verhalten zurück, das selbst jetzt noch kleine Feuerwerke in meinem Bauch explodieren ließ.

Eigentlich hätte ich mir um das Ergebnis meiner Bio-Prüfung Gedanken machen sollen. Mir war klar, dass ich nicht sonderlich gut abgeschnitten hatte. Ich konnte von Glück sagen, wenn ich nicht durchfiel. Dennoch machte es mir mehr Sorgen, dass Ky mir nicht aus dem Kopf ging.

Als ich ins Klassenzimmer kam, begegnete ich sofort Blakes Augen, die mich magnetisch anzogen. Er saß am Fenster neben Jack und als er mir freundlich zuwinkte, nagten die Schuldgefühle an mir. Ich winkte zurück. Der Anblick seines Lächelns erinnerte mich daran, dass ich ihm treu bleiben musste, wenn es zwischen uns noch irgendeine Hoffnung geben sollte.

Nachdem ich mir einen Platz auf der

gegenüberliegenden Seite des Raums gesucht hatte, rief ich mir Emmies Worte ins Gedächtnis: *Vielleicht ist der Unfall von Ky nicht ohne Grund passiert … damit Blake und du eine zweite Chance bekommt.*

Der gleiche Gedanke war mir auch schon mehrmals gekommen und jetzt hielt ich mich an ihm fest. Innerlich schimpfte ich mit mir selbst, weil ich mich von Ky noch immer so sehr aus der Fassung bringen ließ, obwohl Blake die ganze Zeit über für mich da gewesen war.

Bald wurde ich von Sara abgelenkt, die den Raum betrat. Normalerweise fürchtete ich ihre Nähe, aber nach unserer Konfrontation am Morgen war zur Abwechslung mal ich diejenige, die die Oberhand hatte, und ich genoss diese neu gewonnene Selbstsicherheit.

„Das Schuljahr ist noch nicht vorbei", bemerkte Miss Bromley stirnrunzelnd zu Sara. „Und du bist zu spät!"

Sara verdrehte die Augen und murmelte: „Na und?", laut genug, dass es alle hören konnten. Die ganze Klasse schwieg schockiert und starrte Sara an. So war ihr mal wieder die Aufmerksamkeit von allen sicher. Aber wie sie damit bei Miss Bromley durchkommen wollte, hatte sie wohl nicht bedacht.

Der strenge Blick unserer Lehrerin folgte Sara,

als sie sich zu einem freien Platz begab. „Miss Hamilton, wir sehen uns heute nach der Schule zum Nachsitzen."

„Was? Aber das ist die letzte Schulwoche!" Sara stöhnte laut auf. „Und außerdem habe ich schon einen Termin."

„Das ist nicht mein Problem", entgegnete Miss Bromley mit scharfer Stimme. „Wenn du dagegen protestieren willst, kannst du das in der Pause mit Mr. Fitzgerald besprechen."

Sara antwortete nicht. Niemand sonst wagte es, einen Ton von sich zu geben. Ich unterdrückte das Kichern, das in meiner Kehle aufstieg. Miss Bromley ignorierte Saras schmollende Miene und hob eine dicke Mappe hoch, die auf ihrem Tisch gelegen hatte.

Sie schwenkte sie vor uns in der Luft, während sie sprach. „Ich habe damit begonnen, eure Aufsätze von gestern zu korrigieren. Ich bin noch nicht ganz fertig, aber ich hoffe, dass ich sie euch Ende der Woche wiedergeben kann, wenn nicht schon eher."

Ihre Worte ließen alle aufhorchen, denn jeder war gespannt auf sein Ergebnis.

„Ich muss sagen, dass das, was ich bisher gelesen habe, mich sehr beeindruckt hat", sagte Miss Bromley zufrieden. „Ich hatte gehofft, dass

Cyber-Mobbing ein gutes Thema sein würde, aber ich hätte nicht erwartet, dass ich dabei derartige Einblicke bekomme."

Ich setzte mich aufrechter hin und fragte mich, ob sie meinen Aufsatz schon gelesen hatte und sich unter anderem darauf bezog. Ich versuchte, mich zu erinnern, was ich geschrieben hatte. Aber in den letzten vierundzwanzig Stunden war so viel passiert, dass es mir nur verschwommen im Gedächtnis war.

„Ich habe eure Aufsätze auch mit denen der Schüler aus den anderen Klassen verglichen und dabei ist mir einer besonders aufgefallen."

Mein Körper spannte sich an. Könnte sie mich meinen? Mein Blick flog durch den Raum und es schien, als würden sich alle dasselbe fragen.

„Ich würde ihn gern der Klasse vorlesen", sagte Miss Bromley.

Mir stockte der Atem und ich änderte meine Meinung. Jetzt hoffte ich inständig, dass sie sich nicht auf meine Arbeit bezog.

„Ich werde nicht verraten, wer ihn geschrieben hat", fügte sie an, „aber ich finde, dass alle davon profitieren würden, sich anzuhören, was dieser Schüler oder diese Schülerin zu sagen hat."

Miss Bromleys Blick streifte die Klasse, doch ihre Augen blieben auf niemandem ruhen. Jeder war jetzt neugierig und wartete darauf, dass sie anfing.

Sie sah auf die offene Mappe in ihren Händen herunter und begann zu lesen. „An ihrer Stelle würde ich mich umbringen!“

Als sie diese Worte aussprach, blieb mir der Mund offen stehen. Ich sollte mich geehrt fühlen, dass ausgerechnet die Lehrerin, die am schwersten zufriedenzustellen war, mich ausgewählt hatte. Dennoch hätte ich nicht erwartet, dass mein Werk laut vorgelesen werden würde. Was ich geschrieben hatte, war sehr persönlich ... fast wie ein Tagebucheintrag. Es war nichts, was ich mit der ganzen Klasse teilen wollte.

Ich warf einen Blick zu Chelsea auf der anderen Seite des Zimmers. Ihr Blick hing an den Lippen unserer Lehrerin. Wusste Chelsea es? Hatte sie erkannt, dass ich ihre Worte zitiert hatte ... die Worte, die sie an dem Morgen vor der Englischprüfung verwendet hatte?

Miss Bromley schaute wieder auf ihre Mappe und wiederholte den ersten Satz, wobei sie ihn besonders betonte.

„An ihrer Stelle würde ich mich umbringen! Das waren die ersten Worte, die ich hörte, als ich die

Schule betrat. Leider waren sie nicht an irgendjemanden gerichtet, sondern an mich. Die Erkenntnis traf mich wie ein Schlag. *Suizid*. Für einige mochte das etwas dramatisch scheinen, für andere war es der einzige Ausweg. Würde ich es tun? Bisher hatte ich nicht einmal darüber nachgedacht. Aber nachdem ich am eigenen Leib erfahren hatte, was Cyber-Mobbing bedeutete, verstand ich, was manche vielleicht durchmachen mussten."

Ich schaute mich um. Alle Augen waren auf Miss Bromley gerichtet. Eine unbehagliche Atmosphäre hatte sich im Raum ausgebreitet, sobald das Wort *Suizid* gefallen war. Sie las weiter und abgesehen von ihrer Stimme herrschte absolute Stille. Immer wenn sie eine kurze Pause machte, hätte man eine Stecknadel fallen hören können.

Nach einer Weile ließ meine Anspannung nach. Ein paar Schüler blickten in meine Richtung, aber es schien, dass niemand sicher wusste, wer den Aufsatz geschrieben hatte. Es war ein anonymes Werk, dessen Botschaft jeden fesselte.

Als Miss Bromley sich dem Ende näherte, konzentrierte ich mich wieder auf den Klang ihrer Stimme. Sie betonte besonders wichtige Sätze und Aussagen und die vertrauten Worte hallten in mir nach.

„Ich bin selbst ein Opfer von Cyber-Mobbing und weiß jetzt aus erster Hand, wie verheerend es sein kann.

Es ist *erniedrigend* und *beschämend.*

Man möchte danach *nie mehr* in die Schule gehen, nicht einmal mehr das eigene Zimmer verlassen.

Man glaubt, *alle* reden über einen, und selbst wenn sie es nicht tun, ist man überzeugt, dass das Gelächter und der Spott einem selbst gelten.

Wenn ich jemals erfahren würde, dass ich *durch meine Beteiligung an Cyber-Mobbing den Tod eines Mitschülers mitverursacht* hätte, wüsste ich nicht, was ich tun würde.

Die Gelegenheit dazu gibt es jeden Tag: *Indem wir etwas teilen, kommentieren, markieren und liken, was gemein oder unangebracht ist, jemanden demütigt oder beschämt … das alles gehört zum Cyber-Mobbing dazu.* Wenn wir uns nur die Folgen unserer Handlungen bewusst machen würden, wäre das Leben von so vielen Menschen nicht in Gefahr.

Das ist kein Spiel. Es ist real. Und die Konsequenzen können *lebensbedrohlich* sein."

Als Miss Bromley fertig gelesen hatte, hing eine drückende Stille in der Luft.

Ihre Augen überblickten die Klasse. „Das regt zum Nachdenken an, nicht wahr?"

Noch immer sprach niemand. Schuldbewusstsein stand in einigen Gesichtern. Manche blickten in meine Richtung, aber viele auch zu anderen Schülern. Wahrscheinlich gab es in unserer Klasse schon mehrere, die Opfer von Cyber-Mobbing gewesen waren. Und die Worte hätten auf jeden von uns zutreffen können.

„Möchte irgendjemand etwas dazu sagen?", fragte Miss Bromley und schaute einzelne Schüler an, um sie zum Antworten zu ermuntern. Doch keiner hob die Hand.

„Nun, ich hoffe, dass dieser Aufsatz wenigstens ein paar Diskussionen zwischen euch anregt. Nicht darüber, wer ihn geschrieben hat. Das ist nicht relevant; es hätte jeder in eurer Klasse sein können. Ich möchte, dass ihr euch über die Auswirkungen von Mobbing bewusst werdet, sei es online oder offline. Dies ist eine ernste Angelegenheit, und wenn einer von euch auf irgendeine Weise daran beteiligt sein sollte, hoffe ich, dass ihr damit aufhört und euch einmal ganz genau überlegt, was ihr damit anrichtet."

Sie hielt einen Moment inne, bevor sie fortfuhr. „Und wenn es unter euch einige gibt, die gerade

Probleme dieser Art haben, dann könnt ihr jederzeit zu mir kommen. Wenn euch das nicht behagt, ist unsere Schulpsychologin, Miss McCarthy, die beste Ansprechpartnerin. Sie ist jung und sehr nett. Ihr könnt euch einen Termin bei ihr geben lassen. Wir möchten dieses Problem aus der Welt schaffen, aber wir können euch nicht helfen, wenn ihr uns nicht einbezieht. Bitte behaltet so etwas nicht für euch. Und denkt daran, dass wir für euch da sind." Ihre Augen verweilten kurz auf mir, bevor sie jeden Schüler im Raum einzeln anschaute.

Ich sah zu Sara, doch sie blickte mit ausdruckslosem Gesicht nach vorn. Wie gern hätte ich in diesem Moment Gedanken lesen können, um herauszufinden, was in ihrem Kopf vorging. Aber das blieb meiner Fantasie überlassen. Und ich fragte mich, ob sie auch nur eine Spur von Schuld oder Reue verspürte.

Chelsea und Aria, das Mädchen neben ihr, waren nicht so gut darin, ihre Gefühle zu verstecken. Ich sah, wie sie unbehagliche Blicke austauschten und diskret in meine Richtung schauten. Ich hielt ihrem Blick stand und hob dic Augenbrauen. Ich hatte es mit Sara aufgenommen - da konnten mir diese zwei auch keine Angst mehr machen.

Jetzt schämte ich mich nicht mehr dafür, dass meine Arbeit vor der Klasse vorgelesen worden

war, sondern war stolz darauf. Obwohl ich immer noch lieber anonym bleiben wollte, hatte Miss Bromley meine Botschaft in die Welt getragen. Hoffentlich würden es sich die Leute in Zukunft zweimal überlegen, bevor sie sich an Cyber-Mobbing beteiligten.

Ich hatte erwartet, dass unsere Lehrerin noch mehr Aufsätze vorlesen würde, doch sie legte ihre Mappe zurück auf den Tisch. War meiner wirklich der einzige, der es ihrer Meinung nach wert war, geteilt zu werden? Bestimmt gab es auch noch andere, die etwas Wichtiges zu sagen hatten, oder nicht?

Stattdessen hob Miss Bromley jetzt einen anderen Stapel Blätter hoch und erklärte uns unsere nächste Aufgabe. „Also gut, da das Schuljahr fast vorbei ist, möchte ich, dass ihr alle das hier ausfüllt. Diese Aufgabe stelle ich am Ende jedes Jahres. Die anderen Klassen bekommen sie auch.“

Interessiert schaute ich sie an. Ich hatte mich auf eine langweilige Wiederholungsstunde eingestellt, aber offenbar hatte sie etwas anderes im Sinn.

Sie schwenkte die Blätter in der Luft. „Diese Arbeitsblätter sind in Abschnitte unterteilt, die jeweils mit dem Namen eines eurer Klassenkameraden beschriftet sind. Es gibt ein

Kästchen für jeden Schüler und genug Platz, damit ihr eine Bemerkung über diese Person hineinschreiben könnt. Abgesehen davon gibt es nur zwei Regeln: Ihr sollt in jedes Kästchen ein *Kompliment* schreiben - außer natürlich in euer eigenes. Es reicht, wenn es nur ein paar Worte sind, aber sie müssen positiv sein. Und es darf nicht anonym sein. Ihr müsst euren Namen dazuschreiben."

Ein kollektives Aufstöhnen ging durch die Klasse und sofort schossen einige Arme in die Höhe.

Miss Bromley deutete auf Aria, die ganz hinten saß. „Was, wenn wir nichts Positives über diese Person zu sagen haben?"

Miss Bromleys Blicke hätten töten können. Aria schien in ihrem Stuhl zu versinken und lief rot an.

„Lasst euch etwas einfallen!", entgegnete Miss Bromley nur.

Ein Junge in der gegenüberliegenden Ecke hob seine Hand. „Was, wenn wir nicht wissen, zu wem die Namen gehören? Es gibt ein paar Leute in dem Kurs, mit denen ich noch nie gesprochen habe."

„Dann bitte jemanden, sie dir zu zeigen", erwiderte Miss Bromley geduldig. „Und finde

irgendetwas Positives an ihnen. Das kann ihre äußere Erscheinung betreffen, ihren Charakter, ihre Talente … Solange es sich um ein Kompliment handelt, ist alles erlaubt. Wenn ihr fertig seid, schneidet ihr die Kästchen aus, faltet jedes in der Mitte und schreibt den Namen der Person noch einmal auf die Außenseite. Dann legt ihr die Zettel in diese Tüten hier."

Sie holte einige Drahtgestelle hinter dem Schreibtisch hervor, an denen sie braune Papiertüten mit Klammern befestigt hatte. An jeder stand ein Name.

„Es gibt für jeden Schüler eine", erklärte sie.

„Müssen wir alle mitmachen?", rief ein Junge namens Cade aus der Mitte des Raums.

Miss Bromley nickte. „Ja, das müsst ihr. Und nur damit ihr es wisst … ich bekomme jedes Jahr die gleiche Reaktion. Aber wenn ihr schließlich am letzten Schultag eure Tüten erhaltet, werdet ihr überrascht sein, was ihr darin findet. Ich versichere euch, dass es eine schöne Überraschung sein wird."

Stella, ein Mädchen mit langem, gelocktem Haar, das immer ganz vorne saß, hob die Hand. „Was, wenn jemand uns doch einen negativen Kommentar hinterlässt? Das würde mich bestimmt total runterziehen."

Miss Bromley seufzte. „Ihr seid doch alle alt genug, um diese Aufgabe mit der nötigen Reife zu bewältigen. Ich habe euch gerade einen Aufsatz über Cyber-Mobbing vorgelesen. Diese Dinge gelten für alle Arten von Mobbing, nicht nur für das, was im Internet gepostet wird. Vergesst nicht, es sollen Komplimente sein … Äußerungen, die darauf ausgelegt sind, jemandem ein gutes Gefühl zu geben. Und ihr müsst euren Namen darunterschreiben."

Sie fing an, die Blätter auszuteilen. „Fangt an, wenn ihr nicht bis in die Pause bleiben wollt. Und übrigens, falls ihr eine Bemerkung für jemanden aus einer anderen Klasse hinterlassen wollt, könnt ihr sie in eine der leeren Kästchen schreiben. Ich habe hier Tüten für jede Klasse und werde sie den entsprechenden Lehrern weiterleiten. Wenn ihr sie benötigt, könnt ihr euch bei mir auch noch weitere leere Blätter abholen."

Sofort beschloss ich, dass ich einen Kommentar für Becky schreiben würde. Ich freute mich schon darauf, es in ihre Klassentüte zu werfen. Diese Aufgabe war viel schöner als eine langweilige Wiederholungsstunde. Ich nahm meinen Stift und trug als Erstes Beckys Namen in eines der leeren Kästchen ein. Es fiel mir leicht, für sie etwas zu schreiben.

Du bist eine tolle Freundin und ich bin sooo froh,

dich zu haben. Danke, dass du immer für mich da warst. Es macht so viel Spaß, etwas mit dir zu unternehmen. Ich bin froh, dass wir uns kennen!
Deine Julia :xx

Ich lächelte und wollte mit dem ersten Kästchen auf dem Blatt weitermachen. Doch als ich Chelseas Namen las, erstarb mein Lächeln. Ich schielte hinüber zu dem schwarzhaarigen Mädchen, dessen viele Ohrpiercings ich bis hierher sehen konnte.

Sie kicherte und plauderte mit Aria, vermutlich über die Komplimente, die sie schreiben wollte. Für Aria würde es leicht sein, etwas Nettes über Chelsea zu sagen. Sie waren beste Freundinnen. Aber für mich war Chelsea eine Feindin. Ich erinnerte mich noch gut an ihre höhnischen Bemerkungen in der Mädchentoilette und war mir ziemlich sicher, dass sie etwas mit den Schmierereien dort zu tun hatte. Wahrscheinlich hatte sie auch die Facebook- und Instagram-Posts geteilt.

Mir fielen eine Menge fiese Bemerkungen über sie ein. Aber wenn ich mich an die Regeln halten wollte, musste ich wenigstens versuchen, etwas Positives an ihr zu finden.

Nachdenklich tippte ich mir mit dem Stift an die Wange. Da hatte ich eine Eingebung und fing an zu schreiben.

Mir gefällt dein Kleidungsstil. Du trägst echt coole Klamotten. Julia

Ich starrte auf die Worte und nickte. Ich war kein Fan von Chelseas Piercings oder ihrem Augen-Make-up, aber ich bewunderte ihre schwarzen Stiefel und den engen roten Rock, den sie heute trug. Auch wenn ich es nur ungern zugab, war ich neidisch auf ihr Outfit.

Ich ging zum nächsten Kästchen über. Jared Alcott. Das Genie der Klasse. Das würde leicht sein.

Du bist richtig schlau und ich bin total beeindruckt, wie viel du dir merken kannst. Ich bewundere deine Intelligenz! Julia

Ich lächelte, als ich mir die Sätze erneut durchlas. Dann machte ich weiter mit Stella, dem etwas streberhaften Mädchen mit dem welligen Haar, das immer ganz vorne saß.

Da ich nur mit wenigen Leuten aus meinem Englischkurs wirklich befreundet war, fiel mir diese Aufgabe nicht leicht, aber wie Miss Bromley gesagt hatte, konnten wir unseren Mitschülern auch einfach ein Kompliment über ihr Aussehen machen. Also schrieb ich das Erste auf, was mir in den Sinn kam.

Ich finde, dass du sehr klug bist. Außerdem hast du schöne blaue Augen. Julia

So ging ich die Reihen weiter durch. Wenn ich zu einem Namen kam, den ich nicht kannte, fragte ich Hannah, ein hilfsbereites Mädchen neben mir. Als ich Sara Hamiltons Kästchen erreichte, hätte ich am liebsten meinen Kugelschreiber durch das Blatt Papier gebohrt. Ein Kompliment für Sara zu finden würde die größte Herausforderung von allen sein.

Ich beschloss, später noch einmal darauf zurückzukommen, und machte weiter mit Jack Hillman. Hier musste ich zum Glück nicht lange nachdenken.

Du bist total lustig und auch ein sehr talentierter Rapper. Du bist ein toller Freund und es macht Spaß, mit dir abzuhängen. Julia

Ich fragte mich, was Emmie schreiben würde, wenn sie hier wäre, und schmunzelte bei der Erinnerung an ihr romantisches Wiedersehen mit Jack.

Doch dann sah ich Blakes Namen vor mir und sofort wurde mir die Ironie dieses Gedankens bewusst. Ich hatte gehofft, dass er und ich ein Pärchen sein würden, genau wie Emmie und Jack, und dass wir zu viert unsere Freizeit miteinander verbringen könnten. Ich wünschte, ich könnte ihm all die romantischen Dinge schreiben, die Emmie zu Jack sagen würde. Hatte ich diese Chance ein für alle Mal verspielt?

Ich hoffte es nicht, aber ich war mir nicht sicher.

Unschlüssig ging ich verschiedene Möglichkeiten durch. Sollte ich ihm ein allgemeines Kompliment machen oder doch etwas Persönlicheres schreiben? Wir kannten uns schon so lange und ich beschloss, mich nicht zurückzuhalten. Das war die Gelegenheit, meine wahren Gefühle auszudrücken.

Du bist der wundervollste und hilfsbereiteste Mensch, den ich kenne. Du behandelst alle Mädchen respektvoll, und wer immer am Ende mit dir zusammenkommt, kann sich glücklich schätzen. Du bist der beste Freund, den ich je hatte. Julia :x

Nachdem ich mir die Worte noch einmal durchgelesen hatte, zögerte ich. Wie würde Blake reagieren? War das zu viel? Würde es ihn abschrecken? Würde er mir überhaupt glauben? Ich seufzte und konnte mich nicht entscheiden, was ich tun sollte.

Erneut las ich mir die Worte durch. Sie waren aus meinem Herzen gekommen und vollkommen wahr. Es wurde Zeit, ein Risiko einzugehen und ihm zu zeigen, was ich wirklich empfand. Das war meine Chance. Ich beschloss, nichts zu ändern.

Mit meiner Federmappe bedeckte ich die obere Hälfte meines Blattes, damit niemand lesen konnte, was ich geschrieben hatte, und machte

weiter. Schließlich kam ich wieder zu dem Kästchen mit Saras Namen darin. Was für ein Kompliment sollte mir für dieses Mädchen bitte schön einfallen?

Du hast so viel Talent. Deine Mobbing-Taktiken sind wirklich außergewöhnlich. Du solltest einen Preis dafür bekommen, dass du andere so gut heruntermachst! Julia

Ich wünschte, das könnte ich schreiben. Mit einem frustrierten Seufzer kritzelte ich das Erste hin, was mir in den Sinn kam.

Du hast schöne Haare. Julia

Ich fasste mich so kurz wie möglich. Es war schwer genug, auch nur ein Adjektiv wie *schön* im gleichen Satz wie das Wort *Sara* zu verwenden. Aber wenigstens hatte ich irgendetwas geschrieben. Ich fragte mich, was sie wohl über mich sagen würde.

Dann nahm ich meine Schere und schnitt die Kästchen aus, faltete jedes in der Mitte und schrieb die Namen auf die Außenseite, während ich mit Hannah quatschte. Das war die beste Englischstunde, die ich bei Miss Bromley je gehabt hatte, und es war nicht schwer zu erkennen, dass die anderen ähnlich dachten. Selbst diejenigen, die sich erst über die Aufgabe lustig gemacht hatten, schienen jetzt Spaß daran zu haben. Freundliches Geplauder erfüllte den

Raum, während alle ihre Blätter ausfüllten.

Als ich fertig war, brachte ich meine Zettel nach vorn und warf sie in die Tüten mit den jeweiligen Namen. Mehrere andere Schüler waren ebenfalls damit beschäftigt. Auf einmal fiel vor mir ein Stück Papier zu Boden. Ich bückte mich und hob es auf. Der Zettel war nicht ordentlich gefaltet worden, sodass ich den Text darin lesen konnte. Als ich meinen Namen entdeckte, konnte ich nicht anders, als die Notiz zu überfliegen.

Julia

Du bist ein nettes Mädchen und verdienst es, mit Respekt behandelt zu werden. CA

Ein Lächeln stahl sich auf mein Gesicht, während ich den Zettel wieder zusammenfaltete und mich nach dem Autor umsah. In unserem Kurs gab es drei Leute, deren Vornamen mit C anfingen: Cade, Christina und Chelsea. Ich konnte mich nicht an ihre Nachnamen erinnern, aber die Worte mussten von Christina oder Cade stammen, die beide gerade ihre Zettel einsortierten und nicht bemerkt hatten, dass einer heruntergefallen war. Ich ließ das Blatt in meiner eigenen Tüte verschwinden und machte weiter mit dem Stapel in meiner Hand.

Mein Lächeln hielt noch immer an, als ich zu meinem Platz zurückging. Die Wirkung dieser

simplen Worte war groß. Irgendeine Person, mit der ich nicht eng befreundet war, hatte mir etwas geschrieben, was mir wirklich viel bedeutete. Nach allem, was ich durchgemacht hatte, gab das meinem Selbstbewusstsein einen echten Schub und ich war so dankbar.

Immer wieder sagte ich mir die Worte in Gedanken auf: *Du bist ein nettes Mädchen und verdienst es, mit Respekt behandelt zu werden. CA.* Sie hatten sich bereits in mein Gedächtnis eingebrannt.

Ich lehnte mich zu Hannah und fragte flüsternd: „Kennst du den Nachnamen von Christina oder Cade?“

Sie nickte. „Christina Johnson und Cade Adams.“

Ich lächelte sie an. „Danke. Gibt es sonst noch jemanden hier, der die Initialen CA hat?“

Hannah zuckte mit den Schultern. „Hm, ich bin mir nicht sicher. Ich glaube nicht.“

Das Klingeln der Pausenglocke unterbrach unser Gespräch und Miss Bromley erinnerte uns an den zweiten Teil unserer Englischprüfung, der morgen stattfand.

Ich war mir sicher, dass der Zettel von Cade stammen musste. Als er aus der Tür ging,

erhaschte ich einen Blick auf ihn. Er war beliebt bei den Schülern, bekam aber oft Schwierigkeiten mit den Lehrern, weil er im Unterricht redete, Witze machte und generell störte.

Aber das war mir egal. Cade war einer der beliebtesten Jungs unserer Stufe und er hatte etwas Nettes über mich, Julia Jones, geschrieben, das Mädchen, dessen Fotos im Internet zu sehen waren. Diese großzügige Geste bedeutete mir mehr, als ich mit Worten ausdrücken konnte. Sie hatte eine enorme Wirkung auf mich.

Ich war die Letzte, die den Klassenraum verließ, und als ich an Miss Bromleys Schreibtisch vorbeikam, fing sie meinen Blick ein und lächelte. Die heutige Aufgabe war definitiv unerwartet gewesen, genauso wie ihre Entscheidung, meinen Aufsatz vorzulesen, weil er eine wichtige Botschaft für alle enthielt.

Plötzlich sah ich Miss Bromley nicht mehr als herrisch und gefühllos, als Lehrerin, die herumschrie und langweiligen Unterricht machte. Meine Meinung über sie hatte sich komplett gewandelt. „Danke für die tolle Stunde, Miss Bromley."

„Sehr gern, Julia. Ich danke dir für deinen großartigen Aufsatz! Und ich bin immer da, wenn du reden möchtest." Sie zwinkerte mir

verschwörerisch zu und lächelte.

Ich fühlte mich, als würde ich auf Wolken schweben. Auf dem Flur schaute ich mich nach Blake um, doch er verließ gerade mit Jack die Schule. Ich beschloss, ein andermal mit ihm zu reden, und ging stattdessen auf Becky zu, die aus ihrem Klassenzimmer kam.

Sie hakte sich bei mir unter und grinste. „Das Graffiti ist weg."

Ich sah sie dankbar an. „Ich weiß. Ich habe auf dem Weg zur Englischstunde die Toiletten überprüft. Vielen Dank, Becky."

Sie wirkte genauso froh wie ich, dass es so schnell gegangen war. „Willst du mit uns Mittag essen? Lisa und Beth wollen unbedingt mit uns reden."

Ich nickte begeistert. „Klingt gut!" Ich konnte mir nichts Schöneres vorstellen, als die Pause draußen im warmen Sonnenschein mit meinen Freundinnen zu verbringen. Aber dann dachte ich an Millie und zögerte. „Ist Millie auch dabei?"

„Ich weiß nicht", erwiderte Becky. „Ich habe sie heute Morgen noch nicht gesehen. Aber ist doch egal. Komm schon, gehen wir!" Sie zog mich am Arm weiter.

Ich beeilte mich, mit ihr Schritt zu halten. Becky hatte recht. Wenn ich mit meinen Freundinnen Zeit verbringen wollte, würde ich mir das nicht von Millie vermiesen lassen. Immerhin gab es noch Leute, denen ich nicht egal war.

Meine Liste mit Dingen, für die ich dankbar sein konnte, wuchs rasch an. Ich folgte Becky bereitwillig nach draußen auf den Schulhof. Die Sonne wärmte meine Haut und gab mir ein Gefühl tiefster Zufriedenheit.

Pläne …

Als ich unseren Platz auf dem Schulhof erreichte, sprang Beth auf, um mich zu umarmen. „Julia, es kommt mir so vor, als hätten wir uns ewig nicht mehr gesehen!"

Lisa folgte ihr und ihre Augen glänzten aufgeregt. „Weißt du was?"

„Was?", fragte ich und schaute neugierig auf ihr Smartphone, mit dem sie vor mir herumwedelte.

„Das Profil von *Mädchen die Spaß haben wollen* ist verschwunden. Es wurde gelöscht!"

„Oh mein Gott!", quiekte ich und zog mein Handy aus der Tasche, um mich selbst davon zu überzeugen. „Ehrlich?"

„Ja!" Sie nickte nachdrücklich. „Zuerst ist es mir auf Instagram aufgefallen. Ich wollte der Person eine Nachricht schreiben, dass sie gefälligst damit aufhören soll, aber ich konnte das Profil nicht mehr finden. Und von Facebook ist es auch verschwunden."

Becky setzte sich neben mich auf die Bank und

sah zu, wie ich mich bei Facebook einloggte und den Namen des Profils in der Suchzeile eingab. Abgesehen von einer anderen Seite mit ähnlichem Namen erschienen keine Ergebnisse. Ich ignorierte die vielen Benachrichtigungen und meldete mich bei Instagram an. Dort sah ich eine Liste von Bildern mit dem Hashtag #mädchendiespaßhabenwollen, aber das Profil selbst und die Fotos von mir waren weg.

„Wow!“, murmelte Becky und ihre Augenbrauen schossen in die Höhe. „Hat Miss McCarthy Sara dazu gebracht, die Profile zu löschen?“

„Nein …“ Ich schüttelte den Kopf. „Miss McCarthy ist heute gar nicht da, deshalb konnte ich nicht mit ihr reden.“

Lisa und Beth sahen mich neugierig an. „Du könntest zu Mr. Fitzgerald gehen“, schlug Lisa vor. „Ich an deiner Stelle würde mich an ihn wenden. Shelley hat zwei Wochen Schulverweis bekommen, weil sie diese Facebook-Seite über Miss Bromley ins Leben gerufen hat, weißt du noch? Ich kann immer noch nicht glauben, dass ich deswegen auch suspendiert wurde. Ich habe die Seite nicht mal erstellt. Er würde Sara wahrscheinlich ganz von der Schule werfen, wenn er erfährt, was sie getan hat.“

Offensichtlich wussten Lisa und Beth bereits,

dass Sara hinter dem Cyber-Mobbing stand. Vielleicht hatten Millie oder Becky es ihnen erzählt und das war mir nur recht. Je mehr Leute erkannten, was für ein Mensch Sara war, desto besser. Aber die Sache mit Mr. Hathaway wollte ich immer noch für mich behalten. Solange ich diese Drohung in der Hinterhand hatte, würde Sara mich sicher in Ruhe lassen.

„Ich habe Sara heute Morgen getroffen", erklärte ich meinen Freundinnen, „und ihr gesagt, dass sie die Accounts löschen soll, wenn sie nicht will, dass ich sie melde."

Beth runzelte die Stirn. „Du hättest sie melden sollen, als die Profile noch existiert haben. Jetzt gibt es keine Beweise mehr."

„Ich habe Screenshots von allem", erwiderte ich und hielt mein Telefon hoch. „Jedenfalls scheint es gewirkt zu haben. Ich hoffe, sie hält sich von jetzt an zurück."

Ich wollte ihnen nicht alle Einzelheiten verraten. Nur Becky würde ich später, wenn wir allein waren, in alles einweihen.

Ich holte mein Mittagessen aus meinem Rucksack. Als ich Millies Stimme hörte, blickte ich auf. Sie und Jess kamen auf unseren Tisch zu. Millies Blick suchte meinen, doch ich ignorierte sie und widmete mich stattdessen der Pizza, die ich mir fürs Mittagessen eingepackt hatte.

Lisa, die von der angespannten Atmosphäre zwischen Millie und mir nichts bemerkte, quasselte aufgeregt weiter. „Wisst ihr schon das Neueste? Sara hat die Accounts gelöscht. Julia hat ihr heute Morgen angedroht, sie zu melden, und jetzt sind die Profile verschwunden. Ist das nicht cool?"

Millie warf mir einen beeindruckten Blick zu. „Das ist toll, Julia. Das freut mich!"

Ich nickte, antwortete aber nicht, und als mein Handy eine ankommende Nachricht anzeigte, war ich froh über die Ablenkung. Ich schaute aufs Display und sah eine unbekannte Nummer. Rasch öffnete ich die Nachricht und überflog sie.

Hallo, Julia, hier ist Rhonda von Eliza's Boutique. Sienna hat sich gerade krank gemeldet und ich habe für heute Nachmittag noch keinen Ersatz gefunden. Könntest du zwischen 15 und 18 Uhr arbeiten? Bitte lass es mich möglichst bald wissen. Danke, Rhonda.

Ich quiekte begeistert, was die Aufmerksamkeit der anderen Mädels erregte.

„Was ist los?", fragte Becky und runzelte die Stirn.

„Das war die Geschäftsführerin von *Eliza's*", erklärte ich atemlos. „Sie will wissen, ob ich heute Nachmittag arbeiten kann."

„Was?“ Lisa sah mich überrascht an. „Du hast einen Job bei *Eliza's*? Seit wann das denn?“

Ich lachte auf, erfreut über ihre Reaktion. „Ich war am Wochenende zur Probearbeit dort und bin eingestellt worden. Die leitende Verkäuferin ist heute krank, deshalb hat die Chefin mich gefragt, ob ich einspringen kann.“

„Hast du ein Glück!“, erwiderte Lisa neidisch. „Das ist so ein cooler Laden mit echt tollen Klamotten! Wie ist es so, dort zu arbeiten?“

„Es macht super viel Spaß“, sagte ich und beschloss, das Drama mit Sara für mich zu behalten. Ich wollte nicht, dass Lisa oder die anderen es ausplauderten. „Ich freue mich darauf, endlich Geld zu verdienen, damit ich mir was Schönes kaufen kann“, fügte ich hinzu. „Hoffentlich bekommen wir Mitarbeiterrabatt.“

„Da muss ich dich bald mal besuchen. Vielleicht kriegen wir ja auch einen Rabatt“, deutete Lisa mit einem vielsagenden Lächeln an.

Sofort bereute ich meine Worte und schüttelte den Kopf, um sie von der Idee abzubringen. „Ich weiß noch nicht, wie das mit den Rabatten ist. Ich war ja erst einmal zur Probe dort.“

„Arbeitet Emmie nicht auch heute?“, fragte Millie.

„Ja", erwiderte ich knapp, damit sie ja nicht auf die Idee kam, mir noch mehr Fragen zu stellen. Ich blickte auf mein Handy und tippte eine Antwort an Rhonda.

Hi, Rhonda. Ja, ich kann heute Nachmittag um 3 kommen.

Ich hielt inne und sah an mir herunter, wobei mir meine Zwickmühle bewusst wurde. Ich trug ein Paar Jeansshorts mit ausgefranstem Saum und ein pinkes Top mit Pailettenmuster, außerdem meine schwarzen Chucks. Normalerweise machte ich mir mehr Mühe, wenn ich mir Sachen für die Schule raussuchte, aber an diesem Morgen hatte ich einfach nur schnell das Haus verlassen und den Tag hinter mich bringen wollen. Da konnte ich mich nicht auch noch mit Klamottenauswahl befassen.

Vor mir lag eine Doppelstunde Mathe, dann hatte ich für heute Schluss. Aber wenn ich erst nach Hause fuhr, um mich umzuziehen, würde ich es nicht rechtzeitig zum Einkaufszentrum schaffen.

Am besten klärte ich das mit Rhonda. Also fügte ich meiner Nachricht hinzu: *Das einzige Problem ist, dass ich keine Zeit habe, vorher nach Hause zu fahren und mich umzuziehen. Julia.*

Ich tippte auf Senden und wartete auf Rhondas Antwort. Hoffentlich würde sie so ausfallen, wie

ich es mir erhoffte.

In der Zwischenzeit erklärte Millie den anderen, dass Emmie zurück in der Stadt war. „Sie war mit Jack Hillman zusammen, bevor sie weggezogen ist. Und jetzt sind sie wieder ein Paar. Die beiden sind so süß zusammen!"

Die anderen lauschten Millies Schilderungen gespannt und löcherten sie mit Fragen. Sie waren nicht mit Emmie befreundet gewesen, erinnerten sich aber an sie.

Als mein Handy einige Sekunden später vibrierte, schaute ich auf den Bildschirm und las Rhondas Antwort. *Das macht nichts. Du kannst dir etwas aus dem Laden aussuchen. Bis nachher!*
Rhonda

Ja!, jubelte ich innerlich. Dann widmete ich mich wieder meiner Pizza, während die anderen Mädchen weiterquatschten.

Lisa und Beth erzählten von ihren Erlebnissen auf der Klassenfahrt. „Alle gut aussehenden Jungs waren bei euch in der Gruppe", jammerte Lisa und sah Millic an. „Ihr hattet den ganzen Spaß. Das ist so unfair!"

Millies Wangen wurden knallrot und Lisa, die ihren Fehler wohl bemerkte, schielte zu mir hin. Ich schaute Millie vielsagend an. Es geschah ihr recht, dass sie in Verlegenheit gebracht wurde.

Danach vermied sie jeglichen Blickkontakt zu mir, was mir nur recht war.

Bald wandte sich die Unterhaltung dem Abschlussball am Freitag zu. Ich hatte nicht vorgehabt, hinzugehen, aber sobald die Mädchen das hörten, wollten sie nichts davon wissen.

Becky packte mich am Arm. „Julia, du musst mitkommen! Das wird toll!“

Lisa und Beth nickten zustimmend. „Das ist das letzte Event des Schuljahres. Alle werden dort sein!“, sagte Lisa. Sie wirkte schockiert, dass ich es auch nur in Betracht zog, den Ball zu verpassen. „Du gehst doch hin, oder, Millie?“

Millie nickte, sagte aber nichts.

Becky stieß mich mit dem Ellbogen an und grinste. „Hat Blake dich gefragt, ob du mit ihm gehst?“

Bevor ich antworten konnte, rief Lisa aufgeregt: „Wir haben gehört, dass du und Blake wieder zusammen seid! Das ist ja so romantisch … genau wie bei deiner Freundin Emmie und Jack Hillman. Jetzt könnt ihr auf Doppeldates gehen. Frag doch Emmie, ob sie auch zum Ball kommt! Wenn sie schon eingeschrieben ist, darf sie bestimmt mit dabei sein. Dann können wir sie alle wiedersehen.“

Ich schielte unbehaglich zu Millie, bevor ich erwiderte: „Ja, vielleicht. Ich weiß nicht, was die Jungs für Pläne haben. Bin mir nicht sicher, ob sie überhaupt hingehen."

Millie wirkte noch immer so, als würde sie am liebsten im Boden versinken. Vielleicht fühlte sie sich schuldig. Schließlich war immer noch unklar, ob sich die Dinge zwischen mir und Blake wieder einrenken würden.

Beth grinste Lisa an. „Schade, dass wir keine Leute von anderen Schulen einladen dürfen. Sonst könntest du Joe fragen."

„Ich glaube, ich gehe lieber solo", entgegnete Lisa. „Hashtag Mädelsabend. Wir könnten alle gemeinsam gehen! Uns sogar gemeinsam fertig machen!"

„Tolle Idee!", sagte Beth. „Ihr könnt alle zu mir kommen, wenn ihr wollt."

„Das klingt gut!" Becky nickte begeistert. „Was zieht ihr denn an?"

Ich runzelte die Stirn und dachte über Beths Kommentar nach. Hatte Lisa noch immer etwas mit Joe? Es schien unvermeidlich, dass sie meinem Bruder am Ende das Herz brechen würde.

Was den Abschlussball anging, so war mir eine

Idee gekommen. Ich war mir nicht sicher, ob ich vorher zu Beth gehen wollte, besonders wenn Millie auch dort war. Aber wenn ich Emmie dazu überreden könnte, mitzukommen, wäre das doch eine tolle Gelegenheit, Jack und Blake dort zu treffen. Und vielleicht die perfekte Chance für mich, Blake wieder näherzukommen.

Ich ging in Gedanken meinen Kleiderschrank durch. Wenn ich den Abschlussball besuchte, brauchte ich ein richtig tolles Outfit, das Blake beeindrucken würde. Ich war mir aber nicht sicher, ob ich etwas Geeignetes besaß.

Dann erinnerte ich mich an *Eliza's* und daran, dass ich diese Woche mein erstes Gehalt bekommen würde, und eine kribbelige Vorfreude stieg in mir auf.

Als es klingelte, liefen wir widerwillig zurück zu unseren Klassenzimmern. Vor uns lag eine lange Prüfung und keine von uns freute sich auf die nächsten achtzig Minuten. Lisa und Beth hatten Mr. Hathaway als Lehrer und ich war froh, nicht in ihrem Kurs zu sein. Jedes Mal, wenn ich ihn sah, stellte ich ihn mir mit Sara vor. Ich wusste, dass ich mich in seinem Unterricht nicht würde konzentrieren können.

Sara und er hatten sich anscheinend kennengelernt, weil sie ihn um Nachhilfeunterricht in Mathe gebeten hatte. Als ob sie das nötig hätte! Damals in der Mittelstufe war sie jedenfalls immer sehr gut in dem Fach gewesen. Aber ihr war offenbar jedes Mittel recht, um sich an den gut aussehenden Lehrer heranzumachen, für den so viele Mädchen aus unserer Stufe schwärmten.

Als ich meinen Klassenraum betrat, hörte ich ein paar Schüler hinter mir kichern. Mein Name fiel und da wusste ich, dass sie über die Fotos im Internet redeten. Ich widerstand der

Versuchung, mich umzudrehen und sie böse anzustarren, und begab mich stattdessen in eine Ecke des Zimmers, die weit von ihnen entfernt lag. Dort ließ ich mich auf einen Stuhl fallen und beobachtete, wie der Rest der Klasse eintrudelte.

Als Sara erschien, begegnete sie für den Bruchteil einer Sekunde meinem Blick und wählte dann einen freien Platz in der ersten Reihe. *Eins zu null für Julia,* dachte ich und grinste zufrieden. Normalerweise hätte sie die Gelegenheit genutzt, um mich wieder in irgendeiner Weise zu drangsalieren, doch heute war von ihrer sonst so selbstgefälligen Art nichts zu sehen.

Sie blickte auf, als Blake den Raum betrat, doch er ging an dem freien Platz neben ihr vorbei und setzte sich woanders hin. Hoffentlich würde ich nach der Stunde mit ihm reden können.

Mr. Ryland traf mit einem Papierstapel unter dem Arm ein. Jackie rief ihm zu: „Brauchen Sie Hilfe?"

„Es geht schon, danke, Jacky", erwiderte Mr. Ryland mit einem Nicken.

„Sind Sie sicher? Mir würde es nichts ausmachen."

Mr. Ryland bedachte sie mit einem amüsierten Grinsen und ein paar Schüler lachten. Seit

seinem ersten Tag bei uns hatte Jackie auf jede erdenkliche Weise versucht, mit ihm zu flirten. Sie gab einfach nicht auf. Mr. Ryland wehrte jedoch immer ab, indem er Jackie entweder ignorierte oder irgendeine lustige Erwiderung parat hatte. Ganz anders als Mr. Hathaway mit Sara.

Mr. Ryland hatte sich rasch den Respekt der ganzen Klasse verdient und war bei allen Schülern sehr beliebt. Er hatte im Football-Team seines Colleges gespielt und sprach deshalb oft mit den Schülern über Football und andere Sportarten. Jackie nahm häufig an diesen Unterhaltungen teil, obwohl sie wahrscheinlich die unsportlichste Person im Raum war.

Nachdem er uns die Arbeitsblätter ausgeteilt hatte, verbannte ich alle anderen Gedanken aus meinem Kopf, um mich ganz auf den Test zu konzentrieren.

Die Zeit verging wie im Flug, doch als es klingelte, war ich zufrieden. Ich war schon ein paar Minuten früher fertig geworden, sodass ich noch einmal meine letzten Antworten überprüfen konnte. In Mathe achtete ich immer darauf, jede Aufgabe zweimal nachzurechnen, um eventuelle Fehler zu finden, auch wenn ich dadurch etwas langsamer war.

Ich legte meine Arbeit auf Mr. Rylands Tisch

und eilte in den Korridor, der bereits voller Schüler war. Suchend schaute ich mich nach Blake um und als ich mich umdrehte, stand er auf einmal vor mir. Er schien hier draußen gewartet zu haben. Etwa auf mich? Ich wagte es kaum zu hoffen.

Ich schluckte nervös und zögerte. Jetzt, da meine Chance endlich gekommen war, wusste ich nicht mehr, was ich sagen sollte.

Doch er sprach zuerst. „Wie lief dein Test?“

„Ähm … ganz gut, denke ich. Das hoffe ich jedenfalls. Und deiner?“

„Ja … bei mir auch“, sagte er und nickte.

Wir sahen uns an und öffneten dann gleichzeitig den Mund.

„Blake“, begann ich im selben Moment, als auch er meinen Namen sagte. Ich grinste ihn an. „Du zuerst.“

Er grinste zurück. „Nein, nach dir.“

Da ich nichts zu verlieren hatte, beschloss ich, direkt zur Sache zu kommen. „Ich habe mich nur gefragt, ob du zum Abschlussball gehst.“

„Ach ja?“ Er lachte leise. „Das ist witzig. Ich wollte dich dasselbe fragen.“

Mein Lächeln wuchs in die Breite und ich blickte ihm in die Augen. „Alle sagen, dass es lustig werden wird.“

„Ja, der Abschlussball ist meistens ziemlich cool.“

„Also dann … sehe ich dich dort?“ Ich hob fragend die Brauen.

Seine Augen funkelten und er lächelte auf die Art, die ich an ihm so liebte. „Ja, wir sehen uns dort!“

Ich winkte ihm zu und wandte mich um, während die Schmetterlinge in meinem Bauch einen verrückten Tanz aufführten. „Oh mein Gott“, wisperte ich und wagte einen Blick zurück.

Als ich sah, dass sein hübsches Gesicht immer noch mir zugewandt war, machte mein Magen erneut einen Purzelbaum. Er lachte und winkte mir noch einmal zu, bevor er sich auf den Weg machte.

Meine Haut prickelte. Vor mir lag eine Prüfung in Geografie, aber das störte mich nicht im Geringsten. Ich konnte nur an Freitag denken und an die Zeit mit Blake.

Noch drei Tage.

Dann würden wir wieder zusammen sein.

Neue Entwicklungen ...

Bevor ich die Schule verließ, ging ich noch einmal ins Sekretariat und sagte meinen Termin mit Miss McCarthy ab. Danach lief ich durch das ganze Schulgebäude zurück, um den Hinterausgang zu nehmen. Von dort aus waren es nur etwa zwanzig Minuten zu Fuß bis zum Einkaufszentrum. Da die Schulbusse im Moment nicht fuhren, blieb mir keine andere Wahl, als zu Fuß zu gehen, aber ich hatte noch viel Zeit und musste mich nicht beeilen.

Mittlerweile war der Flur leer und ich hörte nur das leise Tappen meiner Sneakers auf dem glatten Boden. Ich war tief in Gedanken versunken. Bei der Erinnerung an mein Gespräch mit Blake überliefen mich immer wieder kleine Schauer der Freude. Ich war in meiner eigenen Welt und fühlte mich beinahe so, als würde ich schweben. Bis mich der Klang einer vertrauten Stimme aus dem Zimmer vor mir aufhorchen ließ.

„Es kann nicht einfach so enden! Das lasse ich nicht zu!" Der fordernde Tonfall war

unverkennbar und enthielt eine deutliche Warnung.

„Nicht so laut!“, erwiderte die raue Stimme eines Lehrers.

Ich wurde langsamer. Offensichtlich war ich in ein privates Gespräch zwischen Sara und Mr. Hathaway hineingestolpert. Mein Herz pochte nervös und ich überlegte, zurückzugehen und doch den längeren Weg zu nehmen. Aber warum sollte ich mich wegschleichen, nur um Sara einen Gefallen zu tun? Außerdem war nun meine Neugier geweckt und ich wollte herausfinden, um was es ging.

Ich machte einen vorsichtigen Schritt auf die Tür zu, vergewisserte mich, dass niemand in der Nähe war, und lehnte mich daneben an die Wand. Die Stimmen aus dem Zimmer waren zu einem Flüstern übergegangen, das ich nur schwer verstehen konnte.

„Aber ich möchte mit dir zusammen sein!“, wimmerte Sara verzweifelt.

„Es tut mir leid, Sara“, sagte Mr. Hathaway. „Das war alles ein Fehler. Ich könnte meinen Job verlieren. Wir müssen das beenden. Bitte geh, bevor dich noch jemand bei mir sieht.“

„Ich bin eine deiner Schülerinnen und du gibst mir Nachhilfe in Mathe. Warum sollte ich nicht

hier sein dürfen?“

„Sara, es tut mir leid, aber es ist vorbei. Du musst jetzt gehen.“ Seine Stimme war fest.

„Es kann nicht vorbei sein. Du liebst mich. Das weiß ich …“

Ich schlug mir die Hand vor den Mund, um nicht laut nach Luft zu schnappen. Ich konnte kaum glauben, was ich da hörte.

„Sara, lass das bitte!“, sagte Mr. Hathaway jetzt noch bestimmter. „Mach es nicht noch schwerer, als es sowieso schon ist. Es ist vorbei und das ist mein letztes Wort!“

Im nächsten Moment stürmte Sara aus dem Zimmer und bog nach links ab, ohne mich auf der anderen Seite der Tür zu bemerken. Abgesehen von ihren Schritten hörte ich nur ihre erstickten Schluchzer. Wenige Sekunden später rannte sie um eine Ecke und war verschwunden.

Ich wagte einen Blick in den Raum und sah, wie Mr. Hathaway sich mit einer Hand durchs Haar fuhr, während er aus dem Fenster starrte. Mein Kopf schwirrte, während ich mich vorbeischlich und in die gleiche Richtung ging, in die Sara verschwunden war. Ich konnte diese neue Information kaum begreifen.

Erneut hörte ich Saras Worte. *Es kann nicht vorbei*

sein. Du liebst mich. Das weiß ich ... Wenn ich noch irgendwelche Zweifel an ihrer Beziehung gehabt hatte, waren sie nun verschwunden.

Doch der Unterton, der in Saras Stimme mitgeschwungen hatte, war mir nur allzu vertraut.

Wusste Mr. Hathaway, mit wem oder was er sich da anlegte?

Wahrscheinlich nicht.

Sara gab selten nach, wenn sie etwas wollte. Und ich wusste, dass sie auch jetzt nicht so einfach aufgeben würde.

Eliza's …

Als ich bei *Eliza's* ankam, bediente Emmie gerade eine Kundin. Ich konnte es kaum erwarten, ihr zu erzählen, was ich in der Schule erlebt hatte. Aber ich wusste, dass ich damit warten musste, bis wir allein waren.

Nachdem die Kundin gegangen war, kam Emmie hinter der Kasse hervor und umarmte mich herzlich. „Julia! Ist das nicht toll? Heute können wir zusammen arbeiten."

„Ja, echt cool!" Ich lachte und trat dann zurück, um ihr Outfit zu betrachten. Sie trug ein blau-weiß-gestreiftes Kleid aus *Eliza's* Kollektion – das gleiche Modell, das Sara sich gekauft hatte. „Das steht dir richtig gut! Hat Rhonda dir erlaubt, es zu tragen?"

„Sie hat es mir sogar geschenkt! Kaum zu glauben, oder?", jubelte Emmie. „Sie ist gerade in ihrem Büro, aber sie hat mir gesagt, dass wir ab jetzt nur noch Sachen tragen sollen, die hier verkauft werden. Ein Outfit bekommen wir geschenkt und für alles andere kriegen wir Mitarbeiterrabatt."

„Wow!“, erwiderte ich und bewunderte noch einmal Emmies neues Kleid, in dem sie so hübsch aussah.

„Hallo, Julia.“ Beim Klang von Rhondas Stimme drehte ich mich um. „Danke, dass du so kurzfristig einspringen konntest. Alle anderen Mitarbeiter sind entweder krank oder im Urlaub. Du bist meine Rettung!“

Ich lächelte zurück. „Kein Problem, Rhonda, das mache ich gern.“

„Dann wollen wir dir mal ein Outfit besorgen. Eins geht aufs Haus. Das darfst du dir von diesem Ständer hier aussuchen“, sagte sie und deutete auf einen Kleiderständer neben uns, dessen Ware heruntergesetzt war. „Hat Emmie dir schon erklärt, was ihr von jetzt an für Arbeitskleidung tragt?“

„Ja, hat sie“, erwiderte ich eifrig.

„Okay, gut!“ Rhonda lächelte uns beide an. „Wenn die Kunden sehen, dass die Verkäuferinnen unsere Sachen tragen, greifen sie eher zu. Du brauchst für den Anfang nur zwei verschiedene Optionen, außer natürlich du möchtest gern mehr kaufen. Und du bekommst fünfzig Prozent Rabatt auf alles. Wie klingt das?“

„Das klingt fantastisch!“, erwiderte ich. „Vielen

Dank, Rhonda."

„Du bist früh dran, also lass dir ruhig Zeit mit deiner Auswahl. Wenn du heute schon etwas kaufen möchtest, kann ich die Kosten direkt von deinem Wochengehalt abziehen."

Sofort dachte ich an den Schulball am Freitag. Das war die Antwort auf meine Gebete! „Danke, Rhonda!", wiederholte ich. „Ich suche mir gleich etwas von diesen Sachen hier aus. Und wenn dann noch Zeit ist, vielleicht noch etwas anderes."

„Mach nur." Rhonda lächelte. „Der Nachmittags-Ansturm hat ja noch nicht begonnen, sodass Emmie dir helfen kann."

Sobald Rhonda außer Hörweite war, sagte Emmie: „Kaum zu glauben, dass sie uns ein ganzes Outfit spendiert, oder?"

„Echt krass!" Ich kicherte und war ganz hibbelig vor Aufregung, während ich mir die Sachen auf dem Ständer anschaute.

Das Kleid, das Emmie gewählt hatte, gab es noch einmal, doch mein Blick fiel auf ein enges hellblaues Kleid mit rundem Ausschnitt.

„Das hier ist sehr hübsch!" , sagte ich und zog meine Größe heraus, damit Emmie es auch sehen konnte. Ein breiter schwarzer Gürtel war

um den Hüftbereich geschlungen.

„Das steht dir bestimmt super, Julia! Das hier ist auch schön", erwiderte Emmie und suchte ein hellgrünes Kleid mit kurzen Ärmeln und ausgestelltem Rock heraus.

„Okay, ich probiere beide an."

Emmie war genauso aufgeregt wie ich, als wir zu den Umkleidekabinen eilten. Als Erstes zog ich das Kleid an, das Emmie mir gegeben hatte, und erzählte ihr dabei von meiner Konfrontation mit Sara heute Morgen. Auch wenn es mir schwerfiel, musste ich die Neuigkeiten mit Mr. Hathaway noch für mich behalten, bis wir ganz ungestört sein würden.

Als ich aus der Kabine trat, fügte ich hinzu. „Und weißt du was … sie hat die Accounts auf Facebook und Instagram gelöscht. Sie existieren nicht mehr!"

„Oh mein Gott! Das ist ja super, Julia! Ich wünschte, ich hätte ihre Reaktion gesehen!"

„Es war echt unvergesslich!" Ich grinste. Dann blickte ich an dem grünen Kleid herunter. „Es ist ein bisschen zu groß. Was meinst du?"

„Hm, das war die kleinste Größe, die es gab. Zieh mal das blaue an!"

Ich nickte und schloss die Tür hinter mir.

Während ich mich umzog, erzählte ich weiter von meinen Erlebnissen an diesem Morgen. Als ich zum zweiten Mal aus der Kabine kam, lächelte Emmie breit. „Das sieht wirklich toll an dir aus. Es passt perfekt!“

Ich drehte mich zu dem bodenlangen Spiegel an der Wand um und musterte mein Spiegelbild. Das Kleid war figurbetont geschnitten und relativ kurz, aber ich verliebte mich sofort.

„Ich glaube, das wäre passend für die Arbeit“, sagte ich und drehte mich hin und her, um es von allen Seiten zu betrachten. „Außerdem kann man es auch anziehen, wenn man mal etwas Schickeres braucht – dafür habe ich noch gar nichts im Schrank.“

Emmie nickte. „Das liegt am Gürtel. Ich finde, du solltest es nehmen.“

Ich sah nach dem Preisschild. Alles an diesem Kleiderständer war herabgesetzt worden, aber selbst mit dem Mitarbeiterrabatt hätte mich dieses Kleid fast fünfzig Dollar gekostet. Fünfzig Dollar, die ich nicht hatte. Mein Tag wurde immer besser.

Emmie folgte mir zurück in den Laden, um nach weiteren Klamotten für mich zu suchen. Als ich bei den Accessoires vorbeikam, hob ich eine coole Sonnenbrille vom Ständer und setzte sie auf. Dann drehte ich mich lachend zu Emmie

um.

„Selbst mit deinen Chucks siehst du aus wie ein Model!“

„Ja, klar!“ Ich verdrehte die Augen, aber insgeheim freute ich mich über Emmies Kompliment. Ich stellte mir vor, wie ich mein Haar glättete und ein bisschen Make-up auftrug, um den Look zu unterstreichen.

Vorsichtig legte ich die Sonnenbrille zurück und wandte mich dem Kleiderständer hinter mir zu. Ich hatte etwas ganz Bestimmtes vor Augen. Bald fand ich ein eng anliegendes rotes Kleid mit überkreuzten Trägern und hielt es vor meinen Körper.

„Wow!“, rief Emmie. „Die Farbe würde dir bestimmt gut stehen!“

„Es ist ziemlich teuer, aber vielleicht reicht mein Gehalt dafür, wenn man den Rabatt einberechnet. Es wäre perfekt für den Schulball am Freitag.“ Ich sah Emmie an. „Du solltest definitiv auch kommen!“

Emmie lächelte und schüttelte den Kopf. „Jack hat mir schon davon erzählt. Und Millie auch. Aber ich bin mir nicht sicher, ob das passend wäre. Ich bin ja noch nicht offiziell wieder in der Schule.“

„Aber du bist schon angemeldet, also darfst du auch hingehen. Außerdem werden da so viele Leute sein, die du von früher kennst. Die Mädels, mit denen ich befreundet bin, wollen dich alle unbedingt sehen. Und Jack wird da sein." Ich lächelte ermutigend. „Ich hatte gehofft, dass wir beide zusammen hingehen könnten. Ich würde dich wirklich gern dabeihaben!"

Emmie brauchte nicht länger überzeugt zu werden. „Okay, ich komme mit!"

„Jaaa!" Ich grinste und klatschte aufgeregt in die Hände. „Dann müssen wir nur noch ein Outfit für dich finden!"

„Und ich hab da auch schon eine Idee", sagte Emmie und eilte zu einem Tisch in der Mitte des Geschäfts.

Ich sah zu, wie sie einen Stapel bauchfreier trägerloser Tops durchsuchte und ein pinkes in ihrer Größe hervorzog. Von einem Ständer in der Nähe nahm sie einen kurzen schwarzen Rock mit silbernen Knöpfen an der Vorderseite.

Sie hielt die Sachen hoch. „Ich habe Stiefel, die perfekt dazu passen würden! Und wenn du willst, kann ich dir auch ein Paar ausleihen, das mir die Freundin meiner Mom geschenkt hat. Du hast doch die gleiche Schuhgröße wie ich, oder? Ich glaube, sie wären super für dein Kleid."

„Danke, Emmie! Das wäre toll!" Ich lächelte und zog sie zur Kasse, um Rhonda unsere Auswahl zu zeigen.

Rhonda nickte alles ab und erlaubte uns, die zusätzlichen Outfits anzuprobieren. Sobald wir uns überzeugt hatten, dass sie passten, gaben wir sie Rhonda, die sie einscannte und dann beiseitelegte, damit wir sie später mitnehmen konnten. Sie erinnerte uns daran, dass sie den Preis von unserem Gehalt abziehen würde, bevor sie es am Donnerstag überwies. Da ich bisher nur zwei Schichten gehabt hatte, würde nicht viel übrig bleiben, aber das machte überhaupt nichts. Rhonda hatte uns viel Arbeit über den ganzen Sommer versprochen und ich freute mich darauf, bald mehr zu verdienen.

In meinem neuen blauen Kleid half ich Rhonda, die Ware zu sortieren. Sie blickte an mir herab und lächelte anerkennend. „Das war eine gute Wahl, Julia. Es steht dir fantastisch. Die schwarzen Schuhe, die du am Samstag anhattest, würden dazu gut passen … für deine nächste Schicht." Sie schaute amüsiert auf meine Chucks herunter, bevor sie mit ihrer Arbeit weitermachte.

Mein Kopf schwirrte noch immer von allem, was an diesem Tag passiert war. Gedankenverloren summte ich die Musik mit, die im Hintergrund lief. Aber bald füllte sich der Laden mit

Jugendlichen und ich musste mich auf meine Arbeit konzentrieren.

Zum Glück war niemand darunter, den ich kannte. Ich hatte schon befürchtet, dass Lisa hier auftauchen und nach einem Rabatt fragen würde. Emmie hatte mir gesagt, dass wir Freunden keinen Rabatt geben durften, und das würde ich auch Lisa mitteilen, wenn ich sie das nächste Mal sah.

Während ich Emmie dabei half, die T-Shirts auf einem der Tische zu falten, stieß sie mich plötzlich mit dem Ellbogen an. „Kennst du diesen Typen?“, fragte sie und nickte zum Schaufenster.

Ich sah auf und mein Magen überschlug sich. Ihn hätte ich hier am allerwenigsten erwartet! Seine durchdringenden blauen Augen funkelten und auf seinem Gesicht lag ein erfreutes Lächeln. Er winkte mir zu und mein Puls schoss in die Höhe. Ich winkte kurz zurück und sah dann weg. Sobald er mir den Rücken zukehrte, beobachtete ich, wie seine große, sportliche Gestalt in der Menge verschwand.

„Wer war das?“, fragte Emmie. „Er konnte kaum aufhören, dich anzustarren.“

„Was? Echt?“ Ich runzelte die Stirn und holte tief Luft. „Das war Ky Robertson.“

Ihre Augenbrauen schossen in die Höhe. „Warte mal … der Ky, von dem du mir erzählt hast?“

Ich nickte und seufzte.

„Oh … mein … Gott!“, sagte Emmie, als hätte sie gerade ein Wunder miterlebt. „Der ist ja echt heiß!“

„Ja!“, murmelte ich. „Ich weiß!“

Den Rest meiner Schicht bemühte ich mich, Kys lächelndes Gesicht aus meinem Kopf zu vertreiben.

Warum hatte er immer noch so eine Wirkung auf mich?

Ich tadelte mich selbst dafür, während ich gleichzeitig versuchte, eine Antwort auf diese Frage zu finden.

Aber es war unmöglich, ihn aus meinen Gedanken zu verbannen, egal, wie sehr ich es auch versuchte.

Würde ich je über ihn hinwegkommen?

Die Reaktion …

Emmie hatte sich nach der Arbeit mit Jack verabredet und er stand schon vor dem Geschäft, als wir *Eliza's* verließen. Sein Gesicht leuchtete auf, sobald er Emmie sah, und die beiden lächelten sich an.

Ich beobachtete, wie er sich einige Strähnen seines wuscheligen braunen Haars aus den Augen strich und sie in seine starken Arme zog. Für einen Moment spürte ich einen Stich der Eifersucht. Ich freute mich wirklich sehr für meine Freundin. Ich wusste, wie viel er ihr bedeutete, und es war wundervoll, dass er ihre Gefühle erwiderte. Aber bei ihrem Anblick fragte ich mich unwillkürlich, ob es zwischen Blake und mir je wieder so sein würde.

Den Arm um Emmies Schultern gelegt drehte sich Jack zu mir um und grinste fröhlich. „Hey, Julia!"

„Hi, Jack!" Ich lächelte zurück.

„Wie ich sehe, habt ihr schon einige Klamotten gekauft!", sagte er mit einem Blick auf unsere

neuen Outfits und die Tüten in unseren Händen.

„Ja!“ Ich lachte. „Es gibt dort so viele tolle Sachen, dass wir nicht widerstehen konnten. Aber die hier haben wir geschenkt bekommen!“ Ich deutete auf die Kleider, die Emmie und ich trugen.

„Echt? Das ist ja cool!“ Er schaute von mir zu Emmie und sein Blick blieb auf seiner Freundin hängen. Ganz offensichtlich war ich nicht die Einzige, die fand, dass Emmie in dem gestreiften Kleid toll aussah.

Emmie gab ihm einen spielerischen Klaps auf den Arm und hielt ihre Einkaufstüte hoch. „Und ich habe noch ein neues Outfit für den Abschlussball am Freitag.“

„Oh. Was? Du willst doch kommen?“

„Julia hat mich überredet. Es wird bestimmt lustig!“

„Das freut mich!“ Jack lächelte und drückte sie noch fester an sich.

Ich beschloss, dass es an der Zeit war, die beiden allein zu lassen. Rasch verabschiedete ich mich und eilte zur Bushaltestelle. Im Bus setzte ich mich auf den ersten freien Platz und holte mein Handy heraus. Leider war der Akku leer und so verbrachte ich meine Zeit damit, mein neues

Kleid zu bewundern und an Freitagabend zu denken. Ich hatte mir bereits überlegt, dass ich mir die Haare glätten würde. Und mit Emmies Stiefeln als perfekter Ergänzung zu meinem Outfit war ich mir sicher, dass Blake beeindruckt sein würde.

Als der Bus an meiner Haltestelle hielt, sprang ich hinunter auf den Bürgersteig. Vorsichtig sah ich mich um. Zu Hause zu sein erinnerte mich wieder an Barry und ich suchte die Straße nach seinem Dienstwagen ab. Doch zum Glück war davon nichts zu sehen.

Ich stieg die Treppe zu unserer Eingangstür hinauf und wollte gerade meinen Schlüssel einstecken, als die Tür aufging und das besorgte Gesicht meiner Mutter erschien.

„Da bist du ja!“ Sie seufzte erleichtert. „Ich habe mir Sorgen gemacht. Wo warst du denn?“

Ich öffnete den Mund, um etwas zu erwidern, doch sie kam mir zuvor. „Ich habe angerufen und geschrieben, aber du hast nicht geantwortet. Ich war beinahe krank vor Sorge!“

Ein wenig schuldig fühlte ich mich schon. Ich hätte ihr Bescheid sagen sollen, dass ich später nach Hause kommen würde. Aber ich war so daran gewöhnt, allein zu wohnen, dass es mir nicht einmal in den Sinn gekommen war. „Ich habe heute gearbeitet … in meinem neuen Job“,

stammelte ich. „Und mein Handy war aus …“

„Was für ein Job? Davon hast du mir überhaupt nichts erzählt! Wenn du noch einmal später nach Hause kommst, schreib mir gefälligst! Dafür hast du ja schließlich ein Handy.“

Ihre Besorgnis war Zorn gewichen, und mit jedem Wort, das aus ihrem Mund kam, wuchs auch mein Ärger. Sie warf einen bangen Blick auf die Straße, bevor sie mich ins Haus ließ. Dann schloss sie die Tür hinter mir. Was war denn los? War wieder irgendetwas mit Barry vorgefallen?

Ich bekam keine Gelegenheit, nachzufragen, denn schon schimpfte sie weiter. „Warum hast du mir nicht erzählt, dass du einen Job hast? Ich kann nicht glauben, dass du mir so was verschweigen würdest!“ Sie hatte die Hände in die Hüften gestemmt und wartete auf eine Erklärung.

Ich runzelte die Stirn. Es gefiel mir überhaupt nicht, so von ihr verhört zu werden. „Du hast seit Monaten nicht bei uns gelebt. Du hast überhaupt keine Ahnung, was in meinem Leben abgeht, und das hat dir vorher auch nichts ausgemacht. Was willst du eigentlich von mir?“

„Ich will …“, stotterte Mom. „Ich will nicht, dass du einfach so wegbleibst! Ich hatte keine Ahnung, wo du bist, und konnte dich nicht

erreichen. Ich war außer mir."

„Tja, weißt du, ich kann ganz gut auf mich selbst aufpassen. Du musst dich nicht so aufspielen und mich wie eine Fünfjährige behandeln!"

„Wage es ja nicht, so mit mir zu sprechen, junge Dame! Ich war vielleicht eine Weile nicht da, aber ich bin immer noch deine Mutter, und während du unter meinem Dach wohnst, wirst du meine Regeln befolgen!" Sie hielt inne und betrachtete mein Outfit. „Das Kleid sieht teuer aus. Wie kannst du dir das leisten?"

„Ich habe jetzt einen Job, schon vergessen? Und es ist mein Geld; ich kann damit machen, was ich will. Und zu deiner Information, das Kleid habe ich umsonst bekommen."

„Umsonst?" Sie schnaubte. „Wie kann so ein Kleid kostenlos sein? Du hast es doch nicht gestohlen, oder?"

Ich starrte sie mit offenem Mund an. Es kränkte mich, dass sie so etwas auch nur andeuten würde. „Natürlich nicht!" Ich wollte ihr noch so einige Dinge an den Kopf werfen, aber sie machte mich so wütend, dass ich nicht länger in ihrer Nähe bleiben konnte.

Ich schob mich an ihr vorbei und rannte die Treppe hoch, wobei ich mit der Schulter gegen Matt stieß, der gerade herunterkam.

„Huch!“, rief er. „Was ist denn hier los?“

Als ich den oberen Treppenabsatz erreichte, hörte ich Moms Stimme von unten. „Sie glaubt wohl, sie kann hier machen, was sie will? Wie kann sie es wagen, so mit mir zu reden!“

Ich schüttelte angewidert den Kopf, knallte meine Zimmertür zu und ließ mich auf mein Bett fallen. Mein Atem ging in flachen Stößen und ich starrte mein Spiegelbild an der Schranktür gegenüber an.

Sie war echt unglaublich! Und jetzt musste ich mit ihr leben und wieder ihren Regeln folgen.

Ich betrachtete mein neues blaues Kleid, das beim Sitzen etwas nach oben gerutscht war. „Wie kannst du nur glauben, dass ich stehlen würde!!“, schrie ich meine geschlossene Tür an, um meinem Frust und Ärger Luft zu machen.

Welches Recht hatte sie, einfach wieder in unser Leben zu spazieren und zu denken, sie könnte hier die Richterin spielen?

Ich hasste sie.

Sie machte alles kaputt!

Warum hatte sie nur zurückkommen müssen?

Ungebetener Besucher …

Nachdem ich geduscht hatte, verstaute ich das blaue Kleid in meinem Wandschrank. Dann holte ich das neue rote Kleid aus der Tüte und hängte es ebenfalls auf, damit es vor den neugierigen Blicken meiner Mutter verborgen blieb und sie mich nicht noch einmal beschuldigte, eine Diebin zu sein.

Morgen Abend würde mein Dad nach Hause kommen und ich konnte es kaum erwarten. Von meinen Eltern war er es, der immer für uns da gewesen war. Er verstand mich. Im Gegensatz zu meiner Mutter.

Als ich laute Stimmen von unten hörte, öffnete ich meine Tür einen Spaltbreit, um zu lauschen. Mom schimpfte wahrscheinlich wieder wegen irgendetwas mit Matt. Vielleicht hatte er einen Teller in der Spüle liegen lassen. *Unglaublich!* Ich wollte gar nicht daran denken, dass er bald zur Uni gehen und mich mit ihr allein lassen würde! Vielleicht könnte ich dann zu Emmie ziehen.

„Du kannst nicht reinkommen, Barry! Ich habe es dir doch gesagt! Es ist vorbei mit uns!“

Ein Schauer rann mir über den Rücken. Ich öffnete meine Tür weiter, eilte zur Treppe und schlich ein paar Stufen nach unten, wo ich mich hinhockte, um die Szene unter mir unbemerkt zu beobachten.

„Barry, bitte geh! Du bist hier nicht mehr willkommen!“ Ein Hauch Hysterie schwang in Moms Stimme mit.

„Warum nicht?“, fauchte er. „Als es im Haus noch etwas zu tun gab, durfte ich kommen, wie?“ Er gab Mom einen groben Schubs. „Du schuldest mir noch was! Und zwar eine ganze Menge! Und es ist nicht vorbei, bis ich es sage!“

„Hey!“ Matt straffte die Schultern und richtete sich zu seiner vollen Größe auf. „Fassen Sie sie nicht an!“

„Barry, verschwinde oder ich rufe die Polizei!“, rief Mom mit hörbarer Panik in der Stimme.

Barry machte einen Schritt auf sie zu, doch Matt trat dazwischen. „Sie sollten jetzt gehen!“ Matt schob Mom hinter seinen Rücken und packte mit einer Hand die Tür, um Barry den Weg zu versperren.

Barry funkelte die beiden an. „Wir sehen uns wieder!“

Matt knallte die Tür zu und stellte sicher, dass

sie gut verschlossen war, bevor er sich zu Mom umdrehte. Sein Gesicht war rot angelaufen und selbst von meinem Platz aus konnte ich sehen, wie seine Hand zitterte.

Ich rannte die Treppen hinunter. „Matt, ist alles in Ordnung?“

Mom sah mich verstört an. „Deshalb war ich so besorgt, als du nicht wiedergekommen bist, Julia. Ich hatte keine Ahnung, dass er so sein kann. Es tut mir so leid …“ Sie brach in Tränen aus und hielt sich die Hände vors Gesicht.

Matt legte ihr beruhigend einen Arm um die Schultern und sagte ihr, dass alles gut werden würde.

Aber würde es das?

Sie hatte diesen Verrückten in unser Leben gelassen und jetzt hatte sie endlich erkannt, dass er ernsthafte Probleme hatte. In gewisser Weise erinnerte er mich an Sara und ihre Besessenheit mit Mr. Hathaway. Doch hier hatten wir es nicht mit einem jungen Mädchen zu tun, sondern mit einem erwachsenen Mann.

Er hatte Mom bedroht und diese Drohung betraf uns alle. Er wusste, wo wir wohnten, und wir hatten ihn sicher nicht zum letzten Mal gesehen.

Ein Schauer überlief mich.

Dad, bitte komm schnell nach Hause.

Selbstbeherrschung …

Während des Abendessens summte Moms Handy immer wieder mit eintreffenden Nachrichten, bis sie es schließlich stumm stellte.

„Die sind von ihm, oder?“, fragte Matt und zog die Brauen zusammen. „Vielleicht sollten wir die Polizei rufen!“

Mom schüttelte den Kopf. „Ich möchte lieber nicht die Polizei mit einbeziehen. Ich habe ihm schon gesagt, dass euer Vater morgen Abend heimkommt. Daher glaube ich nicht, dass er sich noch einmal hierher traut.“

Ich schnaubte. „Wie kannst du dir da so sicher sein?“

„Julia, bitte lass es einfach!“, sagte Mom nur und stocherte mit der Gabel in ihrem Essen herum. „Und sag mir in Zukunft, wo du bist. Das ist doch nicht zu viel verlangt, oder?“

Ich antwortete nicht. Ich wollte von ihren Regeln nichts wissen und es fiel mir schwer, die Frau, die mir gegenübersaß, überhaupt noch zu

respektieren. Ich merkte, dass Matt Mitleid mit ihr hatte. Aber sie war selbst schuld daran, dass sie jetzt in diesem Schlamassel steckte - genau wie ihre ganze Familie. Ich hatte ihr gesagt, dass ich diesen Mann nicht ausstehen konnte, dass er mir unheimlich war. Sie hatte davon nichts hören wollen. Von Anfang an hatte sie sich von seiner falschen Liebenswürdigkeit blenden lassen. Allein die Vorstellung verursachte mir Übelkeit.

Vor dem Abendessen hatte ich doppelt und dreifach kontrolliert, ob alle Fenster und Türen verschlossen waren. Matt hatte sogar vorgeschlagen, eine Alarmanlage zu installieren. Und das war alles Moms Schuld.

Nach dem Essen, das ich kaum angerührt hatte, ging ich in mein Zimmer, um noch ein wenig für die letzte Prüfung morgen zu lernen. Ich hatte keine Hoffnung auf eine gute Zensur und freute mich nicht gerade auf mein Zeugnis. Aber das Schuljahr hatte nur noch drei Tage und sobald endlich Sommerferien waren, konnte ich das alles hinter mir lassen.

Vorher klopfte ich noch an die Badezimmertür, um Matt zu fragen, ob ich mir sein Ladegerät ausborgen könnte. Ich musste schreien, damit er mich unter der Dusche hörte, und es dauerte ein wenig, bis seine Antwort kam.

Ich brauchte unbedingt ein eigenes Ladegerät und beschloss, mein nächstes Gehalt für Dinge auszugeben, die wirklich notwendig waren - im Vergleich zu Klamotten. Außerdem wollte ich auf ein neues Handy sparen. Vielleicht könnte ich mir eines der neueren Modelle leisten, bei denen man auch einen Vertrag mit höherem Datenvolumen bekam. Ich hatte es so satt, ständig nachzuschauen, wie viel ich diesen Monat schon verbraucht hatte.

Als ich Matts Ladegerät aus der Steckdose neben seinem Schreibtisch zog, fiel mir auf, dass auf seinem Computer Facebook geöffnet war. Vier Chatfenster befanden sich am unteren Bildschirmrand und eins davon enthielt Lisas Namen.

Ich konnte mich nicht zurückhalten, scrollte zum Anfang des aktuellen Chats und überflog die Worte.

Matt > Hey Lisa … wie läuft's?

Lisa > Super. Und bei dir?

Matt > Auch so.

Lisa > Cool. Was machst du so?

Matt > Warte darauf, dass das Schuljahr vorbei ist. Wir haben Donnerstagabend unsere Abschlussparty. Hast du Bock?

Lisa > Oh sorry. Kann nicht. Hab schon was anderes vor.

Matt > Schade. Vielleicht sehen wir uns am Wochenende?

Lisa > Klar. Schreib mir.

Matt > Ok. Freu mich auf dich!

Lisa > Ja, ich auch!

Schnell verließ ich den Raum, um nicht von Matt beim Lesen seiner Nachrichten erwischt zu werden. Nachdem ich sein Ladegerät eingesteckt hatte, setzte ich mich auf mein Bett und dachte über Lisas Verhalten nach. Sie würde niemals eine Einladung zu einer Abschlussparty ausschlagen. Selbst wenn sie der Meinung war, dass sie und Matt *nur* befreundet waren. Es sei denn, sie hatte wirklich etwas sehr Wichtiges vor. Das wäre die einzige Erklärung.

Von Neugier getrieben suchte ich auf meinem Laptop nach der Website von Joes Schule, wo ich erfuhr, dass er am gleichen Tag seine Abschlussfeier hatte wie Matt. Wenn er nicht gerade von seiner Familie in Beschlag genommen wurde, würde er ganz sicher die Nacht durchfeiern. Matt jedenfalls meinte, dass das alle in seinem Jahrgang machen würden.

Konnte es sein, dass Lisa mit Joe zu seiner Party

ging?

Wenn sie nichts von Matt wollte, warum machte sie ihm dann Hoffnungen? Das war nicht fair! Und außerdem war es ein Fehler, sich mit Joe abzugeben, besonders auf einer Party mit jeder Menge Alkohol. Ich kaute auf meiner Unterlippe und fragte mich, ob ich sie warnen sollte.

Letztes Mal, als ich das versucht hatte, hatte sie mir vorgeworfen, eifersüchtig zu sein, und lange nicht mit mir gesprochen. Aber wenn ihr etwas passierte, hätte ich garantiert ein schlechtes Gewissen.

Ich beschloss, erst einmal herauszufinden, ob sie wirklich mit ihm auf die Party gehen wollte, und schob meine Sorgen für den Moment beiseite. Dann holte ich meine Bücher heraus. Doch als kurz darauf mein Telefon summte, ignorierte ich die Bücher und blickte auf mein Smartphone.

Ich lächelte, als ich Emmies Namen auf dem Display sah. Wir schrieben uns täglich und unsere Freundschaft vertiefte sich immer mehr.

Möchtest du am Freitag zu mir kommen, damit wir uns gemeinsam fertig machen können? Du kannst auch nach der Party bei mir übernachten. Dann fahren wir am Samstag gemeinsam auf Arbeit.

Ihr Vorschlag kam genau zur richtigen Zeit. Ohne zu zögern, schrieb ich ihr zurück.

JA! Auf jeden Fall!! Danke, Emmie!!

Meine Mutter kam mir in den Sinn und ich fragte mich, ob sie es mir erlauben würde. Doch dann schnaubte ich verächtlich. Sie würde mich nicht davon abhalten. Wenn es sein musste, würde ich aus dem Fenster klettern. Das wäre nicht das erste Mal. Ich erinnerte mich an die eine Nacht, als ich durch mein Fenster geflohen und zu Millie gerannt war, nachdem mir meine Familie mitgeteilt hatte, dass wir wegziehen würden und dass ich alles zurücklassen musste, was ich kannte und liebte … nur um später das Gleiche noch einmal zu tun, als ich mich an dem neuen Ort einigermaßen eingelebt hatte.

Aber jetzt war Emmie meine Freundin und sie war nach Millie die Erste, mit der ich mich wirklich verbunden fühlte. Ich fand es toll, dass Emmie immer genau zu wissen schien, was ich dachte. Sie war genau zur richtigen Zeit in mein Leben gekommen. Obwohl Emmie vorher eng mit Millie befreundet gewesen war, hoffte ich insgeheim, dass die beiden sich während ihrer Abwesenheit auseinandergelebt hatten. Denn ich wollte Emmie nicht teilen, am allerwenigsten mit Millie.

Ich beschloss, noch einmal kurz meine Social-Media-Seiten zu überprüfen, und meldete mich bei Instagram an. Ein paar neue Nachrichten waren gekommen; ich löschte alle, deren

Absender ich nicht kannte. Dann schaute ich auf Facebook vorbei und machte dort das Gleiche. Als ich mein Telefon gerade weglegen wollte, erschien eine neue Chat-Nachricht auf dem Display.

Hey

Es war nur dieses eine Wort. Aber der Name des Absenders ließ mir das Herz bis zum Halse klopfen.

Ich starrte einige Sekunden lang auf den Bildschirm und wusste nicht, was ich antworten sollte. Da kam eine zweite Nachricht.

Du hast einen Job im Einkaufszentrum? Cool!

Ich erinnerte mich an meine Überraschung, als Ky an *Eliza's* vorbeigekommen war. Auch Emmies Reaktion fiel mir wieder ein: *Der ist ja echt heiß!*

Ja, er sah gut aus, aber das war nicht der einzige Grund, weshalb er mich immer noch so aus der Fassung brachte. Es war so viel mehr als das. Aber warum schrieb er mir plötzlich? Das verwirrte mich.

Ich tippte rasch meine Antwort. *Ja ... es macht Spaß.*

Cool!

Ich starrte auf seine Nachricht und wusste nicht, was ich darauf erwidern sollte. Dann, in einem plötzlichen Anflug von Selbstbeherrschung, meldete ich mich ab. Vielleicht fühlte er sich schuldig wegen Millie und wollte sich wieder mit mir anfreunden. Aber ich könnte niemals mit ihm befreundet sein. Das würde nicht funktionieren. Wenn ich Blake gegenüber fair sein wollte, musste ich den Kontakt ganz abbrechen.

Schließlich legte ich mein Telefon weg, öffnete mein Kunstgeschichtsbuch und konzentrierte mich auf den Text.

Ich hatte mir wegen Ky schon eine meiner Noten versaut, und eine Fünf auf dem Zeugnis war definitiv genug.

Warnung …

Irgendwie schaffte ich es durch die morgendlichen Prüfungen und war erleichtert, als nur noch eine vor mir lag. Kunstgeschichte würde nach der Mittagspause stattfinden. Obwohl ich die praktische Seite von Kunst mochte und bereits eine Arbeitsmappe abgegeben hatte, würde die schriftliche Prüfung nicht einfach werden.

Froh über die Pause trat ich auf den Schulhof, um mich mit Becky und den anderen zu treffen. Ich entdeckte Millie und Jess, die mit Ky und einigen seiner Freunde in Richtung Cafeteria liefen, und stieß einen frustrierten Seufzer aus. So sehr ich auch über Ky hinwegkommen wollte - ich hasste es noch immer, ihn mit Millie zu sehen. Die Eifersucht war schwer abzuschütteln, besonders weil es sich um Millie handelte.

Aber wenigstens würde ich mich in der Mittagspause nicht mit ihr abgeben müssen. Ich war froh, dass ich gestern Abend nicht auf Kys letzte Nachricht geantwortet hatte. Wenn er weiterhin mit Millie ging, wollte ich nichts mit

ihm zu tun haben.

Als ich meine Freundinnen erreichte, diskutierten sie gerade lebhaft über die Trennung von Mila Stanford und Harry Donovan. Die beiden waren eines der heißesten Pärchen unseres Jahrgangs gewesen. Sie waren seit einigen Monaten zusammen und ihre Trennung war in aller Munde.

„Ich habe gehört, dass er sie betrogen haben soll, und sie hat es herausgefunden“, sagte Lisa. „Angeblich mit einem Mädchen von einer anderen Schule. Aber jetzt ist er wieder voll scharf auf Mila und will sie zurück. Kaum zu glauben, oder?“

„Auch wenn er einer der beliebtesten Jungs in unserer Stufe ist, gibt ihm das nicht das Recht, zu betrügen“, meinte Beth verächtlich. „Und Mila ist doch so toll! Wie konnte er ihr das antun?“

„Offenbar denkt sie darüber nach, ihm noch eine Chance zu geben“, sagte Lisa. Sie kannte immer die neuesten Gerüchte und ich fragte mich, woher sie ihre Informationen hatte.

Die Mädchen quatschten noch eine Weile darüber, bis Beth Lisa nach der Party fragte, zu der sie eingeladen war.

„Mein Bruder hat morgen Abend seine

Abschlussparty“, erwähnte ich beiläufig und fing Lisas Blick ein. „Er sagt, dass es die größte Party des Jahres werden wird.“

„Ist das die gleiche Party, auf die du gehst, Lisa?“, fragte Beth.

Lisa wirkte verlegen. Ihr war bestimmt klar, wie vernarrt Matt in sie war. Aber vermutlich war sie sich nicht sicher, wie viel ich wusste. Ich hoffte, er würde sie irgendwann auf frischer Tat ertappen und endlich sehen, wie sie wirklich war.

Auch wenn ich mich darüber ärgerte, wie sie meinen Bruder behandelte, verspürte ich immer noch den Drang, sie zu warnen. Deshalb fragte ich vorsichtig: „Die Party wird bestimmt cool. Mit wem gehst du hin, Lisa?“

Auf einmal richteten sich alle Augen auf Lisa. Beth wackelte mit den Brauen und stupste Lisa am Arm an. „Sie geht mit Joe Taylor. Der ist echt heiß!“, kicherte sie. „Stimmt's, Lisa?“

Lisa verdrehte die Augen und versuchte, Beths Bemerkung abzutun. Aber Beth war nicht mehr aufzuhalten und schwärmte weiter davon, dass Lisa jetzt mit einem Jungen aus der Abschlussklasse zusammen war.

Lisa runzelte die Stirn und schüttelte den Kopf. „Wir sind nicht zusammen! Wir sind nur ein,

zwei Mal miteinander ausgegangen, mehr nicht."

„Ja, und ...? Aber er hat dich zu seiner Abschlussfeier eingeladen. Also muss er dich mögen. Eine Sommerliebe, wie romantisch! Du hast ein Glück!" Beth schlug die Hände vors Herz.

Lisa wurde rot und gab Beth einen kleinen Schubs. Ich war mir immer noch nicht sicher, ob ich etwas sagen sollte. Vielleicht war meine Erfahrung mit Joe ein einmaliges Erlebnis gewesen und zwischen ihm und Lisa war es ganz anders. Aber die Erinnerung ließ mich nicht los.

Er hatte kein Nein von mir akzeptiert, und als ich fliehen wollte, hatte er mich mit seinem ganzen Körpergewicht zu Boden gedrückt. Ich konnte immer noch die Schreie hören, die aus meiner Kehle drangen, auch wenn mir in dem Moment nicht klar gewesen war, dass sie von mir stammten. Schließlich hatte ich es geschafft, ihm zu entkommen – aber würde Lisa auch so viel Glück haben? Ich wusste es nicht.

Als die Pause zu Ende war, sprang ich auf und zog Lisa zur Seite. Ich musste sie einfach warnen. „Lisa", wisperte ich eindringlich. „Du darfst nicht mit Joe auf diese Party gehen. Ich habe ein ganz schlechtes Gefühl dabei."

Sie sah mich eine Weile sprachlos an, als müsste sie meine Worte verarbeiten. „Geht es um Matt? Ich hab' es dir doch schon gesagt, Julia. Matt und ich sind nur Freunde. Ich kann ausgehen, mit wem ich will!“

„Das hat überhaupt nichts mit Matt zu tun“, erwiderte ich und verschwieg ihr, dass Matt durchaus ein Teil des Problems war. „Ich mache mir nur Sorgen um dich. Joe lässt echt nichts anbrennen. Ich … ich habe dir nicht alles verraten, was in der Nacht passiert ist, als er mich nach Hause gefahren hat.“

„Ach, darum geht es!“ Lisa schnaubte. „Julia, hör einfach auf, okay! Ich weiß, was passiert ist. Joe hat mir alles erzählt. Und jetzt kümmere dich um deinen eigenen Kram. Wenn ich mit ihm ausgehen will, dann mache ich das.“

Sie bedachte mich mit einem letzten vernichtenden Blick, bevor sie sich der Menge anschloss, die zum Schuleingang strömte.

Seufzend schüttelte ich den Kopf. Ich hatte es versucht. Mehr konnte ich nicht tun. Ihre zickige Reaktion kränkte mich. Ich wollte doch nur helfen. Aber jetzt lag ihre Sicherheit in ihren eigenen Händen. Ich hoffte nur, dass ich falsch lag und sie diese Nacht unbeschadet überstehen würde.

Doch meine Intuition sagte mir das Gegenteil.

Nach der Schule fuhr ich mit Becky ins Einkaufszentrum, um das Ende unserer Prüfungen zu feiern. Das würde mir auch endlich die Gelegenheit geben, sie in die neuesten Entwicklungen mit Sara einzuweihen. Auf dem Weg schickte ich meiner Mom eine Nachricht, damit sie mich nicht wieder anmotzte, wenn ich später nach Hause kam.

Nachdem Becky und ich an einem Tisch in unserem Lieblingscafé Platz genommen hatten, erzählte ich ihr von meiner Konfrontation mit Sara am Montag. Becky hörte gebannt zu und riss die Augen auf. „Ich wusste, dass du uns nicht alles gesagt hast. Das ist das Beste, was ich je gehört habe. Gut, dass du ihr endlich mal gezeigt hast, wo es langgeht!“

„Ja.“ Ich grinste. „Es hat sich echt gut angefühlt!“

„Ich finde trotzdem, dass wir Mr. Hathaway hätten melden sollen. Jetzt muss ich beten, dass ich ihn nicht nächstes Jahr in Mathe habe.“ Becky verzog das Gesicht. „Bei dem Gedanken gruselt es mich.“

„Tja, rate mal, was noch passiert ist! Gestern Nachmittag hat er mit Sara Schluss gemacht!“

„Was??“ Becky blieb der Mund offen stehen.

„Woher weißt du das?“

„Ich habe sie gehört.“ Ich kicherte. „Es war ganz schön krass. Sara hat geheult und alles.“

„Oh mein Gott!“ Becky griff nach meinem Handgelenk. „Erzähl mir alles von Anfang an!“

Ich hatte es kaum erwarten können, ihr die Neuigkeiten mitzuteilen, und sie reagierte genau so, wie ich es erwartet hatte. Wir bekamen unsere Eisbecher und sie löffelte ihr Eis in sich hinein, während ich redete. Ab und zu machte ich eine Pause, um auch etwas zu essen.

„Das ist ja krass!“, sagte Becky schließlich und ich sah, wie sie versuchte, sich die Szene vorzustellen. „Aber geschieht ihr recht. Nach allem, was sie dir angetan hat. Das ist Karma. Sie verdient es, abserviert zu werden. Aber sie wird nicht gut damit klarkommen. Als Blake mit ihr Schluss gemacht hat, ist sie total ausgerastet.“

„Das macht mir auch Sorgen. Ich bin mir ziemlich sicher, dass sie das nicht einfach so auf sich sitzen lässt.“

„Tja, er ist ein Lehrer. Er sollte sich sowieso nicht mit Schülerinnen abgeben. Wenn er seinen Job verliert, ist das seine eigene Schuld!“

Obwohl ich Becky zustimmte, fragte ich mich dennoch, was Saras Anteil an der ganzen Sache

gewesen war. Mit Sicherheit waren sie in beiderseitigem Einvernehmen zusammen gewesen. Sara hatte vielleicht sogar den ersten Schritt gemacht.

Doch egal, wie es zustande gekommen war, ich wusste mit Sicherheit, dass Mr. Hathaway nicht auf die Rache von Sara Hamilton vorbereitet war.

Die Entscheidung …

Sobald mein Dad an diesem Abend das Haus betrat, machte sich eine innerliche Ruhe in mir breit. Ich schlang meine Arme um seinen Hals und wollte ihn gar nicht mehr loslassen. Seine vertraute Nähe trieb mir Tränen in die Augen, die er sanft wegwischte.

„Ist schon gut, Julia. Ich bin jetzt da. Alles wird gut“, murmelte er und umarmte mich noch einmal.

Ich wollte ihm nicht von der Seite weichen und folgte ihm in die Küche.

Gestern Abend hatte ich ihn endlich am Telefon erreicht und ihm die ganze Geschichte erzählt. Mom hatte ihn zwar bereits eingeweiht, aber nicht in jedes Detail, und ich fand, dass er ein Recht darauf hatte, alles zu erfahren. Wenn sie es ihm nicht sagte, würde ich es tun.

Als er in die Küche kam und Mom am Herd stehen sah, stockte er bei dem vertrauten Anblick, als hätte ihn der Schlag getroffen. Es war so lange her, seit die beiden zusammen im

Haus gewesen waren. Peinliches Schweigen hing zwischen ihnen.

Während wir beim Essen saßen, versuchte Mom durch ständiges Reden die Anspannung etwas zu mildern. Es war der Abend vor Matts Abschlussfeier - ein Ereignis, das wir als Familie feiern sollten. Es fühlte sich aber ganz und gar nicht feierlich an. Matt verdiente etwas Besseres. Das war alles so unfair.

Nachdem wir am nächsten Morgen die Aula der Schule betreten und drei freie Plätze gefunden hatten, suchte ich in der Gruppe der Schulabsolventen nach meinem Bruder. Endlich entdeckte ich ihn inmitten der Masse aus leuchtend blauen Kappen und Talaren und winkte ihm aufgeregt zu.

In zwei Jahren würde ich an seiner Stelle stehen und die gleiche Abschlussuniform in den Schulfarben tragen. Flüchtig fragte ich mich, was mir in der Zeit bis dahin noch alles bevorstand.

Würde Matt die Uni seiner Träume finden und mich mit meiner Mutter allein zu Hause lassen, oder würde er sich für ein örtliches College entscheiden und bei uns bleiben? Ich wusste, welche Option ihm lieber war. Aber ich konnte mir nicht vorstellen, dass er uns verließ.

Die Zeremonie begann und wir ließen einige langatmige Reden über uns ergehen. Als endlich die Abschlusszeugnisse überreicht wurden, richtete ich mich auf und wartete darauf, dass Matts Name aufgerufen wurde. Schließlich betrat er die Bühne. Ich klatschte lauter als alle anderen im Saal. Ein Seitenblick auf meine Eltern zeigte mir, dass Mom Tränen in den Augen hatte und Dad seinen Sohn stolz beobachtete.

Später stellten wir uns alle draußen auf, um Fotos zu machen. Als die Abschlussklasse ihre Kappen in die Luft warf, hielt ich diesen Moment mit meinem Handy fest. Später scrollte ich durch meine Fotos und lächelte über das Bild, auf dem ich neben meinem Bruder stand. Er hatte seine Kappe auf meinen Kopf gesetzt und wir strahlten beide in die Kamera. Ich hatte sofort beschlossen, dass das mein neues Profilfoto auf Facebook werden würde. Es war ein Bild, auf das man stolz sein konnte.

Nach der Zeremonie gab es noch ein Büfett und die meisten blieben, um sich mit den Lehrern und anderen Familien auszutauschen. Ich hielt mich an Dads Seite, während Mom mit den Eltern redete, die sie kannte.

Nachdem Dad und ich einen freien Platz an einem der Picknicktische unter den Bäumen gefunden hatten, legte er mir tröstend die Hand

aufs Knie. „Wie geht's dir, mein Schatz?"

Ich sah ihn an und seufzte. „Mir geht es gut, Dad. Um dich mache ich mir Sorgen."

Er schüttelte den Kopf. „Das musst du nicht. Ich komme klar. Ich habe gestern Abend lange mit deiner Mutter geredet und wir wollen versuchen, die Dinge wieder in Ordnung zu bringen. Es wird Zeit brauchen, aber wir wollen es probieren."

„Also nimmst du sie zurück? Einfach so? Nach allem, was sie dir angetan hat?" Ich starrte ihn perplex an. Wie konnte er nur so verständnisvoll sein?

Er seufzte schwer und sagte: „Menschen machen Fehler, Julia. Das geht uns allen so. Es wird eine ganze Weile dauern, bis ich deiner Mom wieder vertrauen kann, aber ich bin bereit, es zu versuchen. Und da ich so oft auf Dienstreise bin, braucht ihr jemanden, der zu Hause für euch sorgt."

Ich runzelte unwillig die Stirn. „Ich kann für mich selber sorgen! Bis jetzt bin ich auch sehr gut zurechtgekommen!"

Dad nickte und lächelte. „Ja, das bist du, und ich bin sehr stolz auf dich. Du bist ein tolles Mädchen. Deine Mutter und ich haben großes Glück, Kinder wie dich und Matt zu haben."

Ich schnaubte. „Ich glaube nicht, dass Mom das auch so sieht.“

„Sie macht gerade viel durch. Und ich verstehe, dass du ihr nicht verzeihen kannst. Aber gib der Sache etwas Zeit, okay? Tust du das für mich?“

Ich nickte schweigend. Wie konnte ich da Nein sagen? Er war mein Vater, und wenn er Mom wieder zurückhaben wollte, durfte ich ihm nicht im Weg stehen. Außerdem waren wir uns gar nicht so unähnlich. Er konnte seine Gefühle für Mom nicht einfach so abstellen – genau wie ich bei Ky. Sie waren zu besonders, als dass man sie so leicht vergessen konnte.

Ich legte meine Hand in seine und drückte sie. „Ich hab' dich lieb, Dad.“

„Ich dich auch, Julia.“

Ich suchte in der Menge nach Matt, der ebenfalls in dem Moment in meine Richtung schaute. Er lächelte und winkte mir zu.

Ich war stolz darauf, dass dieser gut aussehende Junge mein Bruder war.

Vielleicht hatte Dad recht und alles würde gut werden.

Die Zeit würde es zeigen.

Schockwelle …

Endlich war der letzte Tag des Schuljahres da. Wir würden unsere Zeugnisse bekommen, Filme schauen und uns die Snacks teilen, die wir alle zur Schule mitbringen wollten. Ein perfekter letzter Tag - wenn wir es schafften, einigermaßen gute Noten zu kriegen.

Nach dem Ende der Schule wollte ich direkt zu Emmie fahren. Als ich morgens aus dem Haus trat, hatte ich schon eine Tasche mit allem dabei, was ich für heute Abend brauchen würde.

Matts Auto stand nicht in der Auffahrt und mir fiel wieder ein, dass er bei einem Freund übernachten wollte. Nach der Zeremonie gestern waren wir gemeinsam in seinem Lieblingsrestaurant gewesen. Doch so bald wie möglich hatte er sich verabschiedet, um zu seiner Party zu kommen.

Er hatte erwähnt, dass auch die Schüler einer Nachbarschule, vermutlich Joes, zu der Party eingeladen waren. Es sollte ein riesiges Event werden und sie hatten sogar Sicherheitsleute engagiert, die alles überwachten. Ein großes

Grundstück am Stadtrand war dafür die perfekte Location.

Ich hatte alles über die Instagram-Storys verfolgen können, die er immer wieder aktualisierte. Nach den Partyszenen im Video zu urteilen, war es ganz offensichtlich eine tolle Nacht gewesen. Ich hoffte nur, dass Lisa, wo immer sie sich aufgehalten hatte, gut nach Hause gekommen war.

Sobald ich in der Schule war, ging ich zu meinem Schließfach, um meine Übernachtungstasche zu verstauen. Dann quatschte ich noch kurz mit Becky, bevor ich mich zur ersten Stunde begab. Englisch. Auf dieses Fach freute ich mich am meisten.

Als Erstes händigte uns Miss Bromley unsere Grammatiktests aus und ich sah erfreut die Zwei Plus auf meiner Arbeit. Die Prüfung war ziemlich schwierig gewesen und ich war überrascht, dass ich so gut abgeschnitten hatte. Dann entdeckte ich die große rote Eins Plus auf meinem Aufsatz und freute mich noch mehr. Zusammen mit den Zensuren aus dem ersten Halbjahr würde ich damit insgesamt eine Eins auf dem Zeugnis haben. Ich war mir nicht sicher, ob ich das in den anderen Fächern auch geschafft hatte, aber es war ein sehr guter Anfang.

Doch die Bemerkung, die Miss Bromley auf meinen Aufsatz geschrieben hatte, bedeutete mir am meisten.

Julia, du bist sehr talentiert und hast einen aufschlussreichen Essay verfasst, auf den du stolz sein kannst. Glückwunsch zu diesem hervorragenden Ergebnis!

Am liebsten hätte ich mit dem Papier vor Saras Nase herumgewedelt und ihr gesagt, dass ich das alles ihrem Mobbing zu verdanken hatte. Das wäre die beste Rache gewesen! Aber ich war auch zufrieden damit, mich einfach nur im Stillen über mein Ergebnis zu freuen. Wenigstens eine Note, über die sich meine Mutter nicht beschweren konnte.

Als Nächstes teilte Miss Bromley jedem die Papiertüte mit seinem Namen aus, die die Zettel mit den Komplimenten enthielt. Wir alle nahmen sie enthusiastisch entgegen.

Je mehr Zettel ich auffaltete, desto breiter wurde mein Lächeln. Die ersten Bemerkungen waren recht einfach und kurz gehalten, aber sie ließen dennoch mein Herz höher schlagen.

Du bist sehr klug. Jackson W

Ich mag deine Haare. Ruby

Du bist echt hübsch. Kayla T

Du bist ein nettes Mädchen. Grayson

Dann stieß ich auf einen Zettel, der mit so viel Text beschrieben war, dass er kaum in das Kästchen passte.

Ich kenne dich nicht gut, aber du wirkst echt nett. Und ich wollte dir sagen, dass ich auch oft Schaumbäder nehme. Ich liebe das! Wer immer diese Fotos von dir online gestellt hat, ist nur eifersüchtig. Du bist sehr hübsch, deshalb kann ich es verstehen, aber das ist keine Rechtfertigung dafür. Auf jeden Fall wünsche ich dir schöne Ferien! Kaitlyn

Ich suchte den Raum nach dem Mädchen ab, das diese Worte geschrieben hatte. Kaitlyn hob im Unterricht oft ihre Hand und hatte auch immer etwas Interessantes zu sagen. Sie hatte kein Problem damit, ihre Meinung auszudrücken, und hielt sich nicht zurück. Ich hatte sie oft um diese Fähigkeit beneidet und mir gewünscht, ich wäre auch so selbstbewusst. In meinem Kompliment für sie hatte ich genau diese Eigenschaft gelobt, aber jetzt wünschte ich, dass ich ihr noch mehr geschrieben hätte.

Ich fing ihren Blick ein und lächelte, während ich auf den Zettel in meiner Hand deutete. Sie lächelte zurück und reckte den Daumen in die Höhe. Ich war so voller Dankbarkeit für ihre Worte, dass mir sogar die Tränen kamen.

Ich riss mich zusammen und fischte einen

weiteren Zettel aus meiner Tüte. Diese Bemerkung kannte ich schon. Erneut lächelte ich über Cades Worte.

Du bist ein nettes Mädchen und verdienst es, mit Respekt behandelt zu werden. CA

Doch als ich den nächsten Zettel auffaltete, stutzte ich.

Du bist nicht so eingebildet wie viele andere Mädchen. Das ist echt cool. Cade

Ich las den Satz noch mal und blinzelte. Es war ja toll, dass einer der beliebtesten Jungs in der Klasse etwas Nettes über mich zu sagen hatte. Aber wenn dieses Kompliment von Cade stammte, wer war dann CA?

Ich sah mich stirnrunzelnd um. Abgesehen von Christina Johnson war Chelsea die einzige andere Person, deren Vorname mit C begann – das glaubte ich jedenfalls. Aber ich musste mich wohl irren.

Ich machte weiter. Wenn Chelseas Zettel noch irgendwo in der Tüte war, musste es noch einen oder eine andere CA geben, deren Identität ich noch nicht kannte.

Als ich Saras Botschaft las, verdrehte ich die Augen.

Dein Bruder sieht gut aus. Sara

Offensichtlich war ihr nichts Positives über mich eingefallen, also hatte sie meinen Bruder erwähnt. Doch der Gedanke, dass er ihr aufgefallen war, irritierte mich.

Ich widerstand dem Drang, ihre Nachricht zu einer winzigen Kugel zusammenzuknüllen und in den Papierkorb zu werfen, und machte stattdessen mit den restlichen Zetteln weiter. Der Stapel auf meinem Tisch wuchs. Als ich Beckys Namen auf einem Blatt entdeckte, lächelte ich.

Ich bin so froh, mit dir befreundet zu sein! Du inspirierst mich dazu, für mich selbst einzustehen … ich wäre gern wie du. Becky

Ihre Worte machten mich unheimlich glücklich. Das war bisher das schönste Kompliment von allen.

Nach der Demütigung der Facebook- und Instagram-Posts war es einfach überwältigend, so viele wundervolle Nachrichten zu bekommen, und ich wurde schon wieder emotional. Ich schaute Miss Bromley an und lächelte. Sie zwinkerte mir zu und schien sehr zufrieden damit, wie alle Schüler im Raum reagierten.

Ich hatte noch drei Zettel vor mir. Der erste war von Jack.

Du bist etwas Besonderes und eine tolle Freundin.

Danke dafür, dass du so bist, wie du bist! Jack H

Wieder füllten sich meine Augen mit Tränen. Seine Worte berührten mich zutiefst.

Ich blinzelte und las die nächste Bemerkung. Diese war so magisch, dass mir kleine Schauer über den Rücken liefen.

Du bist das wundervollste Mädchen, das ich je kannte. Ich liebe einfach alles an dir. Blake

Als ich in seine Richtung blickte, schaute er auf und schenkte mir ein strahlendes Lächeln. Es brauchte keine Worte. Wir beide waren überglücklich über die Nachrichten, die der andere geschrieben hatte. Und ich wusste, dass ich seine Worte für immer in meinem Herzen behalten würde.

Dann entfaltete ich den letzten Zettel, in der Erwartung, eine Nachricht von dem mysteriösen CA zu finden. Doch das, was ich sah, hätte ich nie im Leben erwartet.

Die Zeit schien stillzustehen. Der Schock traf mich wie eine Welle, die mich bis ins Innerste erschütterte. Eine vertraute Handschrift überzog das Papier, und während ich ein Wort nach dem anderen las, explodierte ein kleines Feuerwerk in meinem Bauch.

Ich erinnere mich an dein perfektes Lächeln, als du

zum ersten Mal meine Familie getroffen hast.

Ich erinnere mich an das Leuchten deiner wunderschönen Augen, wenn ich dich zum Lachen gebracht habe.

Ich erinnere mich an dein seidiges langes Haar.

Ich erinnere mich an deine weiche Hand in meiner.

Ich erinnere mich an unseren ersten Kuss, den magischsten Moment von allen.

Ich erinnere mich an alles.

Ky

Gänsehaut überzog meine Arme. Ich nahm nichts um mich herum mehr wahr, nur die Worte auf dem Blatt Papier in meiner Hand.

Mein Herz hämmerte unkontrolliert.

Bumm!

Bumm!

Bumm!

Das war alles, was ich hörte, als ich mir seine Worte zum zweiten und dann zum dritten Mal durchlas.

***

Wie es weitergeht, erfährst du in

Julia Jones – Die Teenie-Jahre: Teil 8.

Danke, dass du Julias Geschichte bis hierher verfolgt hast. Wenn dir das Buch gefallen hat, würde ich mich sehr freuen, wenn du mir eine Rezension schreibst oder deinen Freunden von den Büchern erzählst.

Herzlichen Dank,

Katrina :x

Weitere Informationen zu allen Büchern findest du hier:

http://indiesgogerman.com/juliajones/

Möchtest du wissen, was Julia erlebt hat, bevor sie aus Carindale weggezogen ist?

In *Julia Jones' Tagebuch – Der schrecklichste Tag meines Lebens* ist Julia zwölf und hat zum ersten Mal mit Saras Schikanen zu kämpfen.

Auch viele andere bekannte Charaktere wie Blake, Millie und Jack triffst du in ihren Tagebüchern wieder.

Weitere Bücher, die dir gefallen könnten …

Printed by Amazon Italia Logistica S.r.l.
Torrazza Piemonte (TO), Italy

39381422R00087